BIG GOD
in a
Chaotic World

BIG GOD

Other books and studies by **BRUCE B. MILLER**

the **WISDOM**
SERIES

When God Makes No Sense
A Fresh Look at Habakkuk

Sexuality
Approaching Controversial Issues
with Grace, Truth and Hope

Same-Sex Marriage
A Bold Call to the Church in Response
to the Supreme Court's Decision

Never the Same
A Fresh Look at the Sermon on the Mount

❧

Same-Sex Wedding
Should I Attend?

Your Church in Rhythm

Your Life in Rhythm
Your Life in Rhythm Study Guide

The Leadership Baton
The Leadership Baton Group Study Guide
(written with Rowland Forman and Jeff Jones)

"In an environment of increasing secularism and aggressive atheism, Bruce helpfully introduces Daniel as a beautiful devotional commentary on Daniel with helpful charts and historical essays to navigate its prophecy, and a marvelous Study Guide for assisting individual readers or small groups as they mine Daniel's wisdom for daily living."
Dr. Larry Parsley, Senior Pastor—Valley Ranch Baptist Church

"In this book, my good friend, Bruce Miller, transports Daniel's life and godliness into the 21st century, demonstrating that his struggles and challenges are, in many respects, ours as well. But most importantly, Daniel's Big God is also ours! Though separated by thousands of years and living in an entirely different culture, the enduring truths that guided Daniel through a maze of paganism are the same life principles for us today!"
Dr. Gene A. Getz—Professor, Pastor, Author

"In this study of Daniel, Bruce Miller manages to do what most commentators don't: offer an eminently practical reading of the book. Reflecting the fact that the Hebrew Bible groups Daniel not with the prophets, but with the wisdom literature, Miller applies his WISDOM method to great effect. The result is that Daniel no longer seems strange but surprisingly down-to-earth!"
**Dr. Joel White, Director of International Exchanges—
Freie Theologische Hochschule Gießen**

"*Big God in Chaotic World* is a handbook of hope! In this book, Bruce engages the reader through logical reason, historical discovery and personal perspective to reveal the person of God through the words of an ancient sage known as Daniel. This is an incredible blend of wisdom, theology and real-life application that moves the reader into a greater faith-stance! This is a common-sense book about an incredibly uncommon God!"
Charlie Tuttle, Lead Pastor—Genesis Church

"What we need today is a biblical view of God. We need to see Him for who He really is, not who we've made Him out to be. This is the great gift Bruce has given us through this book! He helps us see that our view of God determines our response to God. I love how Bruce writes out of a pastor's heart, bringing a scholarly understanding down to earth, right where we live, in the real world. The supplemental Study Guide, the thoughtful questions toward application, and the QR code teachings are icing on the cake. You don't just read this book, you experience it."
Dr. Jeff Warren, Senior Pastor—Park Cities Baptist Church

BIG GOD
in a
Chaotic World

A Fresh Look at Daniel

the WISDOM SERIES

BRUCE B. MILLER

Dadlin Media
— wisdom for life —

McKinney, Texas

Dadlin Media is the publishing ministry of Dadlin ministries, an organization committed to helping people develop wisdom for life.

For more information please go to: http://BruceBMiller.com.

ISBN-10: 1-68316-000-2
ISBN-13: 978-1-68316-000-7

Dadlin Media
— *wisdom for life* —
McKinney, TX 75070

BruceBMiller.com

To the
Big God-worshipping staff and elders
with whom I have the privilege of serving at
Christ Fellowship.

It is a blessing to serve our Big God with you!

Contents

Introduction

As an 18-year-old college student at The University of Texas, I did an intensive study of Daniel with my close friend, Steve Emmons. Decades later, Daniel still captivates my heart.

The first six chapters of Daniel tell gripping stories of God's power in personal lives showing us that he is The Big God. In the stories, Daniel gives us divine visions that together blast our senses with God's control over nations and the future.

We can identify with Daniel. He was a normal guy working a secular job in an immoral culture. He was not a pastor, priest or missionary. Daniel faced challenges to compromise his convictions, political jealousy, powerful enemies and terrifying fears; just as we do.

It was the sixth century BC when Babylon conquered the Jews and deported some of them. Daniel was one of the exiles. In the first part of the book, we learn that he was a deeply spiritual man of impeccable character and exceptional quality to the point that he was made COO of the entire empire. God gave this amazing man visions from the future that he shared with us.

In an uncertain and chaotic world, Daniel shows us how to live faithfully for God. The key we will discover is not in ourselves, but in God. Studying Daniel opens our eyes to see The Big God, the God who is bigger than all our fears, fires and lions. Although it appears that the world is out of control, The Big God remains in control of the present and the future, of personal lives and nations.

Daniel teaches us humility, faith and courage. In the face of tough situations with unreasonable laws, unjust demands and hatred from his peers, Daniel models for us traits that show us how to honor God in the most difficult times. We will learn just how big our God really is. And when our vision of The Big God expands, we find that we can handle whatever chaos life throws our way.

How do we deal with our fear of the future?

We live in a crazy world. If you follow world news at all, it is incredibly unsettling. Sometimes I don't like to think about all the international threats, but then in sober moments, I know it doesn't help to hide my head in the sand. Let's go on a quick tour. At the time of writing this introduction, here's some of what's happening in the world:

❖ The civil war in Syria devastates average citizens in neighborhoods bombed by both sides. Most scary in Syria is the stash of biological and chemical weapons that someone could get access to and unleash on the world.
❖ North Korea is rattling their swords, breaking the decades old armistice and threatening to bomb America as well as South Korea.
❖ Right next door to us, Mexican drug cartels are raping women and cutting off people's heads. Our fear is that the cartels are crossing the border into America.
❖ Africa is filled with craziness from Joseph Kony's child soldiers, to famine, to civil wars.
❖ Iraq is unraveling in what could result in a civil war and a divided country spilling over into Syria as well.
❖ In our longer-term future, the world worries about China as an emerging superpower. They are building up their military and recently launched cyberattacks on American interests.

What is going to happen in the decades to come? The world is a scary place. And we have not even talked about the fragile global economy or the ecological dangers from massive pollution over centuries.

Because of their fears, some people hesitate to bring children into the world. If the world is such a scary place, where is God? If there is a good and all-powerful God, why doesn't he do something about all the evil and suffering? Why does he let the Hitlers and Konys of this world hurt so many people?

We wonder how it is all going to end. What is going to happen to our world?

Television shows reflect our concern. A recent news report said post-apocalyptic television scenarios are popping up everywhere, from a zombie apocalypse in *The Walking Dead* to *Falling Skies* to *Revolution*, a series about what happens after the loss of all advanced technology. Religious people talk about a coming Antichrist. Is this just crazy talk by nutty people or is there something to it?

What does the Bible really say about the future?

The book of Daniel opens our eyes to see the future. Daniel provides background for the last book of the Bible, the book of Revelation. In this study, we are going to see into the future. Daniel's insights help us deal with our fears in this uncertain world.

The book of Daniel divides into two even halves:

1. Chapters 1–6 are historical accounts
2. Chapters 7–12 share visions of the future

Let me warn you, the second half of Daniel gets crazy. You will encounter grotesque beasts, a river of fire and a little horn with a big mouth. In the second half of the book, we come to a different kind of literature. We intuitively know how to interpret different media genres. You have different expectations for what you see in an animated cartoon versus an ad on Craig's List versus an editorial blog versus a *Saturday Night Live* skit versus color commentary for a basketball game. But you may not intuitively understand how to grasp the genre in which Daniel was written.

The second part of Daniel is called apocalyptic literature. Apocalyptic writing uses symbols and exaggerated metaphors to communicate by analogy. Images are truthful, but not precise. People make outlandish and foolish claims from misreading this kind of literature in an overly literal way.

It bothers me to see billboards such as: "Three days until judgment day." I'm embarrassed by outlandish claims from supposed Christian teachers saying the world is going to end on a certain day or identifying a current political figure with the Antichrist. Some of this gets as foolish as the 2012 Mayan calendar silliness.

Imagine taking anime or Stephen Colbert literally. We need to become more sophisticated and common-sense readers. Rather than reading the Bible over-literally, we need to read it seriously and skillfully with the help of the Holy Spirit according to the type of literature we are reading.

God gave Daniel foresight to see the future and he has shared that insight with us. While his future visions have dark shadows to them, his vision of God outshines the darkness. When we see The Big God of Daniel, our fears shrink. We can face the future with confidence because we know The Big God.

Bruce

A Daniel-inspired prayer

Big God,
Grant me the conviction of Daniel in chapter 1,
the wise insight from chapter 2,
the courage of the three in chapter 3,
the humility before you in chapter 4,
the boldness in chapter 5,
and the prayerful faith in chapter 6.

Grant me a vision of how big you really are over everything
from diet to worship to public prayer;
big enough to face an angry king,
a fiery furnace and hungry lions.
Big God, grant me the grace to dare to be a Daniel
with eyes of faith to see your bigness.

Big God, in a chaotic world,
grant me conviction over compromise;
faith over fear; and
courage over caution.
May I see your greatness over kings and empires,
threats and plots,
even in Babylon.
I praise you for your greatness, your bigness.
You are The Big God.
Amen.

How to benefit from this book

This book provides you with 12 chapters on Daniel that can be read by themselves, and also includes a Study Guide that enables you to gain more insights from Daniel.

The Study Guide follows the 12 chapters. I encourage you to use the Study Guide after you read each chapter to mature further with Christ. In order to accelerate your learning, this Study Guide employs The WISDOM Process© explained below.

Because the Bible is more important to read than my thoughts on it, throughout the book we will direct you to read the relevant biblical passage.

The Bible is food for our souls. When we approach it prayerfully, the Spirit of God transforms our minds and blesses us with divine insights. More than anything else you can do, immersing yourself in the Word of God will grow you spiritually.

When we get alone to engage with God and focus our attention on understanding his Word, he speaks to us. But that doesn't mean we don't grow best in community. Connecting in a group to discuss what you are learning will help you grow even more. Invite a friend to do the study with you. Join a group, or start one of your own and prepare for what God has in store!

The WISDOM Process©

As children of God living in a hostile world, we need to learn how to think like Christ with biblical, spiritual wisdom for life.

Tested by thousands of people and hundreds of groups, the six-step WISDOM Process offers a surprisingly simple and profoundly powerful way to think. Today we are drowning in data and starving for wisdom. We Google for information on any topic, but we cannot find wisdom for life's complex challenges. This simple process can guide you to wisdom.

You will find that you can use The WISDOM Process© not only in this Bible study but also for issues you face in ordinary life.

This process of thinking helps us move from knowing facts to transforming our lives in God's power. Most adults learn differently than children. Research into adult learning and studies of ancient education both show that people learn best when they have a reason to learn: a question to answer, a problem to solve or a mystery to unravel. All of us have these in our lives.

✝ Pray

Role of Prayer
We access the guidance of God's Spirit through prayer and the Word of God. While God wants us to use our minds to study his Word to gain his revealed life direction, the Bible tells us:

> *If any of you lacks wisdom, he should ask God,*
> *who gives generously to all without finding fault, and*
> *it will be given to him* (James 1:5).

Bible study should be covered with prayer. Paul prayed like this for the Colossians:

> *For this reason, since the day we heard about*
> *you, we have not stopped praying for you and asking*
> *God to fill you with the knowledge of his will through*
> *all spiritual wisdom and understanding* (Colossians
> 1:9).

In answer to your prayers, the Spirit will shape your desires and then you will develop the mind of Christ. Rather than prayer being a specific step in The WISDOM Process, it should be threaded throughout the process of your study from start to end.

You will find that as you pray, the Spirit of God will guide you to truth. As a group, if you will prayerfully listen to the Spirit, he will direct your conversation to deep spiritual wisdom, conviction and motivation to honor God in daily life choices.

W Work the issue: *What's really at stake*?

Prepare your heart and mind before engaging God's Word. Take a moment to pray about questions in your life and issues arising from the Scripture you are studying. Consider how the Lord may want to impact you at this time. Bring your questions to your study of God's Word.

I Investigate Scripture: *What does God say*?

God's Word is our authority for life. It is our guide for belief and behavior. Our lives must be grounded in the Word of God. It is our primary source of absolute, divine truth. Spend time prayerfully and carefully considering what the biblical text is saying.

S Seek counsel: *What do wise people say*?

After studying the Scripture for ourselves, it is wise to seek the counsel of others. In Proverbs, Solomon said there is wisdom in a multitude of counselors. Wise people listen to advice (Proverbs 12:15; 13:10; 19:20). We provide you with well-researched input in these chapters to help you understand God's Word better, but of course this counsel itself must be judged by the Word of God. We also provide a video message of each chapter.

D Develop your response: *What do I think?*

We learn best when we actively engage. Writing down answers to questions will deepen your interaction with God's Word. Some questions are designed to increase your focus and understanding of the Scripture; others help you extend your thinking in applying God's Word to your life.

O Openly discuss: *What do we think?*

Life transformation is increased when we sharpen each other in dynamic discussion. You will grow more if you study with a group where you can wrestle together with how to understand and obey God's Word. Together, prepared people led by the Holy Spirit will generate a dynamic in which ideas and wisdom multiply beyond what any individual could produce.

M Move to action: *What will I do?*

Christ calls us to obey all he commands (Matthew 28:20). The point of Bible study is not simply knowledge, but obedience. We are studying God's Word to be more and more conformed to the image of Jesus Christ to grow to maturity. The Bible tells us that hearing the Word without acting on it is like building a house on sand, while acting on the truth is like building a house on rock (Matthew 7:24–27; James 1:22–25). We are in the business of building houses on the Rock! Our study should lead us to move to action in the Spirit's power.

Flow chart of
The WISDOM Process™

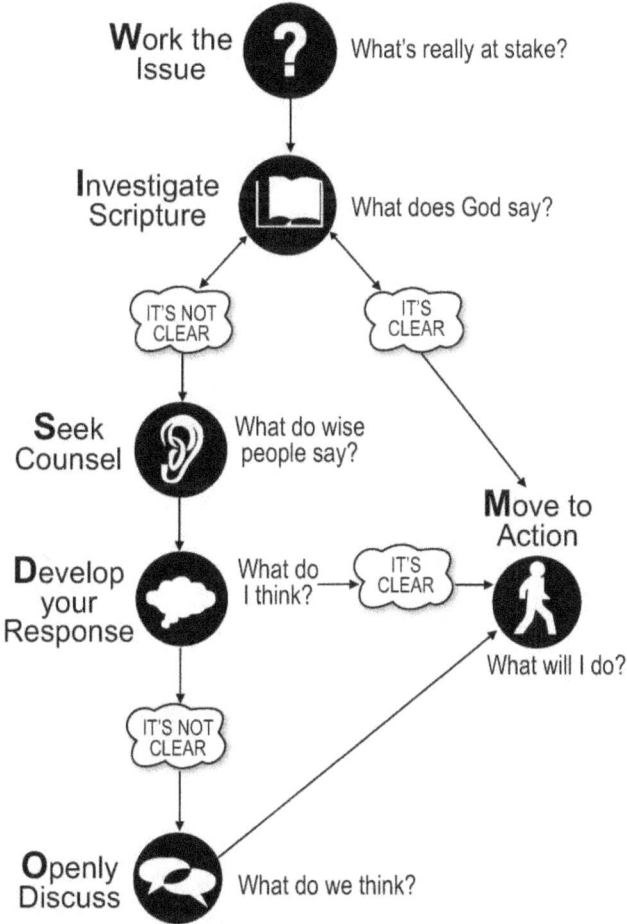

Work the Issue ? What's really at stake?

Investigate Scripture 📖 What does God say?

IT'S NOT CLEAR

IT'S CLEAR

Seek Counsel 👂 What do wise people say?

Move to Action

Develop your Response 💭 What do I think? → IT'S CLEAR → 🚶

What will I do?

IT'S NOT CLEAR

Openly Discuss 💬 What do we think?

Historical background

To understand any book that is historical, it is helpful to understand the context in which it was written. The following briefly surveys these issues.

Daniel, the statesman-prophet

Daniel was born into the nobility of Judah in (roughly) 620 BC. Since Daniel held high office even after the conquest of Babylon by Cyrus the Great in 539 BC, he probably lived to be about 85 years of age. Daniel's name means "God is my judge," and he is mentioned by name four times in the Bible outside of the book of Daniel (Ezekiel 14:14, 20; 28:3; Matthew 24:15). Though some have questioned whether Daniel was an actual historical figure, the matter is conclusively settled by Jesus who plainly spoke of Daniel and his prophecies as historical and authoritative.

Nebuchadnezzar, king of Babylon

Nebuchadnezzar II (c. 634–562 BC) reigned over the Neo-Babylonian Empire from August of 605 BC to 562 BC, a period of 43 years. After Nebuchadnezzar defeated the Egyptians and Assyrians at Carchemish in May–June of 605 BC, his father, King Nabopolassar, the conqueror of the Assyrian capital Nineveh, died in August of 605 BC. Crown Prince Nebuchadnezzar rushed home from the conquest of Jerusalem—bringing Daniel and many others with him—to ascend the throne of Babylon on September 6/7 of 605 BC.

The book of Daniel shows Nebuchadnezzar to be a man of great ability, towering pride and, when thwarted, burning rage. At the time of his choosing, Yahweh (the Hebrew personal name for

God) decisively humbled the king, probably with the result that Nebuchadnezzar gave his allegiance to Yahweh. Such unlikely faith seems indicated by Yahweh calling him "my servant" (Jeremiah 25:9, 27:6, 43:10), a title used only for men such as the Messiah, Abraham, Moses, David, Job and Isaiah. No other foreign person is ever called "my servant" by Yahweh, and the only person who comes close is Cyrus the Great, the Persian conqueror who is called "my shepherd" by Yahweh in Isaiah 44:28 (see also Isaiah 45:1, 45:13).

Nebuchadnezzar's reconstruction of Babylon included the famed Ishtar Gate and the Hanging Gardens, one of the great wonders of the ancient world.

Israel and Judah

The nation that God established by covenant under Moses later divided into two nations—Judah and Israel (see 1 Kings 12)—at the end of Solomon's reign (931 BC). This period (931–586 BC) is often called "the divided kingdom." The divided kingdom may be considered along two lines, devotion to God and commitment to international alliances. Judah often followed the lead of its unfaithful rulers into idolatry, and Israel was much worse. Both Judah and Israel made frequent alliances with regional powers resulting in a steady increase of idolatry.

In the late eighth century BC, the two great world powers were Egypt and Assyria. After many warnings from his prophets, Yahweh brought Assyria to take the northern kingdom of Israel away into bondage. This happened in 722 BC at the fall of Israel's capital, Samaria.

Because of his own reputation and his promises to David, Yahweh gave Judah additional time (2 Kings 19:34, 20:6) by striking against an Assyrian army besieging Jerusalem (2 Kings 19:35) in 701 BC. But Yahweh warned King Hezekiah of Judah that this reprieve would eventually end with the temple treasures and many people being carried away to Babylon, a new power rising in the east (2 Kings 20:17–18). This word was later fulfilled in the deportation that took Daniel and the temple treasures to Babylon (Daniel 1:1–2). However, before Daniel's birth, the Assyrian capital, Nineveh, was overrun by the Babylonians in 612 BC following great internal dissension among the Assyrians. The remaining Assyrians fled west and eventually called for help against the Babylonian expansion from their new ally Egypt.

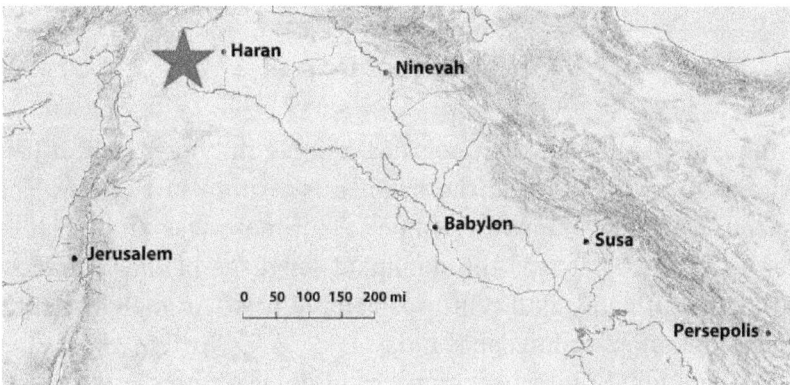

The Battle of Carchemish (605 BC) was fought at the place marked by the star.

Judah wavered between relying on Yahweh or, more frequently, on either fading Assyria or historically dominant Egypt, the ancient regional power. When Pharaoh Necho came up from Egypt to aid the Assyrians at the Euphrates River, King Josiah of Judah blocked him at Megiddo and was killed (2 Kings 23:29). Pharaoh chose his own king for Judah, renamed him Jehoiakim, imposed tribute on Judah (2 Kings 23:34) and then continued northward. However, on the Euphrates River, at a place named Carchemish, Pharaoh Necho and his Assyrian allies were crushed by Crown Prince Nebuchadnezzar of Babylon (May–June of 605 BC). Nebuchadnezzar quickly rushed south toward Jerusalem to deal with the puppet King Jehoiakim of Judah in Jerusalem, the home of a young man named Daniel.

There is no doubt whatever that Nebuchadnezzar believed himself to be in complete control of these events, but he would realize in time that Yahweh was calling the shots. What is more, he said so to the whole empire (Daniel 4)!

Daniel rose quickly to high office under Nebuchadnezzar and survived his death to hold a powerful position under the rule of Cyrus the Great of Persia (c. 600–530 BC).

The book of Daniel

An unusual feature of the book of Daniel is that over half of it is written in Aramaic, while the balance is written in Hebrew. The dialect of Aramaic, known as Imperial Aramaic, was an official or literary dialect that was the dominant language of the Near East during the fifth and sixth centuries before Christ. Aramaic was for a time as dominant as English is today.

Traditional interpretation of Daniel—both Jewish and Christian—has always held that the book of Daniel was written during the sixth century BC by Daniel, a Jew exiled to Babylon, to whom God revealed reliable knowledge of future events. The fact that both Jesus and Ezekiel regarded Daniel and his prophecies as historical, reliable and relevant to future proves convincing.

1

God Honors Convictions

Daniel 1

Imagine you are invited to pray at a public function. Do you pray in Jesus' name? What if they ask you not to use Jesus' name? At President Obama's 2013 inauguration, Atlanta Pastor Louie Giglio withdrew from praying because certain gay rights groups objected to something Louie said in a sermon long before. Should he have withdrawn?

Suppose that your workplace says you can't wear a cross necklace; you can't play Christian music; can't have a Bible on your desk; or can't hang up a Christian poster in your cube. What do you do? What if your son is cast as the lead in the school play but it violates your values? Does he drop out? How will other students respond? How will the theater teacher respond?

Saeed Abedini, a Boise Idaho pastor and father of two young children, was imprisoned in Iran for his religious beliefs. About three years prior to his being arrested in his native Iran, Saeed agreed to no longer do missionary work there. He returned nine times to conduct non-religious, humanitarian work. The last time Abedini traveled to Iran to help build an orphanage, he was arrested by Iran's Revolutionary Guard. How do you live loyally to God in a hostile world? What if not compromising your convictions meant losing a promotion? Getting fired? Failing an exam? Losing a boyfriend? Losing a job? Going to prison? Getting killed?

Back in Babylon

To understand the book of Daniel and get a proper vision of our Big God in this chaotic world, we need to transport ourselves into his world. Daniel was not in Israel, but in Babylon. The time was from about 605–520 BC, 600 years before Christ. This was around the time of democracy in Athens, Greece, 100 years before Socrates.

How did the Jews get there? Put yourself in their shoes. Israel rose to its greatest power under David and Solomon about 350 years earlier. Through a series of kings, they fell away from God. Over and over again, God patiently warned that if they violated his commands, he would judge them. Finally, after hundreds of years, he did. Israel in the north was destroyed and deported by the Assyrians. Later the Babylonians defeated and deported Judah, including Daniel.

We too live in an increasingly hostile, foreign place. We are not at home. The correlations between our situation and Daniel's are close which makes Daniel one of the most intriguing books in the Bible. It shows us how big our God really is, bigger than the chaos in our lives and bigger than all the chaos in the world. Daniel teaches us that in spite of apparent circumstances, God is in control.

God is in control

The world powers at the time were Assyria, Egypt and Babylon. They fought each other until 605 BC when the issue was decided at the famous Battle of Carchemish where the Babylonians won. Years ago, some scholars questioned the historical accuracy of Judah being taken captive by Nebuchadnezzar. But in 1956, writing from a cuneiform tablet was discovered stating "that immediately after the battle of Carchemish in the spring of 605 B.C., Nebuchadnezzar 'conquered the whole area of the Hatti-country.' Wiseman [1961] explains that the geographical term 'Hatti' included, 'at this period, the whole of Syria and Palestine.'"[1]

This area is still in conflict today. An article from the *Bloomberg Businessweek* reported, "Few archaeological sites seem as entwined with conflict, ancient and modern, as the city of Karkemish. . . .The scene of a battle mentioned in the Bible, it lies smack on the border between Turkey and Syria, where civil war rages today. . . . Visible from crumbling, earthen ramparts, a Syrian rebel flag flies in a town that regime forces fled just months ago."[2] Those ramparts could date back to the time of Daniel.

Can you imagine how discouraging it must have been to the Jewish people to be defeated, have their temple destroyed and be deported to a foreign country? Where was God? Was he real? Did he have power over people like the Babylonians? Why did they seem to obviously be winning? We ask similar questions today.

The book of Daniel is a message to people living in exile in a foreign place. They are just like us. We are not living in heaven, just in case you missed that. In many ways, we are living in a foreign place. The Jews were a small minority group in a hostile environment. How could they fit in without being swallowed? How could they remain faithful to God in Babylon? In Psalm 137, the writer sings of this time:

> *By the rivers of Babylon we sat and wept when*
> *we remembered Zion. . . . How can we sing the songs*
> *of the LORD while in a foreign land?* (Psalm 137:1, 4)

As Jews, they thought they heard God promise that they would be a blessing to the nations. How could God use them in captivity in Babylon? How did it even make any sense to be in captivity? Their fundamental theology and basic convictions were being tested to the core.

Babylon offered many other temptations: an opportunity to make a new life, to assimilate into a new culture and to join the reigning power of the world. There were opportunities to make money and experience pleasures unthinkable in Judea. Perhaps some Jews argued to avoid making friendships with the Babylonians for fear of compromise in order to not lose their identity as God's people. We face the same struggles. But it could get much harder in the future.

Our Babylon

Imagine what it might be like many years from now. Nineteen kings ruled over Judah from King David until its fall to Babylon in 586 BC, a total period of 345 years.[3] In the next century, America will be a nation for as long as Judah was. So imagine with me that years from now, the United States has been defeated by the Chinese. You are put on a boat with several others and taken to Beijing where you are put in a three-year school to learn Mandarin and be taught the ways and arts of China so you can serve the Chinese Empire. How do you remain loyal to Jesus Christ? How will you avoid compromising biblical convictions and be able to keep your identity?

The book of Daniel tells us how. It brings encouragement and hope, a refreshed theology for a discouraged people deported to a foreign land. Daniel shows us The Big God in a chaotic world.

Remarkably, Daniel is you. He is not a pastor, priest or prophet. He is not professionally religious. He works in the secular world for the government. He does not have a degree from a seminary, but from a secular university where he studied pagan thought. God worked through Daniel and he can work through you.

Daniel reminds us that God is bigger than any chaos. He shows us how a person who knows The Big God can be loyal to God in a godless Babylon.

Your Babylon may be your local middle school or the business for which you work or the city in which you live. We can avoid compromising our convictions in our Babylon because God is bigger than our fears. When you feel the world is crashing down upon you, when you feel like people around you are opposing your faith, you need the book of Daniel. If you want to live for God with faith and courage, you need Daniel. When we dig deep into the book, we will see that the hero is not Daniel, for whom the book is titled, but the hero is God who is often the unseen power behind events.

Daniel 1:1–21

In the third year of the reign of Jehoiakim king of Judah, Nebuchadnezzar king of Babylon came to Jerusalem and besieged it. ²And the Lord delivered Jehoiakim king of Judah into his hand, along with some of the articles from the temple of God. These he carried off to the temple of his god in Babylonia and put in the treasure house of his god.

³ Then the king ordered Ashpenaz, chief of his court officials, to bring into the king's service some of the Israelites from the royal family and the nobility— ⁴young men without any physical defect, handsome, showing aptitude for every kind of learning, well informed, quick to understand, and qualified to serve in the king's palace. He was to teach them the language and literature of the Babylonians. ⁵The king assigned them a daily amount of food and wine from the king's table. They were to be trained for three years, and after that they were to enter the king's service.

⁶Among those who were chosen were some from Judah: Daniel, Hananiah, Mishael and Azariah.

⁷*The chief official gave them new names: to Daniel, the name Belteshazzar; to Hananiah, Shadrach; to Mishael, Meshach; and to Azariah, Abednego.*

⁸*But Daniel resolved not to defile himself with the royal food and wine, and he asked the chief official for permission not to defile himself this way.* ⁹*Now God had caused the official to show favor and compassion to Daniel,* ¹⁰*but the official told Daniel, "I am afraid of my lord the king, who has assigned your food and drink. Why should he see you looking worse than the other young men your age? The king would then have my head because of you."*

¹¹*Daniel then said to the guard whom the chief official had appointed over Daniel, Hananiah, Mishael and Azariah,* ¹²*"Please test your servants for ten days: Give us nothing but vegetables to eat and water to drink.* ¹³*Then compare our appearance with that of the young men who eat the royal food, and treat your servants in accordance with what you see."* ¹⁴*So he agreed to this and tested them for ten days.*

¹⁵*At the end of the ten days they looked healthier and better nourished than any of the young men who ate the royal food.* ¹⁶*So the guard took away their choice food and the wine they were to drink and gave them vegetables instead.*

¹⁷*To these four young men God gave knowledge and understanding of all kinds of literature and learning. And Daniel could understand visions and dreams of all kinds.*

¹⁸*At the end of the time set by the king to bring them into his service, the chief official presented them to Nebuchadnezzar.* ¹⁹*The king talked with them, and he found none equal to Daniel, Hananiah, Mishael and Azariah; so they entered the king's service.* ²⁰*In every matter of wisdom and understanding about which the king questioned them, he found them ten times better than all the magicians and enchanters in his whole kingdom.*

²¹And Daniel remained there until the first year of King Cyrus.

From Daniel 1:1–21, notice the actions of three people: Nebuchadnezzar, Daniel and God. We will get to Daniel later, but for now, let's contrast Nebuchadnezzar and God.

God's acts directed and overcame Nebuchadnezzar's acts. And there is something fascinating in the Hebrew text that is missed in the English translation. God acted in verses 2, 9 and 17. In each case, the same Hebrew verb is used, *natan*, which means "to give." God's *natan* (giving) thus played a key role in the story's unfolding.[4] In the unseen world, it is God who gave success to Nebuchadnezzar, success to the young men with their diet and success to the men in their final exam. All good things come from God who gives. In this chaotic world, we should resolve not to compromise biblical convictions because God is bigger than our fears. Let's walk through four fears as we unpack this amazing story of our Big God.

God is bigger than our fears

1. God is bigger than any enemy

Look back at Daniel 1:1–2 and notice the contrasts. For the Jews, on the surface it looked bad. People at that time evaluated gods in terms of the prosperity of their country and the success of the army. It looked like the gods of Babylon, such as Marduk, were more powerful than Yahweh, the God of the Jews. The conflicts were cast at the start between:

Jerusalem	Babylonia
The temple of God	The treasure house of Nebuchadnezzar's god
The God	Nebuchadnezzar's god

Nebuchadnezzar was the greatest ruler of the Neo-Babylonian period in Babylon which was the capital of Babylonia. It was situated on the Euphrates River, about 50 miles south of modern Baghdad.[5] Nebuchadnezzar is still famous today for building the magnificent Ishtar Gate, and the Hanging Gardens which was one of the Seven Wonders of the Ancient World.

Like the Jewish people in Babylon, the temple articles were out of place in the treasure house of a Babylonian god. The people could have been tempted to think that God had been defeated.

We are tempted in hard times to question if God is real and if he is truly as powerful as he claims or if he cares. Daniel reminds us that God is big, good and loving. All is not as it might appear. Nebuchadnezzar thought he won, but God gave (*natan*) Judah to Babylon.

When Jesus was bleeding on the Roman cross, it looked as if Satan had defeated him, but God gave his Son to the world and he won the victory on the cross.

God gave his Son

You may be facing an enemy who appears to be winning, who seems much more powerful than you are. God is bigger than any enemy.

2. God is bigger than any authority

Take a look at the next scene in Daniel 1:3–7. Nebuchadnezzar had ordered Ashpenaz, the chief official, to bring some of the young Israelite men into his service. But from the rest of Scripture, we know that God was sending them to Babylon as his representatives to serve him.

When your company sends you to China or Chicago on business, actually God is sending you to China or Chicago to serve him on his business. When circumstances move you to a new neighborhood, city or job, realize that deeper down, God is sending you there to serve not the human "king," but the King of Kings.

Apparently Nebuchadnezzar's intent was not to have been punishment, but political and propaganda. He wanted to convert these young men into Babylonians in every sense of the word. Today, like Nebuchadnezzar, the world tries to pressure us to conform to its ways.

The verse says the men were young—our best historical guess is 15 years old. For Daniel to be as faithful as he was, I imagine his mom and dad did some serious training with him and they must have been amazing role models of faith. How are you preparing your children to go to their Babylon, which could also be called college in our day?

The Babylonians picked the best; guys who were in shape physically and smart, with social savvy. They were to learn the language and literature of the Babylonians. Babylonian literature was extensive. "It was written on clay tablets, using cuneiform (wedge-shaped) impressions made by a wooden stylus" in the Akkadian language.[6] Today archaeology has uncovered thousands of Akkadian cuneiform tablets. Daniel and his friends studied economics, read love poetry and sorcery, including astrology and how to interpret the future from sheep's livers. Daniel did not resist the study. Sometimes we pull so far out of the world that we resist studying secular literature.

At one point in my life, I thought I shouldn't read philosophy, but then I realized that it was part of God's training for me, so I did doctoral work in the history of ideas. We need Christians who are trained in philosophy, business and media as well as sales, law and politics. Daniel demonstrated that you can be faithful to God while studying pagan thought and working in a pagan place. We will come back to Daniel's diet in the next scene.

Notice that Nebuchadnezzar also changed their names. In that day, your name was closely associated with your identity. Originally their Hebrew names related to the true God, but their new names contained allusions to Babylonian gods.

So far we have learned that God is bigger than any enemy and bigger than any authority.

3. God is bigger than any law

I love how 1:8 begins: "But Daniel resolved." Daniel did not leave his decision to the spur of the moment. He determined in advance that he would not compromise his loyalty. The story makes clear that it was not just Daniel who resolved prior to being tested, but all four young men made the same resolution together.

They resolved not to defile themselves. Years before, Joshua declared, "Choose this day whom you will serve . . . but as for me and my house, we will serve the Lord" (Joshua 24:15). Have you resolved not to compromise your biblical convictions, not to compromise your loyalty to God, your identity as a Christ-follower?

There's an old children's song that says, "Dare to be a Daniel." Will you take that dare? Daniel drew a line in the sand that he would not cross. The word "defile" in Hebrew means "to pollute or stain." In this case, Daniel was referring to the king's choice food and wine.

What's clear is that Daniel's stand was a refusal to compromise convictions, an insistence on resisting assimilation. He would not compromise his loyalty or reject his spiritual identity. The pressures then were massive as they are on us today. He could have said, "What choice do I have? The king ordered the menu. They told us to do it; we were just following orders."

Refusing could have hurt their chances to advance in their jobs; worse, it could have led to prison. In addition, the food was from the king's table so it was delicious and very tempting. They were a long way from home and who would know what they ate or drank? Most likely everyone else was doing it. And after all, hadn't God let them down? But Daniel resolved not to defile himself in this way.

Then God stepped in. God caused the official to show favor and compassion. Remember the Hebrew verb is literally "*gave favor*." The word "favor" is *hesed* which is a major concept in the Old Testament depicting God's loving kindness and is paralleled in the New Testament by the great theology of grace. God intervenes with his faithful grace and unfailing love for his people.

God gives favor

The real power did not lie in Nebuchadnezzar, his official, his policies or empire, but in The Big God. The primary point in Daniel 1 is not about how to behave like Daniel, but how to see the bigness of God.

However, we can learn from Daniel's stellar example. He models how to respond well when pressured to compromise. What did he do? He resolved privately, asked permission graciously and then he offered a creative solution.

In standing up for his faith, Daniel had the opportunity to explain why he did so, which gave him the opportunity to spread the truth about God. Daniel showed remarkable faith "to believe that in ten days God would so improve their appearance" that the guard would be convinced. By the power of God, in ten days, it happened.[7]

What kinds of situations like this do we face today? The Bible calls us not to compromise with the world. What about playing soccer on Sunday morning and missing church? What if you are invited to a party where bad stuff will happen? What media is appropriate to avoid? The movie or show may even have won an award but might not be suitable for you. What about the kinds of things the company is asking you to do to get clients or make sales? For you, what would be considered the king's food? What would you do?

Daniel teaches us that conviction does not excuse us from acting with sensitivity, tact and respect. Like Daniel, we should ask permission graciously and bring creative solutions. We have learned that we can resolve not to compromise our biblical convictions because God is bigger than our fears, bigger than any enemy, authority or law.

4. God is bigger than any test

In the last few verses of the first chapter, at the end of their three years, Nebuchadnezzar gave the final exam, but before that in 1:17, God gave them knowledge and understanding far beyond everyone else. Tests and exams can be unnerving. We can get scared. But God is bigger than all our tests. God honors those who honor him. As Daniel will teach us in the chapters to come, honor may not be on earth, but it will come without fail. In the long run, you will never regret honoring God. You will never regret resolving not to compromise.

God honors those who honor him

I imagine these four teenagers were nervous facing King Nebuchadnezzar in his royal palace, but God met them there. God gifted them with wisdom beyond not just the other young men, but above all the other educated men in the kingdom.

In our Babylon, we should hold to biblical convictions with grace because God is bigger than our fears. God is bigger than any enemy, authority, law or test. Our situation today is strikingly similar to Daniel's. We too live in a hostile culture. We live in our own Babylon.

Daniel shows us that our role is not to Christianize our nation. America is not a Christian nation. In fact, there is no such thing as a Christian nation. There are Christian churches that are faithful to God in the Babylons and Romes of our day. We are not to create Christian ghettos in which we avoid as much contact as possible with the world. Rather Jesus sent us into the world to show and tell the love of Christ (Matthew 28:18–20).

Pray for God to grant you the courage not to compromise biblical convictions because God is bigger than our fears. Pray that you will be able to see the greatness of God over all your fears. We serve a Big God!

For further study on chapter 1, see the Study Guide beginning on page 173.

2

God Controls Nations

Daniel 2

Do you have any chaos in your life? Everyone does. Have you noticed any chaos in our world? This world is a crazy place from a guy holding a five-year-old hostage in a bunker to political fights over gun control and to fears of Korea using a nuclear bomb. It is easy to get consumed with fear and anxiety. No wonder so much money is spent on prescription drugs to calm our nerves and help us sleep. Valium is the new aspirin.

We don't need to be convinced that chaos is real; we need to know how to deal with it. We are learning from the book of Daniel that in spite of apparent chaos, we can trust our Big God to be in control. Can you imagine how your life might be different if you could really grasp the bigness of God?

Daniel lived in a chaotic world. In chapter 1, we saw that under King Nebuchadnezzar, Babylon conquered Judah just after the historic Battle of Carchemish in 605 BC. Daniel and three friends had gone through a top-gun executive training program to serve in the Babylonian government where they were foreigners.

Can you imagine how discouraging it must have been to the Jewish people to be defeated and deported? Where was God? Was he for real? How did this horrible situation make any sense? The book of Daniel brings encouragement and hope not merely through seeing the example of Daniel for whom the book is named, but even more important, through encountering The Big God in Daniel's story. When we dig deep into the book, we will see that the hero is not Daniel, but that the hero is God.

As we walk through the story, I encourage you to identify with each character. What would it have been like to be Daniel? What about one of Nebuchadnezzar's advisors? What would it have been like to be Nebuchadnezzar? Look through the eyes of each person. If you have ever had trouble sleeping, then you can identify with Nebuchadnezzar.

We will experience chapter 2 a section at a time, starting with the first 13 verses that set up the escalating conflict between the king and his advisors. Look for the different kinds of chaos experienced by the furious king and by his frustrated advisors.

Daniel 2:1–13

In the second year of his reign,
Nebuchadnezzar had dreams; his mind was troubled
and he could not sleep. ²So the king summoned the
magicians, enchanters, sorcerers and astrologers to
tell him what he had dreamed. When they came in
and stood before the king, ³he said to them, "I have
had a dream that troubles me and I want to know
what it means."
    ⁴Then the astrologers answered the king, "May
the king live forever! Tell your servants the dream,
and we will interpret it."

5The king replied to the astrologers, "This is what I have firmly decided: If you do not tell me what my dream was and interpret it, I will have you cut into pieces and your houses turned into piles of rubble. 6But if you tell me the dream and explain it, you will receive from me gifts and rewards and great honor. So tell me the dream and interpret it for me."

7Once more they replied, "Let the king tell his servants the dream, and we will interpret it."

8Then the king answered, "I am certain that you are trying to gain time, because you realize that this is what I have firmly decided: 9If you do not tell me the dream, there is only one penalty for you. You have conspired to tell me misleading and wicked things, hoping the situation will change. So then, tell me the dream, and I will know that you can interpret it for me."

10The astrologers answered the king, "There is no one on earth who can do what the king asks! No king, however great and mighty, has ever asked such a thing of any magician or enchanter or astrologer. 11What the king asks is too difficult. No one can reveal it to the king except the gods, and they do not live among humans."

12This made the king so angry and furious that he ordered the execution of all the wise men of Babylon. 13So the decree was issued to put the wise men to death, and men were sent to look for Daniel and his friends to put them to death.

Nebuchadnezzar's response

Put yourself in Nebuchadnezzar's shoes. What was his chaos—scary nightmares, impotent religion and manipulative advisors? Have you ever awakened terribly troubled by a dream and you couldn't remember what it was? Because you had such an uneasy feeling, you really did not want to remember it. But, you wondered if your dream was telling you something.

Nebuchadnezzar's heart was pounding. He called in all his advisors: the magicians, enchanters, sorcerers and astrologers. These would be like consultants and psychologists today. They were highly educated. They were the gurus of that day. Some were even involved in black arts to interpret omens.

Dream interpretation was common back then. The language of the day was Akkadian, usually written on clay tablets. We have many ancient Akkadian dream manuals that have survived and we have similar modern manuals today. I pulled out my silicon tablet (iPad) and searched the Internet for "dream interpretation" where I found many online dream interpretation guides including *The Dream Bible*, none of which I endorse.

King Nebuchadnezzar was one smart guy. He was rightfully suspicious of these dream manuals, so he told the advisors he had firmly decided that they would tell him the dream and the interpretation. He was testing them. He remembered enough of his dream to know if they were telling the truth. He used this kind of power to motivate. "If you do not tell me what my dream was and interpret it, I will have you cut into pieces and your houses turned into piles of rubble" (Daniel 2:5b). It was not always great to serve in the royal court.

The advisors asked one more time, perhaps hoping they heard him wrong or that he was just overstating. But Nebuchadnezzar's next reply made it crystal clear. He did not stutter. He accused them of trying to buy time and conspiring to mislead him. He questioned if all previous dream interpretations were a sham. Maybe these enchanters and sorcerers were fake. Their final reply did not help matters. They said, "There is no one on earth who can do what the king asks!" (Daniel 2:10b). The king had confirmed that these guys were a joke. They did not have the power they claimed.

Maybe you have had the terrible experience of realizing that something you had believed was false. You counted on it. You thought it was solid, real, but it has proven to be fake, a lie or a joke. It does not hold water. This can be as simple as a financial retirement plan for your 401(k) that you counted on but has proven foolish, to something much deeper. You may have trusted in a religion you now know to be false, such as Mormonism.

The king went from angry to furious. He ordered the execution of all the wise men of Babylon. While Nebuchadnezzar was a great king, self-control does not appear to have been his strength. To be fair, most of us have been irrationally angry a few times in our lives and have made absolute decrees we later regretted.

Magicians' response

Now put yourself in the shoes of the magicians, enchanters, sorcerers and astrologers. Look through their eyes. What if you were one of these guys? What was their chaos? It kept getting worse: from an impossible demand, to angry threats, to certain death.

Have you ever been issued an impossible demand from your boss, your teacher or coach? It is incredibly frustrating. Then have you ever tried to explain to them that what they were asking was impossible, only to be met with angry threats? If you didn't win that game, if you didn't solve that problem, make that sale, analyze that data, you would be fired, demoted, kicked off the team. Has it ever gone to the next place—certain death? The order was given. They said, "You are fired." The doctor said, "It is terminal." The divorce papers were served or you got the foreclosure notice. How do you respond when the chaos gets this insane? Daniel tells us how.

He and his three friends were facing the same chaos as the other wise men of Babylon, but their response was very different because they knew The Big God. Daniel responded in faith as we see in the next few verses.

Daniel 2:14–23

When Arioch, the commander of the king's guard, had gone out to put to death the wise men of Babylon, Daniel spoke to him with wisdom and tact. [15]He asked the king's officer, "Why did the king issue such a harsh decree?" Arioch then explained the matter to Daniel. [16]At this, Daniel went in to the king and asked for time, so that he might interpret the dream for him.

[17]Then Daniel returned to his house and explained the matter to his friends Hananiah, Mishael and Azariah. [18]He urged them to plead for mercy from the God of heaven concerning this mystery, so that he and his friends might not be executed with the rest of the wise men of Babylon. [19]During the night the mystery was revealed to Daniel in a vision. Then Daniel praised the God of heaven [20]and said:

"Praise be to the name of God for ever and ever;
*   wisdom and power are his.*
[21]He changes times and seasons;
*   he deposes kings and raises up others.*
He gives wisdom to the wise
*   and knowledge to the discerning.*
[22]He reveals deep and hidden things;
*   he knows what lies in darkness,*
*   and light dwells with him.*
[23]I thank and praise you, God of my ancestors:
*   You have given me wisdom and power,*
you have made known to me what we asked of you,
*   you have made known to us the dream of the king."*

Daniel's response

Contrast Daniel's response with the magicians, enchanters, sorcerers and astrologists. Daniel did not freak out. He tactfully sought to understand, prayed to God with his friends and then praised God. Daniel's calmness and confidence is amazing, especially for a very young man, at this time probably 17 to 21 years old. Let's walk through Daniel's three steps:

1. He tactfully sought to understand

He showed no panic or despair. Daniel 2:14 says he spoke with wisdom and tact. Rather than arguing or begging, he first sought to understand. He asked why the king issued such a harsh demand. Then he asked for time, not to stall, but to interpret the dream. Once again, we see great faith on Daniel's part. He knew he served a Big God. So his next step was to pray to God with his friends.

2. He prayed with his friends

In the chaos of our lives, we must pray. It is powerful to pray with friends. This is one of the values of small groups in churches. We can pray together for whatever we are facing in our lives. In response to their prayers, God answered. He gave Daniel the dream and its interpretation. Then what did Daniel do?

3. He praised God

We can so easily forget to thank God when he answers. Daniel did not forget. Daniel 2:22–23 are awesome. Daniel praised the God of heaven. Wisdom and power are his; above any other force, god or source of wisdom. Hear the contrast with the other advisors and their gods. The God is in charge of time and history and kings and empires. We can trust this Big God. He is the revealer of mysteries and deep things. Only God can reveal to you what life is really all about. In response to prayer, he gives wisdom and power, then and now. It might look like the king or the boss has all the power and that his decree is final, but it is not. God has the power. Daniel's amazing praise poem worships God for truths about him that we will also see revealed in the dream and its interpretation. In the next section, we see the resolution.

The resolution: the dream and its interpretation

The action resumed as Daniel and Arioch came before the king. Who would get the credit?

Daniel 2:24–30

Then Daniel went to Arioch, whom the king had appointed to execute the wise men of Babylon, and said to him, "Do not execute the wise men of Babylon. Take me to the king, and I will interpret his dream for him."
²⁵Arioch took Daniel to the king at once and said, "I have found a man among the exiles from Judah who can tell the king what his dream means."
²⁶The king asked Daniel (also called Belteshazzar), "Are you able to tell me what I saw in my dream and interpret it?"
²⁷Daniel replied, "No wise man, enchanter, magician or diviner can explain to the king the mystery he has asked about, ²⁸but there is a God in heaven who reveals mysteries. He has shown King Nebuchadnezzar what will happen in days to come.

Your dream and the visions that passed through your
mind as you were lying in bed are these:
[29]"As Your Majesty was lying there, your mind
turned to things to come, and the revealer of
mysteries showed you what is going to happen. [30]As
for me, this mystery has been revealed to me, not
because I have greater wisdom than anyone else
alive, but so that Your Majesty may know the
interpretation and that you may understand what
went through your mind."

Boldly Daniel contacted Arioch, the chief executioner, probably a large and scary man. Arioch took Daniel to the king and took credit for finding Daniel. When the king asked Daniel: "Are you able to tell me what I saw in my dream and interpret it?" (2:26), Daniel did not say yes. Rather, he wisely protected the other wise men and agreed with them that no man could reveal this mystery. Then I love Daniel 2:28: "But there is a God in heaven who reveals mysteries."

Here is a central theme of the Bible: God is Big and he reveals truth. Although circumstances sometimes look impossible from an earthly standpoint, there is a God in heaven who can do all things. He can solve seemingly unsolvable problems and provide strength for impossible tasks. **God solves** He is The Big God. In a respectful manner, Daniel **problems** was actually telling the king that the religions of Babylon were not worshipping the real God. What follows is one of the most amazing prophecies in the Bible—the prophecy of the statue and the rock. We finally see the dream and its interpretation revealed.

Daniel 2:31–45

Your Majesty looked, and there before you
stood a large statue—an enormous, dazzling statue,
awesome in appearance. [32]The head of the statue was

23

made of pure gold, its chest and arms of silver, its belly and thighs of bronze, [33]its legs of iron, its feet partly of iron and partly of baked clay. [34]While you were watching, a rock was cut out, but not by human hands. It struck the statue on its feet of iron and clay and smashed them. [35]Then the iron, the clay, the bronze, the silver and the gold were all broken to pieces and became like chaff on a threshing floor in the summer. The wind swept them away without leaving a trace. But the rock that struck the statue became a huge mountain and filled the whole earth.

[36]This was the dream, and now we will interpret it to the king. [37]Your Majesty, you are the king of kings. The God of heaven has given you dominion and power and might and glory; [38]in your hands he has placed all mankind and the beasts of the field and the birds in the sky. Wherever they live, he has made you ruler over them all. You are that head of gold.

[39]After you, another kingdom will arise, inferior to yours. Next, a third kingdom, one of bronze, will rule over the whole earth. [40]Finally, there will be a fourth kingdom, strong as iron—for iron breaks and smashes everything—and as iron breaks things to pieces, so it will crush and break all the others. [41]Just as you saw that the feet and toes were partly of baked clay and partly of iron, so this will be a divided kingdom; yet it will have some of the strength of iron in it, even as you saw iron mixed with clay. [42]As the toes were partly iron and partly clay, so this kingdom will be partly strong and partly brittle. [43]And just as you saw the iron mixed with baked clay, so the people will be a mixture and will not remain united, any more than iron mixes with clay.

[44]In the time of those kings, the God of heaven will set up a kingdom that will never be destroyed, nor will it be left to another people. It will crush all those kingdoms and bring them to an end, but it will

itself endure forever. ⁴⁵*This is the meaning of the*
vision of the rock cut out of a mountain, but not by
human hands—a rock that broke the iron, the
bronze, the clay, the silver and the gold to pieces.
    The great God has shown the king what will
take place in the future. The dream is true and its
interpretation is trustworthy.

The giant statue depicted four kingdoms of decreasingly valued metals; all were smashed by a massive rock cut without hands which grew to be a global, eternal kingdom. Now let's look a little closer. Daniel told Nebuchadnezzar that the king's power had been given to him by the God of heaven. He and the Babylonian Empire were the head of gold. Babylon was the world power of its day.

Babylon was then destroyed by the Medo-Persian Empire led by Cyrus the Great (539–331 BC); the two arms suggest the twofold division of Media and Persia. In 332 BC, the armies of Alexander the Great defeated the Medo-Persian Empire in a series of decisive battles. The Greek Empire ruled the world from 331–146 BC. Finally, "the Roman Empire dominated the world from the defeat of Carthage in 146 B.C. to the division of the East and West empires in 395 B.C."[8] This prophecy is so accurate that those who doubt the Bible have insisted that Daniel could not have been written in the sixth century BC. It must have been written much later. But in light of historical and archaeological evidence, that view does not hold water. The amazingly accurate prophecy shows the divine nature of the Bible.

The visions in the book of Daniel may well be one of the greatest proofs of the divine inspiration of the Bible. In chapter 2 and several other chapters, Daniel mapped out the rise and fall of world kingdoms so remarkably that you would think you were reading a history book and not a book of prophecy!

At least three independent sources authenticate that the book of Daniel was written well before the birth of Christ. Flavius

Josephus, court historian for three successive Roman emperors, recorded Alexander the Great receiving a copy of Daniel upon his annexation of Jerusalem in the autumn of 332 BC, immediately following his conquest of Tyre.

When the Septuagint (LXX) was translated from Hebrew into Greek in the third century BC, Daniel was included. Daniel was also included in the Dead Sea Scrolls dating around 200 BC. There is absolutely no way that Daniel could have been written "after the fact." He did indeed see what God saw—the future.

Now what about the feet? This was the only part of the statue that was mixed, iron and clay. This mixed part may have looked to a future kingdom or a loose federation of nations with some connection to ancient Rome. It's amazing how many English expressions come from the Bible. Our expression "feet of clay" comes from Daniel 2.

What is more significant is the rock. "Several features of the rock would have impressed Nebuchadnezzar, (1) Its origin was supernatural . . . (2) The rock had extraordinary power" and "(3) Its scope was worldwide."[9]

Babylon would not rule forever, nor would any other human kingdom. Our confidence is that God will come and rule the world in an eternal kingdom. In spite of current chaos, God is coming. The Rock will come and rule the world. From the rest of Scripture, we know that this Rock is none other than the Messiah, Jesus Christ, the King of Kings. The book of 1 Peter quoted the prophet Isaiah when he wrote:

> *For in Scripture it says:*
> *"See, I lay a stone in Zion,*
> *a chosen and precious cornerstone,*
> *and the one who trusts in him*
> *will never be put to shame."*
> *Now to you who believe, this stone is*
> *precious. But to those who do not believe,*
> *"The stone the builders rejected*

> *has become the cornerstone,"*
> *and,*
> *"A stone that causes people to stumble*
> *and a rock that makes them fall."*
> *They stumble because they disobey the*
> *message—which is also what they were*
> *destined for* (1 Peter 2:6–8).

Jesus Christ is the Rock. You can trust in him as the foundation of your life or you can fall over him. What did Nebuchadnezzar do? His response in Daniel 2:46 is remarkable.

Nebuchadnezzar responded in faith

Picture the scene with the Jewish young man, Daniel, who was taken captive standing in the royal court of the most powerful man on earth.

Daniel 2:46–47

> *Then King Nebuchadnezzar fell prostrate*
> *before Daniel and paid him honor and ordered that*
> *an offering and incense be presented to him. ⁴⁷The*
> *king said to Daniel, "Surely your God is the God of*
> *gods and the Lord of kings and a revealer of*
> *mysteries, for you were able to reveal this mystery."*

King Nebuchadnezzar fell down before Daniel and ordered offering and incense. Then he made an amazing declaration: "Surely your God is the God of gods and the Lord of kings and a revealer of mysteries" (2:47). He learned that God is bigger than all the chaos because he is The God of gods, the Lord of kings and the revealer of mysteries. His advisors apparently did not get it. We hear nothing from them. But in that moment, Nebuchadnezzar realized that God was bigger than his chaos.

God is bigger than scary nightmares, impotent religions and manipulative advisors. The point for each of us is to trust God because he is bigger than our chaos. For Nebuchadnezzar, this was a first-time experience. For Daniel and his friends, it was growth in learning to trust God more.

In a world of chaos, will you trust in The God who is bigger than all your chaos? Will you turn from trusting in power, religion or anything else to trusting in God alone? We find peace and confidence when we give up our empires and advisors for the true Big God. Jesus said,

> *Now this is eternal life: that they know you, the only true God, and Jesus Christ, whom you have sent* (John 17:3).

If you have never done so, I invite you as Peter did at Pentecost: repent, believe and be baptized. Baptism is a great statement to your family and friends of your choice to believe in Jesus. Just as Nebuchadnezzar symbolized his faith by bringing incense and offerings, baptism is a way of physically expressing the choice in your heart to trust in Jesus Christ as the true King of Kings.

At the end of the story, Daniel was promoted and he did not forget his friends.

Daniel 2:48–49

> *Then the king placed Daniel in a high position and lavished many gifts on him. He made him ruler over the entire province of Babylon and placed him in charge of all its wise men. [49]Moreover, at Daniel's request the king appointed Shadrach, Meshach and Abednego administrators over the province of Babylon, while Daniel himself remained at the royal court.*

God honors those who honor him. We should trust God because he is bigger than our chaos since he is The God of gods, the Lord of kings and the revealer of mysteries, and as we will see, he is also the one who rescues from the fire.

For further study on chapter 2, see the Study Guide beginning on page 185.

3

God Delivers through the Fire

Daniel 3

We are learning just how big our God really is, bigger than all our chaos. We are learning from Daniel that we can trust our Big God to be in control. In Daniel 3, we will see that God is bigger than the fire. Imagine how your life might be different if you could really grasp the bigness of God. What confidence and courage you would have.

What kinds of fires do we face today? Let's get a bit more specific. What pressures do we face to honor other gods? To answer that question, we have to consider what other gods exist today and then what it can look like to honor them. So let's ask both. First what "gods" or "idols" exist today? Idols can be mental as well as metal. You can define a "god" as what is most important to you. Sometimes we make ourselves into little gods. Sex can be a god, as can money, pleasure, success, sports and movie stars. There is even a fairly popular television show called *American Idol.* Anything you place above God in your affections can be an idol.

So, next question, how do we honor our modern-day gods or idols? We spend money on them. We dress like them. We buy symbols to represent them. We go to events, scream, jump up and down, and buy their merchandise.

Let's increase the temperature. We know we have idols today and we can picture a bit of what it looks like to honor them. Now, what are possible consequences of not honoring them? What pressures do we face today that push us to honor other gods? Peer pressure is huge.

When our son, Jimmy, was in high school, we were excited that he was nominated to the homecoming court because neither I nor my wife, Tamara, came anywhere close to the homecoming court; in fact, we had nothing to do with that part of high school, but we were happy for Jimmy. As part of that nomination, he was invited to a float-making party for the homecoming parade, but he did not want to go. Tamara gave him a really hard time because she wanted him to enjoy high school, and she had never been invited to such a party.

It sounded really wholesome to be making parade floats. Jimmy told us that was not what was going to happen at that party. Everyone would be getting drunk. He insisted on not going. Since we had received a notice about the party from the school, Tamara thought this was certainly not the case, so she called. They told her that since it was an off-campus event, they had no idea what would be happening and they also had no control. Jimmy did not go to the party. He was right. Everyone got drunk. What pressure do you imagine Jimmy faced to go to that party? He might have been the only homecoming nominee who did not attend.

What if you resist pressure at work? What if you refuse to wear short shorts and tight shirts? I've talked with ladies who were fired because they refused to dress a certain way. What if you resist pressure to buy everything the neighbors are buying for their children because you want to avoid honoring the god of con-sumerism? What if you resist the digital god with her powers of instant, always-on, always-connected communication and enter-tainment? What pressure do you face not to turn off her devices?

Daniel's friends, Shadrach, Meshach and Abednego, faced incredible pressure to honor a false god and they would face terrible consequences if they refused. It was about 600 years before Christ in the greatest empire of the world, Babylon. Daniel and three friends had been deported to Babylon where they were re-educated and were serving in the Babylonian government. A text has been found listing "more than fifty officials" during Nebuchadnezzar's reign which seems to include the names of these three men with different spellings.[10]

Daniel 3 presents a dramatic conflict, amazing courage and huge faith in the face of dire threats. The story puts us in the position of the three men: What would we do if we were in their situation? Would we stand or would we bow? We will walk through the chapter a section at a time beginning with the order to worship the image in the first seven verses.

Daniel 3:1–7

King Nebuchadnezzar made an image of gold, sixty cubits high and six cubits wide, and set it up on the plain of Dura in the province of Babylon. ²He then summoned the satraps, prefects, governors, advisers, treasurers, judges, magistrates and all the other provincial officials to come to the dedication of the image he had set up. ³So the satraps, prefects, governors, advisers, treasurers, judges, magistrates and all the other provincial officials assembled for the dedication of the image that King Nebuchadnezzar had set up, and they stood before it. ⁴Then the herald loudly proclaimed, "Nations and peoples of every language, this is what you are commanded to do: ⁵As soon as you hear the sound of the horn, flute, zither, lyre, harp, pipe and all kinds of music, you must fall down and worship the image of gold that King Nebuchadnezzar has set up. ⁶Whoever

*does not fall down and worship will immediately be
thrown into a blazing furnace."
   ⁷Therefore, as soon as they heard the sound of
the horn, flute, zither, lyre, harp and all kinds of
music, all the nations and peoples of every language
fell down and worshiped the image of gold that King
Nebuchadnezzar had set up.*

In chapter 2, God gave Nebuchadnezzar a vision of a statue
with a gold head. Perhaps the king distorted that vision into a
desire to create a gold-plated statue to his own honor. The statue
was massive—90 feet, about nine stories high, probably set on a
massive base. In the area where the plain of Dura may have been,
archaeologist Julius Oppert found "a large brick square, forty-five
feet on a side and twenty feet high, which he believes was the
foundation for this very image."[11] Most pictures depict the statue as
being of Nebuchadnezzar and that is possible, but look again at the
text. It never says what the image depicted. It could have been a
statue of a Babylonian god such as Marduk or an image of
Nebuchadnezzar himself. In any case, religion and politics were
united in a huge state affair full of pomp and circumstance.

Where was Daniel? We are not told, possibly he was in
another part of the empire on business or he was ill.

How do people today do what Nebuchadnezzar did with the
image? How do we create images of our idols? What about
trophies? Could a certain house or a car become a symbol that
honors the god of consumerism, success or excess? Could certain
clothes honor a designer, or the god of popularity, the god of
beauty or the god of fashion or the seductive god of self? How do
we draw attention to ourselves and get people to see how great we
are? Here is the heart of much sin. We want praise for ourselves. In
many subtle ways, we want people to think well of us.

I get frustrated with myself around the house. I'll do
something simple such as taking out the trash and I mention it to
Tamara so she will know what an awesome husband I am. "Hey, did

you notice, I changed the light bulbs. That was me. And I swept off the porch. That was me. I did that." I can be such a little boy. "Look I trimmed the trees. Did you notice? Don't they look good? I mean that was probably as good, or better, than a professional, right?" Affirm me. Tell me I am great. We too build our statues, our images that draw attention to us and invite people to honor us.

The two repeated lists of kinds of officials who were present and the kinds of musical instruments used heightened the tension as it signaled the importance of the ceremonies. Probably this was the royal orchestra decked out in colorful, elaborate costumes. This was like the swearing-in ceremony for the president or the opening of the Olympics. It was a really big deal, a spectacle. Music was a big part of it. In most cultures, music draws attention to religious and political ceremonies and to worship.

In our time, where do you see music connected with honoring gods of our day? How about music and sexuality? People usually do not have parties without music. Every parade, convention and huge event has music. Politicians recruit famous bands to play at their events. At musical concerts, people throw themselves at their idols, the stars of the day. Religions use music from chanting to organs. Music itself is neither positive nor negative. The issue is, what god are you worshipping? What idol is your music honoring—the god of revenge, pleasure, racism, greed or love?

Apparently, near the amazing royal orchestra was a massive blazing furnace. We don't usually have furnaces at the opening of the Olympics, just a burning torch. Nebuchadnezzar used his power to coerce; many dictators have done that. He said, when you hear the music, bow down and worship or I will throw you into a blazing furnace. Hitler was not the first one to burn people. Likely this furnace was a massive kiln that had been used to smelt metal for gold plating and perhaps to fire the bricks used to build the base for the statue. We know it was big enough for four people to walk around in. Honor the idol or die in the fire. That's pressure. But it got worse. In the next section, we see the accusation and the rage.

Daniel 3:8–15

*At this time some astrologers came forward
and denounced the Jews. ⁹They said to King
Nebuchadnezzar, "May the king live forever! ¹⁰Your
Majesty has issued a decree that everyone who hears
the sound of the horn, flute, zither, lyre, harp, pipe
and all kinds of music must fall down and worship the
image of gold, ¹¹and that whoever does not fall down
and worship will be thrown into a blazing furnace.
¹²But there are some Jews whom you have set over
the affairs of the province of Babylon—Shadrach,
Meshach and Abednego—who pay no attention to
you, Your Majesty. They neither serve your gods nor
worship the image of gold you have set up."*

*¹³Furious with rage, Nebuchadnezzar
summoned Shadrach, Meshach and Abednego. So
these men were brought before the king, ¹⁴and
Nebuchadnezzar said to them, "Is it true, Shadrach,
Meshach and Abednego, that you do not serve my
gods or worship the image of gold I have set up?
¹⁵Now when you hear the sound of the horn, flute,
zither, lyre, harp, pipe and all kinds of music, if you
are ready to fall down and worship the image I made,
very good. But if you do not worship it, you will be
thrown immediately into a blazing furnace. Then
what god will be able to rescue you from my hand?"*

If the astrologers had not accused them, then the three guys
might have just gone on with their day without a problem. I
imagine it was a massive event spread out over a huge area. The
fact that they did not bow might have been missed. But, the
astrologers really didn't like Shadrach, Meshach and Abednego.
Notice their language: "There are some Jews" (3:12). They addressed them racially, not by their titles or names. Have you ever
had someone address you by your race—"There are some white
guys over there; some black men; some Asians"? Then they said to

the king, the men "whom you have set over the affairs of the province of Babylon . . . pay no attention to you" (3:12). These guys were jealous. Maybe the three guys were promoted over them or had a higher salary or a better office. Have you ever had someone in your workplace be jealous of you and then try to undermine you? That hurts.

The word "denounced" in 3:8 literally means to "eat the pieces of." They ripped apart Shadrach, Meshach and Abednego. Then they exaggerated by accusing the guys of not paying any attention to Nebuchadnezzar. Where did that come from? The truth is they did not bow to the statue when the music played, but the accusation was much more than that. Have you ever had that happen to you? People exaggerated against you or just made up stuff on top of a little bit of truth.

The accusers appealed to Nebuchadnezzar's vanity and it worked. He was furious with rage. He could not believe they would not bow so he gave them one more chance. His own pride was attacked and he was embarrassed because the accusers had made it a public issue. Nebuchadnezzar ended his speech with a challenge: "Then what god will be able to rescue you from my hand?" (3:15). We have our versions of this challenge today: "Your soul may belong to God, but...." People obsessed with power want to believe that they can control you.

Nebuchadnezzar was about to learn the surprise answer to what he thought was an angry rhetorical retort. The next section is the turning point of the story as we see the three guys respond to the king and make an amazing faith-filled courageous stand.

Daniel 3:16–24

*Shadrach, Meshach and Abednego replied to
him, "King Nebuchadnezzar, we do not need to
defend ourselves before you in this matter. [17]If we are
thrown into the blazing furnace, the God we serve is
able to deliver us from it, and he will deliver us from*

> *Your Majesty's hand. ¹⁸But even if he does not, we want you to know, Your Majesty, that we will not serve your gods or worship the image of gold you have set up."*
>
> *¹⁹Then Nebuchadnezzar was furious with Shadrach, Meshach and Abednego, and his attitude toward them changed. He ordered the furnace heated seven times hotter than usual ²⁰and commanded some of the strongest soldiers in his army to tie up Shadrach, Meshach and Abednego and throw them into the blazing furnace. ²¹So these men, wearing their robes, trousers, turbans and other clothes, were bound and thrown into the blazing furnace. ²²The king's command was so urgent and the furnace so hot that the flames of the fire killed the soldiers who took up Shadrach, Meshach and Abednego, ²³and these three men, firmly tied, fell into the blazing furnace.*
>
> *²⁴Then King Nebuchadnezzar leaped to his feet in amazement and asked his advisers, "Weren't there three men that we tied up and threw into the fire?"*
>
> *They replied, "Certainly, Your Majesty."*

We are not told if any others resisted honoring the image. These three may have stood alone. That is hard. It would have been so much easier just to rationalize and bow down with everyone else. Imagine the kinds of pressure they faced. Their leader, Daniel, was not there. It's harder when your spiritual leader is not present. They were in the vast minority. Everyone else was doing it. Obviously they were facing a horrifying punishment. They were also killing any career advancement. It looked like their jealous accusers were getting what they wanted.

Notice their first response to the king. They did not defend themselves. It's hard not to get defensive when you are accused, especially falsely. Then they made their famous amazing declaration in 3:17. Can you imagine saying this?

Daniel 3:17–18

If we are thrown into the blazing furnace, the
God we serve is able to deliver us from it, and he will
deliver us from Your Majesty's hand. ¹⁸But even if he
does not, we want you to know, Your Majesty, that we
will not serve your gods or worship the image of gold
you have set up.

They resisted honoring the idol because they knew God was able to deliver them, because they knew he would ultimately deliver them; and because they knew that even if he chose not to deliver them from this particular fire, God is The God, therefore they would not serve any other god or honor the image of gold. Period. This is a deep place to get to in our devotion to God—to get to the place where we trust and honor God whether he protects us or not. Our honor of him is not dependent on what he does for us. These three guys knew that God is The Big God. He is bigger than the fire so they would not bow down.

God is trustworthy

The threat of idolatry today is often more subtle and thus potentially more seductive. Will you refuse to honor the gods of power, materialism, sex, pleasure, sports or money? If your boss demands you to work on Sunday, what will you do? If your team is taking the client to a gentlemen's club, what will you do? If everyone else in the office is wearing designer clothes; if the other parents are buying their children the popular toys; if everyone else is seeing the latest movie or the show, will you too honor that god by watching their show or wearing their clothes? I am not really talking about external actions alone; God is driving to our hearts. What we do with our money and our time expresses what we worship. For one person, watching the latest movie or wearing designer clothing may mean something different than it does for

39

another person. In our community, some people worship sports by putting playing or watching them above church and family.

Are you willing to courageously stand when the entire crowd is bowing down? Will you refuse to honor other gods? Will you honor God whether he delivers you from the furnace or not? For Shadrach, Meshach and Abednego, they worshipped and obeyed God because he is The Big God, not because of what he would do for them. While God does honor those who honor him, we must resist the distortion of truth that says if you obey God, you will always be rescued from the fire, you will get the job, earn more money, be healed and everything will go great for you. This is not true on earth, however this is true in eternity. We can stand courageously, refusing to honor other gods because God can deliver us, will ultimately deliver us and the bottom line is, he is The God.

God is The God

At this point, Nebuchadnezzar totally lost it. He went ballistic. The text says his attitude changed which means his face got red and his eyes flashed with fire. He became irrationally angry, ordering the fire as hot as they could make it and getting the strongest soldiers to throw the fully clothed guys into the fire. His order to make the fire as hot as they could cost him some good soldiers who were burned up as they came close to the furnace in their haste to obey angry orders. The next section brings the amazing divine rescue. Nebuchadnezzar shifted from furious rage to utter amazement.

Daniel 3:25–30

He said, "Look! I see four men walking around in the fire, unbound and unharmed, and the fourth looks like a son of the gods."
26Nebuchadnezzar then approached the opening of the blazing furnace and shouted,

"Shadrach, Meshach and Abednego, servants of the Most High God, come out! Come here!"

So Shadrach, Meshach and Abednego came out of the fire, ²⁷and the satraps, prefects, governors and royal advisers crowded around them. They saw that the fire had not harmed their bodies, nor was a hair of their heads singed; their robes were not scorched, and there was no smell of fire on them.

²⁸Then Nebuchadnezzar said, "Praise be to the God of Shadrach, Meshach and Abednego, who has sent his angel and rescued his servants! They trusted in him and defied the king's command and were willing to give up their lives rather than serve or worship any god except their own God. ²⁹Therefore I decree that the people of any nation or language who say anything against the God of Shadrach, Meshach and Abednego be cut into pieces and their houses be turned into piles of rubble, for no other god can save in this way."

³⁰Then the king promoted Shadrach, Meshach and Abednego in the province of Babylon.

Rather than delivering the three *from* the fire, God delivered them *through* the fire. In our own lives, sometimes God does not stop us from being thrown into the fire, but he joins us in the fire and protects us right in the furnace. Often God does not deliver us from the fire, but through the fire.

This huge group, which Nebuchadnezzar assembled to witness his greatness symbolized by his statue, were treated to being witnesses of The Big God's greatness. God is bigger than the fire. We would prefer not to be thrown in the fire, but that is often where God does his greatest work. He forms our character, shows us he can be trusted and shows everyone watching that he is greater than the fire. The prophet Isaiah said:

When you walk through the fire, you will not be burned; the flames will not set you ablaze. For I am the LORD *your God, the Holy One of Israel, your Savior* (Isaiah 43:2–3).

God came to be with his people in the fire. This is his way. The fourth person was either an angel or the pre-incarnate Christ. But in any case, the point is that God was present with them in the fire. God is with us in every fire in our lives. No matter what you are going through right now, no matter how hot the fire, God is with you.

God is with us

When you face fires, sometimes God delivers you from the fire thus building your faith, other times God delivers you through the fire thus refining your faith and sometimes God delivers you by the fire into his arms, thus perfecting your faith.[12] God can and will rescue you from any and every fire because God is bigger than the fire.

This amazing divine rescue led to the new declaration and decree in the conclusion of the story.

Daniel 3:28–30

Then Nebuchadnezzar said, "Praise be to the God of Shadrach, Meshach and Abednego, who has sent his angel and rescued his servants! They trusted in him and defied the king's command and were willing to give up their lives rather than serve or worship any god except their own God. [29]Therefore I decree that the people of any nation or language who say anything against the God of Shadrach, Meshach and Abednego be cut into pieces and their houses be turned into piles of rubble, for no other god can save in this way."
[30]Then the king promoted Shadrach, Meshach and Abednego in the province of Babylon.

The king, who commanded all to honor the statue, then commanded all to honor the God of Shadrach, Meshach and Abednego.

These three guys faced a rough situation. They were denounced by their peers, interrogated by the king and then thrown into the fire. But The Big God gave them courage, delivered them and promoted them.

The arrogant king was humbled and the faithful Jews were exalted. They made a huge impression on the king. Imagine your boss or CEO saying about you, "Bob, Mary and Jose' trusted in God and defied my orders and were willing to give up their lives rather than honor any god except their own God." People may not share your faith, but they often respect people with the courage to take a stand for their God.

So, what is God saying to us in this chapter? Courageously refuse to honor other gods even against a direct command, even if it costs your life, because The Big God is able to deliver you, because The Big God will deliver you and because God is The God Most High.

When situations seem utterly hopeless, you can trust God to vindicate you and to rescue you one way or the other. Courageously refuse to honor other gods even at great cost because God is bigger than the fire.

For further study on chapter 3, see the Study Guide beginning on page 197.

4

God Humbles the Proud

Daniel 4

Are you super humble? I mean really humble. We want to applaud all the super humble people. Ridiculous, right? Seriously, I hate pride because it keeps sneaking back into my heart. All my life I have struggled with pride. Of course, I know not all pride is sinful. Mom told me to be proud of my first crayon artworks, as sad as they were.

There is something healthy about satisfaction in doing well. But most of the time, the serpent of pride whispers that we are great. We think we deserve more credit. In fact, more people should recognize what we have done. Our families sure don't give us the recognition we deserve for what we do around the house nor do the people at work give us enough credit for our accomplishments.

How can we grow in humility? The point, of course, is not to aim for low self-esteem, to talk about what pathetic worms we are. Rather the key to humility is not found in who we are at all. The secret to humility is found in who God is. A proper view of us comes from a proper view of God. When you can see how Big God is, then you can see yourself and discover humility. In this chapter, we will see how God is bigger than the chaos in our own souls, the pride that distorts our hearts and twists our minds.

To different degrees, we all view ourselves at the center of the universe. As a little child, the entire world revolves around us. Some of us have grown a bit beyond that, but we still think we are pretty important. Children are so proud of their sandcastles, dollhouses and tree forts that they build and so proud of their school awards. We grown-up children are proud of our beautiful homes, our awards at work and accomplishments in our circles.

In my own little circle, I have been proud of early success. In 1989, at 28 years old I was the youngest professor at Dallas Theological Seminary, and I looked really young. In the first session of every class, a brave student would raise his hand and ask, "How old are you?!" The question both irritated me and fed my pride.

In suburban America, many of us live in brick houses or apartments, drive nice cars and buy whatever we want at the grocery store. It is easy to ignore God. We are managing life on our own. We are making it. We work hard and provide for our families, and we are proud of it. What will it take for us to recognize that God is really big so we can become more humble?

God helps us in Daniel 4. Daniel lived in a chaotic world. He served as a foreigner in the Babylonian government under the great King Nebuchadnezzar. After several decades, I imagine that the Jews could have wondered if God was really in charge. He was, as he proved once again. By this time, Daniel was probably 50 years old, having served for 30 years in Babylon.

Daniel 4 is utterly unique in the Bible. Remarkably, it is written in the first person by King Nebuchadnezzar as his confession. It is the only chapter in the Bible written by a pagan king. The chapter begins and ends with doxologies of praise to God by Nebuchadnezzar. The opening stirs our curiosity to wonder how

King Nebuchadnezzar got to this point in his heart. He had experienced a conversion, a major leap forward with God. And the story of how he got there is not pretty. He looked like an idiot in the story, and yet he told it. Are you willing to tell the story of your life in which you look pretty foolish, but God is clearly big?

As we unpack the story scene by scene, consider what God is saying to you. In speaking of the Old Testament, Paul said in the New Testament:

> *Now these things occurred as examples to keep*
> *us from setting our hearts on evil things as they did*
> (1 Corinthians 10:6).

The point from this story is to renounce prideful sin and acknowledge The Big God because he rules eternally over all kingdoms and humbles the proud. This point is clearly stated three times, in verses 17, 25 and 32. Let's start our amazing story with the introduction in which we hear that the Most High God is Big! Nebuchadnezzar made an official address to all the empire.

Daniel 4:1–3

> *King Nebuchadnezzar,*
> *To the nations and peoples of every language,*
> *who live in all the earth:*
> *May you prosper greatly!*
> *² It is my pleasure to tell you about the miraculous*
> *signs and wonders that the Most High God has*
> *performed for me.*
> *³ How great are his signs,*
> *how mighty his wonders!*
> *His kingdom is an eternal kingdom;*
> *his dominion endures from generation to*
> *generation.*

Notice that this is a proclamation to everyone in the whole earth. The Babylonian kings thought of themselves as ruling the known world.

Since Nebuchadnezzar is a mouthful of a name, we are going to nickname him, "Neb." In 4:2, Neb said it is "his pleasure" to tell this story. It is such a joy to tell stories of the great wonders God does in our lives. I never get tired of hearing the stories of what God has done. At our last men's retreat, so many guys shared what God did in their lives that the time which was scheduled for one hour went for nearly two hours. We need to tell more stories of our Big God, even when we look dumb in the story. Neb's story was about another dream, a terrifying dream.

Daniel 4:4–18

I, Nebuchadnezzar, was at home in my palace, contented and prosperous. ⁵I had a dream that made me afraid. As I was lying in bed, the images and visions that passed through my mind terrified me. ⁶So I commanded that all the wise men of Babylon be brought before me to interpret the dream for me. ⁷When the magicians, enchanters, astrologers and diviners came, I told them the dream, but they could not interpret it for me. ⁸Finally, Daniel came into my presence and I told him the dream. (He is called Belteshazzar, after the name of my god, and the spirit of the holy gods is in him.)

⁹I said, "Belteshazzar, chief of the magicians, I know that the spirit of the holy gods is in you, and no mystery is too difficult for you. Here is my dream; interpret it for me. ¹⁰These are the visions I saw while lying in bed: I looked, and there before me stood a tree in the middle of the land. Its height was enormous. ¹¹The tree grew large and strong and its top touched the sky; it was visible to the ends of the earth. ¹²Its leaves were beautiful, its fruit abundant, and on it was food for all. Under it the wild animals found shelter, and the birds lived in its branches; from it every creature was fed.

¹³"In the visions I saw while lying in bed, I looked, and there before me was a holy one, a messenger, coming down from heaven. ¹⁴He called in a loud voice: 'Cut down the tree and trim off its branches; strip off its leaves and scatter its fruit. Let the animals flee from under it and the birds from its branches. ¹⁵But let the stump and its roots, bound with iron and bronze, remain in the ground, in the grass of the field.

"'Let him be drenched with the dew of heaven, and let him live with the animals among the plants of the earth. ¹⁶Let his mind be changed from that of a man and let him be given the mind of an animal, till seven times pass by for him.

¹⁷"'The decision is announced by messengers, the holy ones declare the verdict, so that the living may know that the Most High is sovereign over all kingdoms on earth and gives them to anyone he wishes and sets over them the lowliest of people.'

¹⁸"This is the dream that I, King Nebuchadnezzar, had. Now, Belteshazzar, tell me what it means, for none of the wise men in my kingdom can interpret it for me. But you can, because the spirit of the holy gods is in you."

Look back at 4:4. How was Neb feeling—"contented and prosperous"? Imagine he is living in the suburbs, his children swimming in the community pool, bills are paid, working out at the fitness center; all is well. He is living in a better place than his parents had. He is in great danger and does not know it.

Then he had a dream that scared him to death. He was terrified. At first, none of the other wise men could interpret it or they didn't want to tell the king what it likely meant. Then Daniel walked in, also called Belteshazzar which was his Babylonian name.

Notice Neb knew that Daniel had "the spirit of the holy gods" (4:18). He knew there was something special about Daniel, something spiritual, even supernatural. Do people know that about you? Do they sense something different about you, something spiritual? Do they ask you to pray for them? Or to help them with issues in their lives that scare them?

In Neb's nightmare, a holy one, a messenger, came from heaven and gave an announcement in a loud voice that the tree would be cut down. The word for messenger means "to watch." These are supernatural watchmen. There is an unseen, supernatural, spiritual world. Angels are watching us.

Pay attention to 4:17 because it expresses the theme of the chapter:

Daniel 4:17b

So that the living may know that the Most
High is sovereign over all kingdoms on earth and
gives them to anyone he wishes.

This line is repeated in verses 25 and 32. We must come to know that the Most High is sovereign. The original word—"sovereign"—means to have authority, rule or power over. We must come to know that The Big God rules over all kingdoms and gives authority to anyone he wishes. Neb lost sight of who was really the King.

Notice one more detail in 4:17. This verdict was not just for Neb, but "so that the living may know." God is always concerned about more than just us. The world did not revolve around Neb and it does not revolve around me or you. God works in us not just for our sake, but for the sake of others as well. He wants all the living to know who he is.

Daniel was in the delicate spot of giving the king the alarming interpretation of the terrifying dream.

Daniel 4:19–27

Then Daniel (also called Belteshazzar) was greatly perplexed for a time, and his thoughts terrified him. So the king said, "Belteshazzar, do not let the dream or its meaning alarm you."

Belteshazzar answered, "My lord, if only the dream applied to your enemies and its meaning to your adversaries! ²⁰The tree you saw, which grew large and strong, with its top touching the sky, visible to the whole earth, ²¹with beautiful leaves and abundant fruit, providing food for all, giving shelter to the wild animals, and having nesting places in its branches for the birds—²²Your Majesty, you are that tree! You have become great and strong; your greatness has grown until it reaches the sky, and your dominion extends to distant parts of the earth.

²³"Your Majesty saw a holy one, a messenger, coming down from heaven and saying, 'Cut down the tree and destroy it, but leave the stump, bound with iron and bronze, in the grass of the field, while its roots remain in the ground. Let him be drenched with the dew of heaven; let him live with the wild animals, until seven times pass by for him.'

²⁴"This is the interpretation, Your Majesty, and this is the decree the Most High has issued against my lord the king: ²⁵You will be driven away from people and will live with the wild animals; you will eat grass like the ox and be drenched with the dew of heaven. Seven times will pass by for you until you acknowledge that the Most High is sovereign over all kingdoms on earth and gives them to anyone he wishes. ²⁶The command to leave the stump of the tree with its roots means that your kingdom will be restored to you when you acknowledge that Heaven rules. ²⁷Therefore, Your Majesty, be pleased to accept my advice: Renounce your sins by doing what is right,

> *and your wickedness by being kind to the oppressed.*
> *It may be that then your prosperity will continue."*

Daniel was alarmed because apparently he had grown to highly respect King Nebuchadnezzar. He was concerned for him. Do we have similar concern for those in authority over us even if they are egomaniacs? Daniel showed courage in being remarkably direct: "Your Majesty, you are that tree!" (4:22a). This was probably what Neb feared.

Notice that in 4:25 we see the point which is repeated in 4:17: To acknowledge that the Most High rules over all. After sharing the interpretation as it applied personally to Neb, Daniel dared to offer him advice.

God rules eternally

Daniel 4:27b

> *Renounce your sins by doing what is right, and*
> *your wickedness by being kind to the oppressed. It*
> *may be that then your prosperity will continue.*

The word for "renounce" means to break with, "tear away or break off."[13] This is the first step in getting help—recognizing that you have a problem. This is the first step in recovery whether in AA (Alcoholics Anonymous) or in a Christ-centered recovery ministry. This is the first step to salvation: repentance. This step requires humility, to admit you have been wrong. Neb needed to face that he had not done right nor been kind to the oppressed. Are you willing to take this step? Have you ever repented of your sin and turned to trust in Jesus Christ alone to save you? Today, as a Christian, are you stubbornly remaining in pride or are you willing to renounce your sin and acknowledge that The Big God rules?

Most of us have sensed that God has been trying to get our attention. God often gives us time, but then if we don't respond, he speaks louder to get our attention. That's what happened to Neb as the prophetic dream was fulfilled in real life.

God often gives us a long time to repent, but when we don't, the discipline can be swift.

Daniel 4:28–33

> All this happened to King Nebuchadnezzar. [29]Twelve months later, as the king was walking on the roof of the royal palace of Babylon, [30]he said, "Is not this the great Babylon I have built as the royal residence, by my mighty power and for the glory of my majesty?"
>
> [31]Even as the words were on his lips, a voice came from heaven, "This is what is decreed for you, King Nebuchadnezzar: Your royal authority has been taken from you. [32]You will be driven away from people and will live with the wild animals; you will eat grass like the ox. Seven times will pass by for you until you acknowledge that the Most High is sovereign over all kingdoms on earth and gives them to anyone he wishes."
>
> [33]Immediately what had been said about Nebuchadnezzar was fulfilled. He was driven away from people and ate grass like the ox. His body was drenched with the dew of heaven until his hair grew like the feathers of an eagle and his nails like the claws of a bird.

Twelve months later, Neb had apparently not listened well to Daniel's warning. Being on his roof would have been normal. They often had flat roofs that functioned as huge balconies.

At this point, Babylon was at the height of its glory. It was surrounded by a system of double walls, the outer one of which was 17 miles long and wide enough for chariots to pass on its top. Of the city's eight gates, the most celebrated was the Ishtar Gate. The main "processional street was about 1,000 yards long, and it was decorated on either side by enameled bricks, showing 120 lions (Ishtar symbol) and 575 dragons and bulls (Marduk and Bel symbols). More than fifty temples crowded within the city walls. The Greeks considered the 'hanging gardens' within the city one of the seven wonders of the world."[14]

I don't know about you, but I cringe when I read 4:30: "Is not this the great Babylon *I* have built as the royal residence, by *my* mighty power and for the glory of *my* majesty?" [emphasis added]. You want to scream, "No, stop!" Can't you identify? Our accomplishments are smaller than a massive empire, but we are still proud.

I planted some St. Augustine grass in my backyard in a 12 foot by 12 foot square that I nursed back to life after a drought. I would sit on my back porch and say, "Look at that grass I grew."

I've also written a few books and I am tempted to be proud of it. Our church, Christ Fellowship, has grown to be a fairly large church. I'd be lying not to confess that over the years I have struggled with the evil thought: I did this. I built this amazing church. Idiot!

I play racquetball in a local league at the neighborhood fitness center. We have a small tournament at the end of the league. Do I ever dare wear the shirt I won that says, "Champion" in large letters? If I wear it, what will be happening under the shirt in my heart? Where does pride trip you?

While the words were still on his lips, judgment came from God. Neb's royal authority was removed in a day until he acknowledged that the Most High rules. We don't know exactly what happened to Neb. Did he lose his mind—literally go mentally insane? Possibly. Was this a disease sent from God? Possibly. We know he was banished from human society. The one who had authority over the animals ate like an ox. We don't know how long seven times is. It could be seven months or seven years. It was long enough for his nails to grow into claws like those of a bird.

In a sense, he was already insane in that he was acting like he was the eternal king and that God did not exist. His outward mental disease manifested the delusion of which he was already a victim. I found a nice quote by D.N. Fewell (1988): "A man who thinks he is like a god must become a beast to learn that he is only a human being."[15] It was only in the later years of his life that Neb got it. It is not too late for you. However old you are, it is not too late to bow before The Big God.

In our earthly success, we can ignore God. In our pride, we think that we can handle life ourselves. Our superficial happiness and security delude us into thinking we can ignore The Big God. In a moment, your whole life can get turned upside down. You can be eating grass like a cow.

I shared that at 28 years old I was the youngest professor at Dallas Theological Seminary. But two years later, after being assured that my job was secure, I was released, let go, fired—and it was not done well. I'll never forget having a fellow professor stop me in the hallway and say, "I am so sorry." He did not know that I did not know. That was awkward. Since the seminary enrollment and income were down, the last hired was the first fired. For a while my world was shattered. I was furious, embarrassed, ashamed and confused. When God reminds you that you are not in charge, when he humbles you, it usually hurts but it is a good hurt for which later you are thankful.

My wife and I are at a new stage of parenting. As a parent of adult children, you realize at a deeper level that you have no control over what your children do when they leave home. It's a very helpless feeling. If you try to exercise control, it backfires, so I am learning to trust God more and am so glad that he is in control.

The end of the story is awesome as we see Neb transformed by the power of God. He praised the eternal Big God!

Daniel 4:34–37

*At the end of that time, I, Nebuchadnezzar,
raised my eyes toward heaven, and my sanity was
restored. Then I praised the Most High; I honored and
glorified him who lives forever.*

*His dominion is an eternal dominion;
his kingdom endures from generation to
generation.*
*35All the peoples of the earth
are regarded as nothing.*
*He does as he pleases
with the powers of heaven
and the peoples of the earth.*
*No one can hold back his hand
or say to him: "What have you done?"*
*36At the same time that my sanity was restored,
my honor and splendor were returned to me for the
glory of my kingdom. My advisers and nobles sought
me out, and I was restored to my throne and became
even greater than before. 37Now I, Nebuchadnezzar,
praise and exalt and glorify the King of heaven,
because everything he does is right and all his ways
are just. And those who walk in pride he is able to
humble.*

Neb's restoration began "with the simple gesture of looking
to heaven—a cry for help and the recognition" of God's suprema-
cy.[16] Will you take that step? It takes humility. If God is speaking to
you, don't wait for the nightmare to come true
like it did for Neb. Renounce your sin and acknowledge The Big God who rules all kingdoms
and humbles the proud. Humble yourself before
God and trust in Jesus Christ alone as your King.

**God humbles
the proud**

Chapter 4 calls us to surrender our pride
and humbly acknowledge that God is big because he rules all the

kingdoms of the world and humbles the proud. We each need to take the next step for us in renouncing our prideful sin.

We need to acknowledge and praise our Big God. Twice Nebuchadnezzar used three words for emphasis: he said he praised, honored and glorified God in 4:34 and then in 4:37, he praised, exalted and glorified. These are on-going actions that we need to do as well. Do we honor God as Neb did in these last verses?

In the end, Neb realized that everything God does is right and just, even going through his period of insanity. God rules. He is fully capable of humbling those who walk in pride. Neb found someone bigger than himself to live for, bigger than his mighty empire. In Jesus' terms, he found life in the life-giver (John 11:25). God's desire is to bring us to repentance, not to hurt us, but to free us from the rotting disease of pride so in humility we acknowledge The Big God who rules eternally over all kingdoms. God is Big.

Pastor Tim Keller has said, "Pride ultimately is cosmic plagiarism. We try to take credit for a gift that has been given to us." The cure for prideful sin is to acknowledge our Big God. You may want to write down what you have been proud of and give it to God. You may want to write down for what you have wrongly taken credit. Or perhaps you want to give to God your insanity time. Perhaps you have been reduced to an ox eating grass and you want to give that to God. Let's echo Nebuchadnezzar in acknowledging our Big God.

For further study on chapter 4, see the Study Guide beginning on page 209.

5

God has the Last Word

Daniel 5

I have to admit that I am a bit of an aggressive driver, so when I see a yellow warning light, my instinct is not to hit the brake and slow down, but to hit the gas and make it through just before it turns red.

Have you ever been warned? Maybe a friend warned you not to get involved with a certain person. Your mom may have warned you not to touch the hot stove. A boss or teacher may have warned you that if you kept doing what you were doing, you were going to fail or be fired. Warnings by nature are not fun. They are meant to be taken seriously, and yet as human beings, we often ignore them.

Some warnings come from the example of other people's lives. Growing up, you may have heard your dad say, "See what happened to that guy? He was drinking and driving and he wrecked his car. Don't drink and drive." Why is it hard to learn from others' examples? Some of us seem determined to learn the hard way. For some strange reason, we want to touch the hot stove ourselves. The apostle Paul said Old Testament stories are given to us as examples so we will not get in the same messes as those characters did (1 Corinthians 10:11).

In this chapter, we enter a story with a wild party and see the example of a man full of pride. This guy mistreated God's holy things. Can we identify at all with this kind of behavior? At some time in your life, have you had too much alcohol to drink? Have you gone to a party to lose yourself in the music and chaos of the night? Have you ever treated God and his church with disregard? We can identify. Pride and pleasure tempt all of us.

But what if we took the warning of The Big God's judgment seriously? How might we live differently if we really understood how Big God is and the seriousness of his judgment? Have you ever seen someone else face such severe consequences for their behavior that you determined never to do what they did? What decisions might you make today if you had a clear, vivid image of The Big God's judgment right in front of you?

God judges

Our text today brings us a warning; The Big God has the last word. Chapter 5 stands in sharp contrast with chapter 4. Each chapter presents an arrogant king, but one repents and one does not. The results are dramatically different. By the time we get to Daniel 5, King Nebuchadnezzar had died (562 BC). None of his successors would match his achievements, and Babylon's glory soon began to fade.[17]

Daniel had become an older man of about 81 years, largely forgotten by the new generation ruling in the palace. The new king was Belshazzar. For years, scholars who did not see the Bible as God's Word said that no such person as Belshazzar existed. But there is now ample historical evidence that he did exist. In fact, this entire chapter is heavily substantiated by ancient documents.

We read how Babylon was defeated by the Medes and Persians. This fact is attested by other historical records. According to the ancient historians Herodotus (1.190–91) and Xenophon, the Persians killed the Babylonian king, a riotous, indulgent, cruel and godless young man. They entered the city while the Babylonians were partying.[18]

Let's unpack the story scene by scene. We will see that the main point is to humbly repent of our arrogant, blasphemous sin because The Big God will judge us. Try to imagine the scene with a wild party in the palace. People drinking, wearing party clothes, loud music and general craziness were interrupted in a terrifying way: drinking wine was halted by fingers writing on a wall.

Daniel 5:1–9

King Belshazzar gave a great banquet for a thousand of his nobles and drank wine with them. [2]While Belshazzar was drinking his wine, he gave orders to bring in the gold and silver goblets that Nebuchadnezzar his father had taken from the temple in Jerusalem, so that the king and his nobles, his wives and his concubines might drink from them. [3]So they brought in the gold goblets that had been taken from the temple of God in Jerusalem, and the king and his nobles, his wives and his concubines drank from them. [4]As they drank the wine, they praised the gods of gold and silver, of bronze, iron, wood and stone.

[5]Suddenly the fingers of a human hand appeared and wrote on the plaster of the wall, near the lampstand in the royal palace. The king watched the hand as it wrote. [6]His face turned pale and he was so frightened that his legs became weak and his knees were knocking.

[7]The king summoned the enchanters, astrologers and diviners. Then he said to these wise men of Babylon, "Whoever reads this writing and tells me what it means will be clothed in purple and have a gold chain placed around his neck, and he will be made the third highest ruler in the kingdom."

> *⁸Then all the king's wise men came in, but they could not read the writing or tell the king what it meant. ⁹So King Belshazzar became even more terrified and his face grew more pale. His nobles were baffled.*

This great banquet or wild party was likely held in the largest room in the palace complex, a room that has been excavated by archaeologists. Why did Belshazzar throw this wild party? By the way, we are going to nickname him "Shaz" for short. So, what was this drinking party about? We do not know for sure. It could have been a holiday like New Year's Eve where many people get drunk. Sometimes a party is designed to build morale for the business. Sometimes it is just to show off a person's money and power. Sometimes it is to distract us from dealing with the serious matters of life. People go to "Happy Hour" as their way to deal with the stress of work or to avoid the stress of home. It's an escape.

Notice how many times in the story Daniel mentioned drinking. The word for drinking carries the idea of feeling the effects. Often in those times, the king was hidden from his guests, but here Shaz was leading the way in drinking. Drinking and music sometimes go together. They were praising gods of gold, silver, bronze, iron, wood and stone, the stuff of the creation, of nature. Picture drunken people loudly singing Babylonian karaoke. They were partying hard.

Then it got worse. Shaz called for the gold and silver goblets that Nebuchadnezzar had taken from the temple in Jerusalem. What was he thinking? Even pagan people would have seen these goblets as sacred, not to be messed with. Likely they had not been touched but were kept in secure storage. This was like shaking his fist at God. Maybe Shaz was trying to show everyone he was greater than Nebuchadnezzar, even though he was not nearly as great a king. Maybe he was trying to show his power over the Jews and their God. Or maybe he was just being a drunken idiot. This was like spitting on the American flag, only worse.

In our home, we have a memory box that is really precious to us. My wife Tamara's Uncle Tom gave his life at Pearl Harbor. He was awarded a Purple Heart medal. We have that medal in a glass memory case hanging on a wall in our home. Can you imagine if a drunken person broke the glass and took out the Purple Heart to play with? How do you think we would feel if he tried to pin it on his shirt? He would be desecrating something precious to us.

Shaz was taking the holy gold goblets that had been dedicated to worship the one true God and filling them with alcohol to toast false gods of other religions. This is blasphemy, sacrilege. Perhaps he was saying to God, "You may have humbled Nebuchadnezzar, but not me."

Shaz was defying the third of the Ten Commandments: "You shall not misuse the name of the LORD your God" (Exodus 20:7a).[19]

What today could be analogous to the holy gold goblets from the temple? We know that our bodies are temples of the Holy Spirit and members of Christ, so to use our bodies immorally is to use what was designed for worship and give it to gods of sexuality, gluttony or abuse. We know that the church is the body of Christ and temple of the Holy Spirit, so how do we disregard the church as if it did not matter? How do we approach the Word of God, the Lord's Supper, baptism and coming to worship services? Some people casually skip worship because they stayed up late the night before or because it is raining. Do we honor the holy Big God by going to church, or do we ignore him?

When we dishonor God deliberately, sometimes he stops us in our tracks as he did Shaz in Daniel 5. The room which had been drowned in noise now became deathly silent, with fear gripping everyone.[20] When divine fingers appeared and wrote a message on the wall for all to see, evidently Belshazzar screamed for his "wise men."[21] All the laughing was sucked out of the room.

Have you ever received a spiritual or supernatural message that scared you? Maybe right in the midst of major sin, you suddenly felt massive conviction or knew that you were in danger from God himself. Let's see what happened next in our story. The king was not getting help from his wise men. They couldn't read the message or figure out what it meant which made Shaz even more terrified. Then the queen stepped in and endorsed Daniel and the king inquired about him.

Daniel 5:10–16

The queen, hearing the voices of the king and his nobles, came into the banquet hall. "May the king live forever!" she said. "Don't be alarmed! Don't look so pale! ¹¹There is a man in your kingdom who has the spirit of the holy gods in him. In the time of your father he was found to have insight and intelligence and wisdom like that of the gods. Your father, King Nebuchadnezzar, appointed him chief of the magicians, enchanters, astrologers and diviners. ¹²He did this because Daniel, whom the king called Belteshazzar, was found to have a keen mind and knowledge and understanding, and also the ability to interpret dreams, explain riddles and solve difficult problems. Call for Daniel, and he will tell you what the writing means."

¹³So Daniel was brought before the king, and the king said to him, "Are you Daniel, one of the exiles my father the king brought from Judah? ¹⁴I have heard that the spirit of the gods is in you and that you have insight, intelligence and outstanding wisdom. ¹⁵The wise men and enchanters were brought before me to read this writing and tell me what it means, but they could not explain it. ¹⁶ Now I have heard that you are able to give interpretations and to solve difficult problems. If you can read this writing and tell me what it means, you will be clothed in purple and have a gold chain placed around your neck, and you will be made the third highest ruler in the kingdom."

The queen was most likely not Shaz's wife, but his grand-mother. She was the queen mother who knew Daniel and she had courage. [Note: Do not underestimate the wisdom and power of grandmothers.] She knew all about Daniel and possibly she had converted, as her husband Nebuchadnezzar had, to worship the true God.

This timeframe is about 23 years after Nebuchadnezzar's death and still Daniel's reputation lived on. He had been faithful to The Big God all his life. I want to be like Daniel. What a model of lifelong faithfulness. What was his secret? He knew and wor-shipped The Big God. He saw how big God is and so he could stay faithful through multiple kings and empires. How will you stay faithful to God through changing bosses, companies, teachers and locations?

Meanwhile Shaz treated Daniel with a condescending atti-tude. He called him one of the exiles, used his Jewish name and said he had heard that Daniel had *some* ability. He badly misjudged Daniel. The next scene is the center of the story. Daniel confronted Shaz. He told him essentially that he had messed up.

Daniel confronted Shaz in two parts. First, he told Shaz he should have learned from Nebuchadnezzar, then he laid out his five-fold failure:

Daniel 5:17–21

> Then Daniel answered the king, "You may keep your gifts for yourself and give your rewards to someone else. Nevertheless, I will read the writing for the king and tell him what it means.
> [18]"Your Majesty, the Most High God gave your father Nebuchadnezzar sovereignty and greatness and glory and splendor. [19]Because of the high position he gave him, all the nations and peoples of every language dreaded and feared him. Those the king wanted to put to death, he put to death; those he

*wanted to spare, he spared; those he wanted to
promote, he promoted; and those he wanted to
humble, he humbled. ²⁰But when his heart became
arrogant and hardened with pride, he was deposed
from his royal throne and stripped of his glory. ²¹He
was driven away from people and given the mind of
an animal; he lived with the wild donkeys and ate
grass like the ox; and his body was drenched with the
dew of heaven, until he acknowledged that the Most
High God is sovereign over all kingdoms on earth and
sets over them anyone he wishes."*

Daniel rejected Shaz's condescending attitude by refusing all
his gifts. Daniel may have thought something such as, "Keep them
for yourself. By the way your majesty, although King Nebuchadnezzar was much greater than you are, he received all his power
and greatness as a gift from the Most High God. As great as Neb
was, when his heart became arrogant and hardened with pride,
God humbled him, stripping him of everything until he
acknowledged that the Most High God rules over all kingdoms."
The implied point is clear: Shaz, did not learn anything from
Nebuchadnezzar's example. He would have to learn it the hard way.
Next Daniel courageously and directly laid out the five-fold failure
by Shaz:

Daniel 5:22–24

*But you, Belshazzar, his son have not humbled
yourself, though you knew all this. ²³Instead, you have
set yourself up against the Lord of heaven. You had
the goblets from his temple brought to you, and you
and your nobles, your wives and your concubines
drank wine from them. You praised the gods of silver
and gold, of bronze, iron, wood and stone, which
cannot see or hear or understand. But you did not
honor the God who holds in his hand your life and all*

your ways. [24]Therefore he sent the hand that wrote the inscription.

Do you see the five-fold failure? What did Shaz do?

1. He did not humble himself although he knew better
2. Set himself up against the Lord of heaven
3. Drank wine from the temple goblets
4. Praised the gods of silver and gold who were nothing
5. Did not honor the God who held his life in his hands

Daniel was blunt. Would you dare to be a Daniel by confronting a person in sin? Would you warn a person of God's coming judgment? On the other side, how would you respond if you were Shaz being confronted?

Recently I showed up at the door of a friend of mine who was considering leaving his wife. With two other friends, we warned him that he was setting himself up against God. He knew it was wrong, but just didn't care anymore. He said he was tired of life and marriage the way it was. He knew better, but refused to humble himself under God's Word.

"Blasphemy is the act of dishonoring God through speech or actions."[22] When you deliberately go against God, even though you know better, you are putting yourself in serious danger. My friend told me he was sorry he was disappointing me; I replied that he didn't disappoint me as much as I was scared for him.

Gods of this world are nothing. They can't see, hear or understand and yet we bow to them, worshipping the creation over the Creator. When we give ourselves to wine, parties and pride, we bow down to false gods. We dishonor the one Most High Big God who gives us our very breath, who holds our lives in his hands. When you willfully and knowingly turn against God, you put yourself in grave danger.

We see the danger for Shaz in the last scene of the story where Daniel interpreted the words. Essentially he told Shaz, "You are doomed." And Daniel was right.

Daniel 5:22–31

"But you, Belshazzar, his son, have not humbled yourself, though you knew all this. ²³Instead, you have set yourself up against the Lord of heaven. You had the goblets from his temple brought to you, and you and your nobles, your wives and your concubines drank wine from them. You praised the gods of silver and gold, of bronze, iron, wood and stone, which cannot see or hear or understand. But you did not honor the God who holds in his hand your life and all your ways. ²⁴Therefore he sent the hand that wrote the inscription.

²⁵*"This is the inscription that was written:*
MENE, MENE, TEKEL, PARSIN
²⁶*"Here is what these words mean:*
Mene: God has numbered the days of your reign and brought it to an end.
²⁷*Tekel: You have been weighed on the scales and found wanting.*
²⁸*Peres: Your kingdom is divided and given to the Medes and Persians."*
²⁹*Then at Belshazzar's command, Daniel was clothed in purple, a gold chain was placed around his neck, and he was proclaimed the third highest ruler in the kingdom.*
³⁰*That very night Belshazzar, king of the Babylonians, was slain, ³¹and Darius the Mede took over the kingdom, at the age of sixty-two.*

"The message literally read, 'Numbered, numbered, weighed, and divided.'"²³ *Mene* means your kingdom's reign has been numbered. It has been determined that it is ending soon. *Tekel*: You have been weighed on the scales and found too light. You do not have enough righteousness or moral good. *Peres*: Your kingdom will be divided and taken away from you.

The inscription announced divine judgment. You are doomed. It is over. Your arrogant, blasphemous partying is done. That very night Shaz died and his kingdom was defeated by the Medes and the Persians. That night shifted rapidly from drunken laughter to terror and ultimately, to death.

According to an historical document called the *Nabonidus Chronicle*, the date was the sixteenth of the month Tishri, which "most scholars agree would have been October 12, 539 B.C. The banquet may have been held on the night before, October 11, 539 B.C." [24] According to ancient historians Herodotus and Xenophon, the soldiers diverted the Euphrates River and were able to wade in the river under the walls to enter the city. Xenophon said the city was invaded while the Babylonians were partying.

The Persian enemy armies must have been making their way into the city even as the party was happening. Little did the partiers know, their fun was about to end horribly. Our English expressions, "Your days are numbered!" and "The handwriting is on the wall!" come from this chapter. Often these are expressions of fate rather than the hand of God. Does God judge today as he judged Shaz in Daniel 5? God is the same holy God. He does not tolerate prideful sin any more today than he did back then.

The prophet Isaiah wrote a warning to Babylon that could apply directly to us today:

> *Now then, listen, you lover of pleasure,*
> *lounging in your security*
> *and saying to yourself,*
> *"I am, and there is none besides me"...*
> *You have trusted in your wickedness*
> *and have said, "No one sees me."*
> *Your wisdom and knowledge mislead you*
> *when you say to yourself,*

> *"I am, and there is none besides me."*
> *Disaster will come upon you,*
> > *and you will not know how to conjure it*
> > *away.*
> *A calamity will fall upon you*
> > *that you cannot ward off with a ransom;*
> *a catastrophe you cannot foresee*
> > *will suddenly come upon you*
> (Isaiah 47:8–11).

God judges. We do not. Since we are not God, we cannot know with certainty when suffering or death is God's judgment and when it is not. Not all suffering and death come from God's judgment, but some does. Our role is not to judge, but to warn people of God's judgment, starting with ourselves.

The biblical principle is clear; if you set yourself up against God, he will bring you down, no matter how powerful or wealthy you are. If you sin against the holy God, you will be weighed and found wanting. The ultimate consequence is death. Sin leads to death. Hell is eternal death, final separation from the life-giver. We have all sinned, and a holy, righteous God cannot and should not overlook sin. So what are we to do?

There is nothing we can do to save ourselves. That is why God sent Jesus Christ. Only God can save us from our mess. God became one of us to save us from ourselves. Jesus Christ paid the penalty. In our | **God saves us** place, he died the death we deserve. No one made him do it. We did not ask him to do it. He came and died out of love. It was not nails, but love that held him to that cross. We cannot earn our salvation; we cannot forgive ourselves, but God can, based on the high price Jesus paid (John 3:17).

The call to us is clear in the striking contrast between Daniel 4 and 5. Both Nebuchadnezzar and Belshazzar were arrogant, sinful men. Both were confronted with a message from God. One humbled himself and the other did not. One was saved and the other was destroyed. The point of Daniel 5 is a clear warning: Humbly repent of your arrogant, blasphemous sin because The Big God will judge you. Apart from Jesus Christ, you will be weighed and found too light. You cannot live a righteous enough life to earn forgiveness. When you trust in Jesus Christ alone to save you from your sin, he does.

We must continually heed the warning to humble ourselves. We must resist the temptation to go back to partying and wine, being full of pride and setting ourselves against the Lord of heaven. As those keenly aware of The Big God, we must live to honor him because The Big God has the last word.

For further study on chapter 5, see the Study Guide beginning on page 221.

6

God Tames Lions

Daniel 6

How can we live faithfully for God in Babylon? Babylon represents this chaotic, fallen world with its allures, pressures and evil. Most of us do not work in a Christian environment. You work in a Babylon. We do business in Babylon as we go about our lives buying groceries and arranging for the plumber to fix our leaks. We play in Babylon at the country club, fitness club or the YMCA. So let me ask again: How can we live faithfully for God in Babylon? We need a model.

Thankfully, we have one. Daniel shows us how to live faithfully for God in Babylon. He models three character traits that we can emulate. We need to understand Daniel's model for how to live for God as an exile in a foreign place.

These first six chapters all take place in Babylon. Daniel and others were not at home in the Promised Land, but living as exiles. So are we. We are not at home, but living for God as exiles in this strange and difficult world.

In our study, we have seen Daniel hold to his convictions in chapter 1 as he resisted eating the king's choice food. Then we've seen him respectfully serve King Nebuchadnezzar in chapter 2 by interpreting the vision of the giant statue. Chapter 6 parallels chapter 3 where Daniel's three friends resisted an order of the king to worship a false god and were thrown in a furnace to be burned alive, but were rescued by God. In contrast, in chapter 6 Daniel resisted an order to stop praying to the true God and was thrown to lions to be eaten alive. In chapter 4, Daniel respectfully confronted King Nebuchadnezzar and then in chapter 5 confronted King Belshazzar. Now in chapter 6, we meet a third king, Darius the Mede, also known as Cyrus (his Persian name).

Let's step into this famous story. Daniel was an older man, in his early 80s and he still served in a high position in the government. This guy was in shape; Daniel must have played racquetball! Seriously, we sometimes drastically underestimate the contribution of our 80-something men and women. Seniors, let Daniel challenge you—you are not done serving God until you see Jesus face to face. I hope I can be like Daniel when I am in my 80s.

In chapter 6, we find a major conflict: God's law versus the law of the Medes and Persians. Daniel had to choose between the two laws with horrific consequences. Political adversaries created a trap using a legal apparatus that seemed foolproof. If we want to know how to live faithfully for God in Babylon, we need to study Daniel's example. We are going to see three Danielic character traits that we can develop to live faithfully in Babylon as we unpack the story scene by scene. In this first scene, we will see the first character trait:

1. Exceptional quality

In Babylon, Daniel's exceptional quality represents The Big God who is bigger than political enemies. Look for this character trait as we read the opening scene.

Daniel 6:1–9

It pleased Darius to appoint 120 satraps to rule throughout the kingdom, ²with three administrators over them, one of whom was Daniel. The satraps were made accountable to them so that the king might not suffer loss. ³Now Daniel so distinguished himself among the administrators and the satraps by his exceptional qualities that the king planned to set him over the whole kingdom. ⁴At this, the administrators and the satraps tried to find grounds for charges against Daniel in his conduct of government affairs, but they were unable to do so. They could find no corruption in him, because he was trustworthy and neither corrupt nor negligent. ⁵Finally these men said, "We will never find any basis for charges against this man Daniel unless it has something to do with the law of his God."

⁶So these administrators and satraps went as a group to the king and said: "May King Darius live forever! ⁷The royal administrators, prefects, satraps, advisers and governors have all agreed that the king should issue an edict and enforce the decree that anyone who prays to any god or human being during the next thirty days, except to you, Your Majesty, shall be thrown into the lions' den. ⁸Now, Your Majesty, issue the decree and put it in writing so that it cannot be altered—in accordance with the law of the Medes and Persians, which cannot be repealed." ⁹So King Darius put the decree in writing.

Daniel demonstrated such exceptional quality in his work that the king planned to set him over the whole kingdom. He was that good. Daniel's peers were not excited about his promotion. Their jealousy led to seeking grounds for charges against Daniel. They started scheming about how they could undermine Daniel. By the way, a "satrap" is an official governmental position.

I talked to a lady at our church who said, "This goes on all the time at my workplace. Most everyone is jockeying for position; undermining others; spreading gossip; buttering up important people." For most people, it is difficult not to get pulled into this kind of junk. You wonder if you will survive if you don't get a bit dirty yourself. It's really tough when they throw you under the bus. I've had false accusations thrown against me several times and it hurts.

This little group put out their spy network to get dirt on Daniel. The private investigator couldn't find anything. Nothing showed up on the wiretaps or phone records. A computer guru couldn't find anything suspicious in his digital footprint; nothing on Babylonian Facebook, Twitter or email. There was no porn on his hard drive; no Internet searches for bad stuff. He was clean. If a group of people determined to get rid of you, what would they find on you?

So these guys decided to go after Daniel for his devotion to God. They came up with a clever trap. Playing on the vanity of the king, they got King Darius to establish an unbreakable law that would trap Daniel. They lied, saying that everyone had agreed to this new law. In those times, people often approached a god through a priest. They suggested that King Darius make a law that for 30 days no one could approach any god except through Darius. They manipulated the king to set a law they knew Daniel couldn't keep.

They knew that the Medes and the Persians set up a system where a law put in writing by the king could not be changed. This is like the Pope being infallible *ex cathedra*. Once a law was officially enacted by the king, no one could change it, not even the king. Evil people through time often have used the law unjustly to get their way, cleverly manipulating the system for selfish gain.

The quality of Daniel's work was so exceptional that the king intended to make him COO of the entire kingdom. Specifically, we learn that he had no corruption in him. He had integrity. Then we learn that he had no negligence. He was a hard worker.

Fundamentally he was trustworthy and faithful. How would you like an employee like Daniel? How about a boss like Daniel? In fact, this could be your new hiring practice: We will only hire Daniel-like people. In our work, we should all be like Daniel.

A key way that we live faithfully to God in Babylon is by developing exceptional quality. You should be an exceptional employee. I hope Christians regularly are recognized as "employee of the month" and "number one salesperson" because they do excellent work. That exceptional quality extends to our attitude and our integrity. We live faithfully for God in Babylon by emulating Daniel in exceptional quality because God is bigger than our political enemies.

Notice that these other guys knew about Daniel's spiritual commitment and habits. Daniel did not hide his faith. He was not a secret believer. Do people at work know you follow Jesus? If I interviewed them, would they tell me that you follow Jesus? How would they know?

Secondly, how did these guys know their trap would work? What made them think that Daniel would not compromise his faith? You see, Daniel led such a model life of commitment to God that these guys were sure Daniel would hold to his spiritual commitments.

Daniel is an amazing model of how to live faithfully for God in Babylon. In the next scene, we see a second Danielic character trait we can emulate. Not only did Daniel show exceptional quality, but he also prayed regularly to The Big God who is bigger than unjust laws.

2. Prayed regularly

Look carefully at how Daniel responded to the trap they had set.

Daniel 6:10–18

Now when Daniel learned that the decree had been published, he went home to his upstairs room where the windows opened toward Jerusalem. Three times a day he got down on his knees and prayed, giving thanks to his God, just as he had done before. 11Then these men went as a group and found Daniel praying and asking God for help. 12So they went to the king and spoke to him about his royal decree: "Did you not publish a decree that during the next thirty days anyone who prays to any god or human being except to you, Your Majesty, would be thrown into the lions' den?"

The king answered, "The decree stands—in accordance with the law of the Medes and Persians, which cannot be repealed."

13Then they said to the king, "Daniel, who is one of the exiles from Judah, pays no attention to you, Your Majesty, or to the decree you put in writing. He still prays three times a day." 14When the king heard this, he was greatly distressed; he was determined to rescue Daniel and made every effort until sundown to save him.

15Then the men went as a group to King Darius and said to him, "Remember, Your Majesty, that according to the law of the Medes and Persians no decree or edict that the king issues can be changed."

16So the king gave the order, and they brought Daniel and threw him into the lions' den. The king said to Daniel, "May your God, whom you serve continually, rescue you!"

17A stone was brought and placed over the mouth of the den, and the king sealed it with his own signet ring and with the rings of his nobles, so that Daniel's situation might not be changed. 18Then the king returned to his palace and spent the night without eating and without any entertainment being brought to him. And he could not sleep.

It would not surprise me if Daniel had become aware that this group was spying on him and plotting against him. You don't live to your 80s through multiple political administrations without being deeply connected and aware. Of course, once the decree was published, Daniel clearly understood the implications. He knew the law. So would he now continue to pray, and so seem to fall into their trap? Or would he be wiser to cease praying for the 30 days? What about trying to pray secretly so no one would see him? Or he could have flaunted his beliefs by going out in the middle of the public square to pray. Daniel neither hid nor flaunted his devotion. He simply continued his normal practice. What about you? Have you struggled with either showing off your spiritual devotion, or with hiding it?

We hear no tension from Daniel, no angst or anxiety or fear. He simply continued his prayers to The Big God. He refused to stop praying to Yahweh, the true God of Israel. He would not pray through Darius, even though he was the king and even though that was now the law. Daniel was captive to a higher law, to a greater King. "In a word, Daniel would rather be eaten by lions than stop praying to God."[25]

Wow. Talk about a strong model to follow. Will we trust God to that level? To live faithfully in Babylon, we must follow Daniel in regular prayer to The Big God who is bigger than unjust laws. We must stay faithful in prayer in the face of legal manipulation and in the face of death threats.

Three verbs are used of Daniel and they are all participles indicating continuing action: bowing, praying and thanking. This is not an emergency prayer by Daniel, but his daily habit. And Daniel was praising God. How amazing that he was giving thanks in light of a soon, certain meeting with hungry lions. And this was no joke.

Daniel was confident in the living God. His giving thanks reminds me of Paul's command in 1 Thessalonians:

> *Rejoice always, pray continually, give thanks in*
> *all circumstances; for this is God's will for you in*
> *Christ Jesus* (1 Thessalonians 5:16–18).

Daniel modeled regular prayer and praise in the face of opposition and trouble. What a model for us. No matter what your circumstance, give thanks in prayer.

In our lives, there may come times when we must make a choice between obeying human laws or obeying God. It happened to the early Christians. In Acts 5, we read the story of Peter who was falsely accused by Jewish leaders. In a court setting they said:

> *We gave you strict orders not to teach in this*
> *name, yet you have filled Jerusalem with your*
> *teaching and are determined to make us guilty of this*
> *man's blood. Peter and the other apostles replied:*
> *"We must obey God rather than human beings"* (Acts
> 5:28–29).

Will we show this Daniel-like courageous faith when we must choose?

We must be careful in applying this truth because the example of Daniel has been co-opted to support American culture wars. Remember there is no such thing as a Christian nation. Daniel did not try to make Babylon Christian; rather, he worked with exceptional quality for Babylon and demonstrated spiritual commitment to the true God as he served in the royal palace. He did not advocate prayer before Babylonian council meetings or for prayer in Babylonian public schools. I'm not saying those are wrong in America, but we must be careful about how we apply the biblical text. We are not to go to war for Christ. He will do that just fine himself when he returns.

For instance, we are opposed to abortion, but that does not mean we bomb abortion clinics or withhold a portion of our federal taxes that may go to support abortion. However, if a government official legislated that you have an abortion (as has happened in China), then you must obey God instead and courageously refuse to do it.

Daniel was forbidden to pray at all. If we are ever forbidden to have Bibles, we should refuse to give up our Bibles. This can get very personal in our homes. Sometimes a spouse or a parent tries to control your faith. They do not like your devotion to Jesus. In these situations, you need great wisdom. If your husband demands that you not go to a Bible study on Thursday night because he wants to spend time with you, you might agree to that. If he demands that you quit praying or reading the Bible, you must refuse. To live faithfully for God in Babylon, we must regularly pray to The Big God even against unjust laws.

The corrupt officials were delighted. Their trap worked. They went to the king as a group. Before they said a word about Daniel, because they knew the king liked him, they got King Darius to reaffirm the decree and that it was unalterable. Then they sprung the trap and tried to pull the race card by calling Daniel a Jewish exile. He was a Jew, not really one of them.

King Darius was distressed. We are not told why. Perhaps he was mad that he was manipulated; angry that his top guy Daniel might be killed; maybe he was worried that he might be getting into trouble with The Big God over this. He tried everything he could to get out of the situation, but no clever lawyer could even find a way out. It was a good trap. At sunset, the group came back, since laws were to be carried out that day, and reminded the king that this decree couldn't be changed. So Darius did it. But as he did, he gave a wish or a prayer to Daniel:

> *May your God, whom you serve continually, rescue you!* (16b).

He had a shred of faith.

The soldiers put a stone over the mouth of the lion's den which was likely a huge pit or cave. Then they sealed it with the king's own signet ring and the rings of the nobles. Daniel seemed doomed, but don't count out The Big God.

In the next scene, we see the third Danielic character trait. Not only did Daniel show exceptional quality and pray regularly, but he also confidently trusted in The Big God who is bigger than hungry lions.

3. Confidently trusted

Daniel 6:19–24

At the first light of dawn, the king got up and hurried to the lions' den. ²⁰When he came near the den, he called to Daniel in an anguished voice, "Daniel, servant of the living God, has your God, whom you serve continually, been able to rescue you from the lions?"

²¹Daniel answered, "May the king live forever! ²²My God sent his angel, and he shut the mouths of the lions. They have not hurt me, because I was found innocent in his sight. Nor have I ever done any wrong before you, Your Majesty."

²³The king was overjoyed and gave orders to lift Daniel out of the den. And when Daniel was lifted from the den, no wound was found on him, because he had trusted in his God.

²⁴At the king's command, the men who had falsely accused Daniel were brought in and thrown into the lions' den, along with their wives and children. And before they reached the floor of the den, the lions overpowered them and crushed all their bones.

As Daniel's friends were not preserved from the furnace, Daniel was not preserved from the lion's pit. Daniel was actually thrown into the lion's den. God often does not deliver us from the pit, but meets us in the pit—he joins us in the lion's den and protects us there. As he did in

God delivers in the pit

the fiery furnace with Daniel's friends, God sent an angel to be with Daniel in the lion's pit. No matter what pit you are in, God is with you. If you are in the pit right now, if you hear roaring lions, know that God is with you in the pit. You are not alone. God may not deliver you *from* the pit, but he will deliver you *in* the pit.

Amazingly, King Darius called Daniel "the servant of the living God" (20b). The word "living" puts God in contrast to the dead idols of Babylon. And Darius knew that Daniel continually served the living God. Do people know that about you? Would they say that you continually serve God? Even from the lion's den, Daniel spoke respectfully to the king and assured King Darius that he was innocent and had never done wrong to his majesty. From deep distress, King Darius shifted to being overjoyed.

Daniel was lifted from the den with no wounds. I love the last line of 6:23: "Because he had trusted in his God." Here is the third character trait of Daniel that we should emulate. Daniel confidently trusted in The Big God who is bigger than hungry lions. No matter what hungry lions are threatening to eat you, trust God to shut their mouths.

In the end, these corrupt officials who set a trap were caught in their own trap. According to Persian custom, their wives and children were punished with them. Moms and dads, the principle is that our choices affect our children. Whether we are faithful or unfaithful to God will have an impact on our children.

The last scene of the story reminds us of King Nebuchad-nezzar's response after God's deliverance from the fiery furnace. He made a decree to the whole kingdom. Darius did the same, but it was even stronger. Nebuchadnezzar decreed that no one should speak against the true God; Darius commanded everyone to fear and revere The Big God. In the final scene of the first six chapters, we hit the crescendo. Our living eternal Big God deserves worship because he rescues his people.

Daniel 6:25–28

> Then King Darius wrote to all the nations and peoples of every language in all the earth:
> "May you prosper greatly!
> 26"I issue a decree that in every part of my kingdom people must fear and reverence the God of Daniel.
>
> "For he is the living God
>   and he endures forever;
> his kingdom will not be destroyed,
>   his dominion will never end.
> 27He rescues and he saves;
>   he performs signs and wonders
>   in the heavens and on the earth.
> He has rescued Daniel
>   from the power of the lions."
>
> 28So Daniel prospered during the reign of Darius and the reign of Cyrus the Persian.

Worship The Big God because he is the living God who endures forever. His kingdom will never end. He rescues and he saves. This is our Big God. As a result of living faithfully for The Big God in Babylon, Daniel prospered. God honors those who honor him, if not here on earth, for sure in eternity.

We began by asking how we could live faithfully in Babylon. Daniel has shown us that we can live faithfully by developing three Danielic character traits: exceptional quality, regular prayer and confident trust. We can faithfully live for God in a chaotic world by representing The Big God with exceptional quality, even in the face of political pressure because God is bigger than political enemies; by regularly praying to The Big God with steady discipline, even against legal pressure, because God is bigger than unjust laws; by confidently trusting the Big God with quiet confidence, even when facing lions, because God is bigger than hungry lions. Fundamentally, we can live faithfully because we worship the living, eternal Big God who rescues his people.

God rescues his people

I want to show you something amazing: a connection between Daniel and another man hundreds of years after Daniel. Daniel, an innocent man, was set up by political opponents who spied on him. Many years later, spies were sent to catch another man in something he said, but they could not do it because he was innocent. They set him up by using the law against him. Another political ruler, long after Darius, thought the man was innocent and tried to free him, but the official was trapped, so he condemned him to death. Just like Daniel, the man was arrested while he was praying in a private location where he often prayed. After he was executed, he was put into a grave with a stone rolled over the entrance and a seal to secure it. Three days later he rose alive on Easter Sunday. The Big God is amazing and so is his book.

On the basis of his death and resurrection, Jesus offers life to every person on earth. He promises to free us from the eternal pit which we all deserve because of our sin. The only way to a relationship with The Big God as your Father is by trusting in Jesus Christ. If you have never made that step, I urge you to do so. This is the most important decision you will ever make.

God lives

Despite the apparent chaos in our world, The Big God is in control. He is bigger than political enemies, unjust laws and hungry lions. When we worship The Big God, we realize that all is well with our souls.

As a pastor, I have heard the crushing pain of many people, and yet while I feel their pain, I know that God is bigger still. God is bigger than all their chaos. God is bigger than all our chaos put together. He is The Big God!

Our faith in The Big God gives us the courage to live faithfully in Babylon no matter the consequences. Open your eyes to our amazing Big God!

God endures forever

King Darius ended chapter 6 with a powerful declaration of The Big God. Let's affirm our faith in The Big God. Let's declare that he is the living God who endures forever. He rescues and he saves. He is The Big God!

For further study on chapter 6, see the Study Guide beginning on page 233.

7

Four Great Beasts

Daniel 7

Without the reality of God's power, the future might terrify us, but it need not. Daniel's opening vision in chapter 7 reveals with uncanny accuracy the empires to come in the centuries after he would die. According to Daniel, it is not the details of the future but the character of our Big God that gives us confidence to face tomorrow.

Many commentators agree that chapter 7 is the most important chapter of the book of Daniel. It is the turning point of the book and has enormous significance prophetically. It is the most frequently quoted chapter in the New Testament. Let's jump into Daniel 7 to see what we can learn about the future and about our Big God.

Daniel's first vision occurred during the first year of Belshazzar, king of Babylon (likely 553 BC), when Daniel was about 67 years old. Everything in the vision is on a worldwide scale. It gives keys to understanding history and the future in an international scope. Let me point out upfront that the complexity of images has led to varying interpretations. Despite differences in views of the details, the main point is clear and helps us deal with our fears in this scary world.

You are about to meet a few major characters which we will identify soon: the beasts, the little horn, the Ancient of Days and the Son of Man. Be prepared; the vision is emotionally disturbing.

Get ready to pay close attention. Read straight through the entire chapter which will take about five minutes. Imagine you are Daniel seeing this vision. Don't be discouraged. It will not be clear to you at first. It was not to Daniel either.

Daniel 7:1–28

In the first year of Belshazzar king of Babylon, Daniel had a dream, and visions passed through his mind as he was lying in bed. He wrote down the substance of his dream.

2Daniel said: "In my vision at night I looked, and there before me were the four winds of heaven churning up the great sea. 3Four great beasts, each different from the others, came up out of the sea.

4"The first was like a lion, and it had the wings of an eagle. I watched until its wings were torn off and it was lifted from the ground so that it stood on two feet like a human being, and the mind of a human was given to it.

5"And there before me was a second beast, which looked like a bear. It was raised up on one of its sides, and it had three ribs in its mouth between its teeth. It was told, 'Get up and eat your fill of flesh!'

6"After that, I looked, and there before me was another beast, one that looked like a leopard. And on its back it had four wings like those of a bird. This beast had four heads, and it was given authority to rule.

7"After that, in my vision at night I looked, and there before me was a fourth beast—terrifying and frightening and very powerful. It had large iron teeth; it crushed and devoured its victims and trampled underfoot whatever was left. It was different from all the former beasts, and it had ten horns.

⁸"While I was thinking about the horns, there before me was another horn, a little one, which came up among them; and three of the first horns were uprooted before it. This horn had eyes like the eyes of a human being and a mouth that spoke boastfully.

⁹"As I looked,

> "thrones were set in place,
>> and the Ancient of Days took his
>> seat.
> His clothing was as white as snow;
>> the hair of his head was white
>> like wool.
> His throne was flaming with fire,
>> and its wheels were all ablaze.
> ¹⁰A river of fire was flowing,
>> coming out from before him.
> Thousands upon thousands attended
>> him;
>> ten thousand times ten thousand
>> stood before him.
> The court was seated,
>> and the books were opened.

¹¹"Then I continued to watch because of the boastful words the horn was speaking. I kept looking until the beast was slain and its body destroyed and thrown into the blazing fire. ¹²(The other beasts had been stripped of their authority, but were allowed to live for a period of time.)

¹³"In my vision at night I looked, and there before me was one like a son of man, coming with the clouds of heaven. He approached the Ancient of Days

and was led into his presence. ¹⁴ He was given authority, glory and sovereign power; all nations and peoples of every language worshiped him. His dominion is an everlasting dominion that will not pass away, and his kingdom is one that will never be destroyed.

¹⁵"I, Daniel, was troubled in spirit, and the visions that passed through my mind disturbed me. ¹⁶I approached one of those standing there and asked him the meaning of all this.

"So he told me and gave me the interpretation of these things: ¹⁷'The four great beasts are four kings that will rise from the earth.

¹⁸"'But the holy people of the Most High will receive the kingdom and will possess it forever—yes, for ever and ever.'

¹⁹"Then I wanted to know the meaning of the fourth beast, which was different from all the others and most terrifying, with its iron teeth and bronze claws—the beast that crushed and devoured its victims and trampled underfoot whatever was left. ²⁰I also wanted to know about the ten horns on its head and about the other horn that came up, before which three of them fell—the horn that looked more imposing than the others and that had eyes and a mouth that spoke boastfully. ²¹As I watched, this horn was waging war against the holy people and defeating them, ²²until the Ancient of Days came and pronounced judgment in favor of the holy people of the Most High, and the time came when they possessed the kingdom.

²³"He gave me this explanation: 'The fourth beast is a fourth kingdom that will appear on earth. It will be different from all the other kingdoms and will devour the whole earth, trampling it down and crushing it. ²⁴The ten horns are ten kings who will come from this kingdom. After them another king will arise, different from the earlier ones; he will subdue

*three kings. ²⁵He will speak against the Most High
and oppress his holy people and try to change the set
times and the laws. The holy people will be delivered
into his hands for a time, times and half a time.*

*²⁶"But the court will sit, and his power will be
taken away and completely destroyed forever. ²⁷Then
the sovereignty, power and greatness of all the
kingdoms under heaven will be handed over to the
holy people of the Most High. His kingdom will be an
everlasting kingdom, and all rulers will worship and
obey him.'*

*²⁸"This is the end of the matter. I, Daniel, was
deeply troubled by my thoughts, and my face turned
pale, but I kept the matter to myself."*

The vision rocked Daniel. Let's unpack the dream and its interpretation by identifying the four main characters and what we learn about God and the future from each.

The beasts = four historical empires

Emotionally, the four beasts are horrifying. Four grotesque, cruel beasts come up out of the stormy sea. They are mutants. One follows the other, giving us a pattern of evil empire following evil empire.

The first beast was like a lion with the wings of an eagle. Archaeology has uncovered statues of winged lions in the ruins of Babylon and we know lions decorated the famous Ishtar Gate. The lion is Babylon.

Then came the one like a bear raised on one side with three ribs between its teeth. This symbolizes Media and Persia with the higher side symbolizing Persia who rose to dominance in the alliance. The bear is Media-Persia.

The third mutant beast is like a leopard with four wings and four heads. A leopard is fast and has an insatiable thirst for blood.

The leopard stands for Greece. Alexander the Great invaded "in 334 B.C. and within ten short years (by the age of thirty-two) had conquered the entire Medo-Persian Empire to the borders of India."[26] After Alexander died in 323 BC, his generals carved the kingdom into four parts. The leopard is Greece with its four heads.

The fourth beast defies any analogy to a known animal. It is terrifying and very powerful with large iron teeth. It crushed and devoured its victims. The fourth beast is Rome who took over the Mediterranean world and much more.

But this fourth beast is different from the others. It has ten horns. Three horns are uprooted by an eleventh little horn that rose up with eyes like a human and a boastful mouth. This last image depicts a future version of the fourth beast in a new configuration. We will share more in the next section when we move to the future, but for now let's consider what we learn from the four beasts representing four historical empires.

For those of you who remember Daniel 2, some of this may sound familiar. In chapter 2, Daniel interpreted a dream by King Nebuchadnezzar of a giant statue made of four metals that corresponded directly to the animals in this vision. The gold head matches the lion; the silver chest the bear; the bronze waist the leopard and the iron legs the fourth terrifying beast with iron teeth.

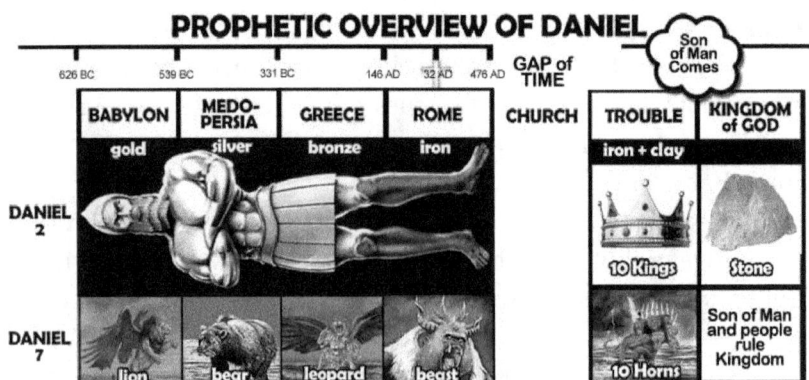

PROPHETIC OVERVIEW OF DANIEL

BABYLON	MEDO-PERSIA	GREECE	ROME	CHURCH	TROUBLE	KINGDOM of GOD
gold	silver	bronze	iron		iron + clay	

626 BC — 539 BC — 331 BC — 146 AD — 32 AD — 476 AD — GAP of TIME — Son of Man Comes

DANIEL 2 — 10 Kings — Stone

DANIEL 7 — lion / bear / leopard / beast — 10 Horns — Son of Man and people rule Kingdom

Through this book, we will add to this chart. Note: For a full color image, go to BruceBMiller.com.

Here's what's amazing. Daniel predicted three empires that would follow the one in which he was living. He did this in 553 BC, hundreds of years before Persia, Greece or Rome existed. Some people argue Daniel must have been written much later because it is impossible for him to have known so much in advance, but the evidence shows the book was written in the 500s BC. Here's the truth we learn about God.

The Big God controls history

What Daniel predicted about empires came true in detail. It happened. You can trust a God with this kind of power. If these prophecies came true in the past, then we can expect that Daniel's predictions about the future will also happen.

The good news is that God controls history, but there is some bad news. Life is not a picnic. The world is not going to get progressively better. The next character in the dream is the little horn. What do we know about this little horn? It uproots three of the ten horns. It has human eyes, which com- municates that it is very intelligent. It is more imposing that all the other horns. It has a mouth that speaks boastfully. It wages war against God's people and appears to be defeating them. It will devour the whole earth, trampling it down and crushing it. It will speak against the Most High and oppress his people. It will try to change the set times and the laws. For a brief time, God's people will be delivered into his hands.

God controls history

Little horn = the Antichrist

Nothing is more dangerous than an evil genius. We know this from shows such as *MegaMind* and *Pinky and the Brain*. Seriously, this little horn, who we can identify from other biblical texts as the Antichrist, will lead a federation of nations that apparently have a connection back to the Roman Empire. He will be brilliant and arrogant. Great evil arises when a charismatic leader rallies people to hate others and call them the enemy.

The word for "oppress" literally means "to wear out." He will try to eliminate set times which probably refers to religious holidays. And he will try to change moral laws. Even today our enemy, the devil, tries to wear us down by harassing us. Exhaustion and discouragement block many Christians from living all in for God. Don't give up. You will come to the end of your human strength, but God's power never ends. You can stand and move forward in God's strength.

The Big God allows evil only for a time

The Bible is realistic. It's going to get worse out there. We live in a fallen world where evil people do terrible things. That's the bad news. Here is the good news.

I love the massive scene shift in 7:9 from the raging sea to a heavenly courtroom.

Ancient of Days = God the Father

Starting in verse 9, Daniel shifted to poetry to describe his vision of the future in heaven. The Ancient of Days takes his seat on the throne. His clothing is white, symbolizing purity; his head is white like wool, symbolizing wisdom. His throne is a blazing fire with a river of fire flowing from before him, symbolizing righteous judgment.

The court is seated and the books are opened. Judgment is about to begin. The great judge, the chief justice of the universe, will judge the beast and all humanity.

Suddenly the terrifying fourth beast will be slain. He will be done. His power will be taken away and he will be completely destroyed forever. It will look like the little horn, the Antichrist, is winning, when suddenly the Ancient of Days ends it. God wins.

The Big God will destroy evil

The little horn with a big mouth will spew out hatred toward God when suddenly God's judgment will silence him forever.

How does this truth impact us today? Here is one of the major answers to evil. God is allowing evil to have its day, but only for a time. We know how it will end. God wins. He totally defeats evil once and for all. When you know how it ends, you can deal with minor defeats and setbacks today.

I'm sure you remember the greatest college football game of all time (in my opinion)—the 2006 Rose Bowl where the mighty Texas Longhorns (my alma mater) defeated the highly-touted USC Trojans, who had been called by a sports network the greatest team ever to play college football, until that game. Riding a 34-game winning streak, USC featured two Heisman Trophy winners in the backfield—quarterback Matt Leinart and running back Reggie Bush. From a human standpoint, USC had everything going for them. With about five minutes to go, USC was ahead 38 to 26.

At USC's last touchdown, two UT players were hurt; one broke his arm. The announcer said, "There is the dagger." It looked like it was over. The other team had won—until UT scored two touchdowns and then with 19 seconds to go, Vince Young scored a two-point conversion, giving UT the 41–38 victory. Watching the game was nerve-wracking, especially if you were watching it with my son Jimmy, a fanatical UT fan. But now Jimmy has the DVD of the game and while re-watching it over and over is still exciting, most of the fear is gone because we know how it ends. Even the setbacks are exciting because they just make the victory all the sweeter. UT wins that game every time.

Let me tell you how the world ends: God wins. In eternity, we may just want to re-watch the DVD of the end of history so we can be reminded over and over again. **God wins** God wins, every time.

every time In the end at the judgment when the books are open and our lives are reviewed by the great judge, how will we fare? We know what happens to the Antichrist and he deserves it. What about you and me? When God reviews everything we have done and not done; everything we have thought; our motivations for what we have done; how will our book read? Not good. It is the last character in the vision who gives us hope of surviving judgment day.

The last character is the Son of Man. Who is the Son of Man? Look back at 7:13–14. We know that he comes with the clouds. He is given all authority and all people will worship him. He will rule an eternal kingdom.

Son of Man = Jesus Christ

Clouds are associated with the appearance of God. The Psalms state he makes the clouds his chariot (Psalm 104:3). Daniel 7:13 is the most quoted verse from Daniel in the New Testament.

Daniel 7:13–14

In my vision at night I looked, and there before me was one like a son of man, coming with the clouds of heaven. He approached the Ancient of Days and was led into his presence. 14 He was given authority,

glory and sovereign power; all nations and peoples of
every language worshiped him. His dominion is an
everlasting dominion that will not pass away, and his
kingdom is one that will never be destroyed.

Jewish readers would have been surprised to see one like a son of man on clouds because this is divine imagery. Ancient Jewish writers identified the Son of Man as the Messiah. Now let's listen with new ears to what Jesus said in his mock trial before the high priest when Jesus quoted Daniel 7:13:

Again the high priest asked him, "Are you the
Messiah, the Son of the Blessed One?" "I am," said
Jesus. "And you will see the Son of Man sitting at the
right hand of the Mighty One and coming on the
clouds of heaven." The high priest tore his clothes.
"Why do we need any more witnesses?" he asked.
"You have heard the blasphemy" (Mark 14:61b–64a).

The high priest understood that Jesus was claiming to be the Messiah, even God himself. Jesus Christ, the Son of Man, will rule over the entire earth as the King of Kings in an eternal kingdom just as real as Babylon, Greece or Rome.

The Big God will rule

We know how it ends. God rules the world forever. He is the victor. Notice in Daniel 7 that the people of the Most High will possess the kingdom forever. God's holy people will reign with Jesus Christ. This is frankly amazing and outrageous. It's one thing to play on a winning football team, but what about playing on the team victorious over the whole world that will reign forever in a kingdom of peace? Wow!

How do we get to be part of that?! The answer is that the Son of Man came to rescue humanity oppressed by evil, humanity destroying ourselves with our own selfishness and greed. He came once and won the decisive battle of Golgotha on the cross and from the empty tomb, he rose from the dead. Today he offers eternal life to those who will repent and believe in him and give him allegiance. You can be on the eternally winning team.

God offers eternal life

This is a heavy vision. Daniel turned pale. The Bible is realistic and sober. Yes, evil is real and it is going to get worse. But deeper still is the confidence we can have in facing the future because we trust The Big God. You can trust The Big God with the uncertain future because he controls history and while today he allows evil for a time, soon he will destroy evil once and for all and will personally rule over the whole world forever. Although it may look for a while like evil has the upper hand, do not be confused, God has it all in his hands. There is no question who wins. I love the famous true saying: "I don't know what tomorrow holds, but I know who holds tomorrow." If you are a believer, then the proper response to Daniel 7 is worship.

> *Therefore, since we are receiving a kingdom that cannot be shaken, let us be thankful, and so worship God acceptably with reverence and awe, for our "God is a consuming fire"* (Hebrews 12:28–29).

For further study on chapter 7, see the Study Guide beginning on page 247.

8

The Ram and the Goat

Daniel 8

News reports of persecution against Christians can seem so distant, until it happens to someone you know personally. One of my longtime friends is Musa Asake from Nigeria. He has been in my home many times. I've visited him in Jos and been to his mom's home in their village.

Musa currently leads the Christian Association of Nigeria (CAN), an umbrella organization over churches in Nigeria. Recently Musa was in Washington, DC meeting with people from the State Department to make the case that the American government should declare Boko Haram a terrorist organization. Boko Haram is a violent Islamic sect that attacks Christians on a weekly basis including bombing churches. In an email to me, Musa wrote:

> "Greetings to you and your family and happy
> Easter. I want to thank God and to also thank you for
> your partnership with us in this great ministry. . . .

"The challenge for the church in Nigeria now is very critical. The Muslim extremist group is busy killing innocent people and burning down places of worship. We Christians in Northern Nigeria are very helpless now. We are crying to our God on a daily basis but also bearing in mind that His timing is different from ours and so we will continue to wait on Him hoping and trusting that this merciless kind of killing will one day stop to His glory. Pray for special protection from above for me and my family as we serve God in this dangerous position of being the spokesperson for the church in Nigeria at this time.

"Pray for the families that have lost their loved ones in this continued crisis. Examples: Mrs. Deborah Shettima from Borno watched her husband killed by the insurgents, they took away her two daughters, ages seven and nine, and she has not heard of them to date. Three months later they came back and killed her remaining 16-year-old son leaving her alone with no place to stay. Hannatu Andrew also lost her husband and four children. In one day their house burnt to ashes and many others. Pray for Pastor Sarna Chindo in Kano who lost eight of his members the evening of 23 of February 2013 to these senseless killers.

"Yesterday there was a mass burial of 28 people that were brutally murdered at the early hours of Sunday at Attakar. I am visiting the scene tomorrow. Pray for my safety as I don't have any protection from the government but from God for sure. Pray that we continue to have the spirit of forgiveness in the midst of these difficult and trying times."

Yours in His service,
Musa and Tabitha Asake

How do we process this kind of violence? How can Musa have so much faith and courage and love? With such terrible things happening, it is easy to wonder what God is doing. You might find yourself questioning whether God is powerful and good. Is he involved in this uncertain world? You would not be the first one to ask questions like these. These are important questions. While we do not receive full answers, we do get perspective from the book of Daniel. Certainly one response is to pray. In fact, please take a moment to pray for Musa and his wife, Tabitha.

In America, physical torture and serious persecution are rare. We usually encounter them only in movies and reports from other parts of the world. From the vantage point of world history, we live in a time and place of unusual peace and prosperity. Most human beings have lived through harder times. It is likely that we, or our children, will face more difficult days ahead. How will we handle harder times? We can gain insight on how to do that by seeing our Big God more clearly in Daniel 8.

Background history

It was about 550 BC. In his vision, Daniel saw himself in the citadel of Susa. Susa "was about 220 miles east of Babylon and 150 miles north of the Persian Gulf."[27] In 1901, archaeologists discovered the famous Code of Hammurabi in Susa. The Code of Hammurabi, a Babylonian law code, is one of the oldest deciphered writings of significant length in the world dating to over one thousand years before Daniel. The biblical characters Esther and Nehemiah lived in Susa where Esther served as queen. We must never forget that we are not dealing with myth and legend but with concrete history of real people in real places.

As we prepare to read chapter 8, get ready to hear about more animals: a ram and a goat and we meet another horn. Is it the same horn as the one in chapter 7? The political references of the ram and the goat will be clear, but the horn is more mysterious. Read the entire chapter to get a sense of the whole.

Daniel 8:1–27

In the third year of King Belshazzar's reign, I, Daniel, had a vision, after the one that had already appeared to me. ²In my vision I saw myself in the citadel of Susa in the province of Elam; in the vision I was beside the Ulai Canal. ³I looked up, and there before me was a ram with two horns, standing beside the canal, and the horns were long. One of the horns was longer than the other but grew up later. ⁴I watched the ram as it charged toward the west and the north and the south. No animal could stand against it, and none could rescue from its power. It did as it pleased and became great.

⁵As I was thinking about this, suddenly a goat with a prominent horn between its eyes came from the west, crossing the whole earth without touching the ground. ⁶It came toward the two-horned ram I had seen standing beside the canal and charged at it in great rage. ⁷I saw it attack the ram furiously, striking the ram and shattering its two horns. The ram was powerless to stand against it; the goat knocked it to the ground and trampled on it, and none could rescue the ram from its power. ⁸The goat became very great, but at the height of its power the large horn was broken off, and in its place four prominent horns grew up toward the four winds of heaven.

⁹Out of one of them came another horn, which started small but grew in power to the south and to the east and toward the Beautiful Land. ¹⁰It grew until it reached the host of the heavens, and it threw some of the starry host down to the earth and trampled on them. ¹¹It set itself up to be as great as the commander of the army of the LORD; it took away the daily sacrifice from the LORD, and his sanctuary was thrown down. ¹²Because of rebellion, the LORD's people and the daily sacrifice were given over to it. It

prospered in everything it did, and truth was thrown to the ground.

¹³Then I heard a holy one speaking, and another holy one said to him, "How long will it take for the vision to be fulfilled—the vision concerning the daily sacrifice, the rebellion that causes desolation, the surrender of the sanctuary and the trampling underfoot of the LORD's people?"

¹⁴He said to me, "It will take 2,300 evenings and mornings; then the sanctuary will be reconsecrated."

¹⁵While I, Daniel, was watching the vision and trying to understand it, there before me stood one who looked like a man. ¹⁶And I heard a man's voice from the Ulai calling, "Gabriel, tell this man the meaning of the vision."

¹⁷As he came near the place where I was standing, I was terrified and fell prostrate. "Son of man," he said to me, "understand that the vision concerns the time of the end."

¹⁸While he was speaking to me, I was in a deep sleep, with my face to the ground. Then he touched me and raised me to my feet.

¹⁹He said: "I am going to tell you what will happen later in the time of wrath, because the vision concerns the appointed time of the end. ²⁰The two-horned ram that you saw represents the kings of Media and Persia. ²¹The shaggy goat is the king of Greece, and the large horn between its eyes is the first king. ²²The four horns that replaced the one that was broken off represent four kingdoms that will emerge from his nation but will not have the same power.

²³"In the latter part of their reign, when rebels have become completely wicked, a fierce-looking king, a master of intrigue, will arise. ²⁴He will become very strong, but not by his own power. He will cause astounding devastation and will succeed in whatever he does. He will destroy those who are mighty, the holy people. ²⁵He will cause deceit to prosper, and he will consider himself superior. When they feel secure, he will destroy many and take his stand against the Prince of princes. Yet he will be destroyed, but not by human power.

26"The vision of the evenings and mornings that has been given you is true, but seal up the vision, for it concerns the distant future."

27I, Daniel, was worn out. I lay exhausted for several days. Then I got up and went about the king's business. I was appalled by the vision; it was beyond understanding.

After seeing this vision, how would you have felt? At first Daniel was terrified and fell on his face. This was likely God's voice echoing through the canal. Before The Big God, we sense our smallness and our sinfulness. An angel named Gabriel gave Daniel the interpretation. This is the first time in the Bible where a holy angel was called by name. It is Gabriel who appeared to Zechariah, the father of John the Baptist, and to Mary, the mother of Jesus. By the end of the interpretation, Daniel was exhausted and appalled by the vision. And yet he went about the king's business even though he did not understand all that he saw.

Before we unpack the truth in this chapter, let's go back to a 50,000 foot level and see how this chapter fits with what we have learned from the visions in chapters 2 and 7.

In chapter 2, we saw the statue with four kinds of metal representing four empires, then ten toes and then a massive stone which crushed the statue, representing the future kingdom of God. In chapter 7, we saw four animals representing the same empires, then ten horns and a little horn rise up, then the Son of Man defeats the horn and he rules with his people forever.

In chapter 8, we meet a ram and a goat that correspond to the second and third of the four empires: Medo-Persia and Greece, followed by a horn that seems similar to the little horn from chapter 7. In each case, we are looking at historical empires followed by a gap of time (in which we are living now), followed by the end of history, and the eternal earthly kingdom of God.

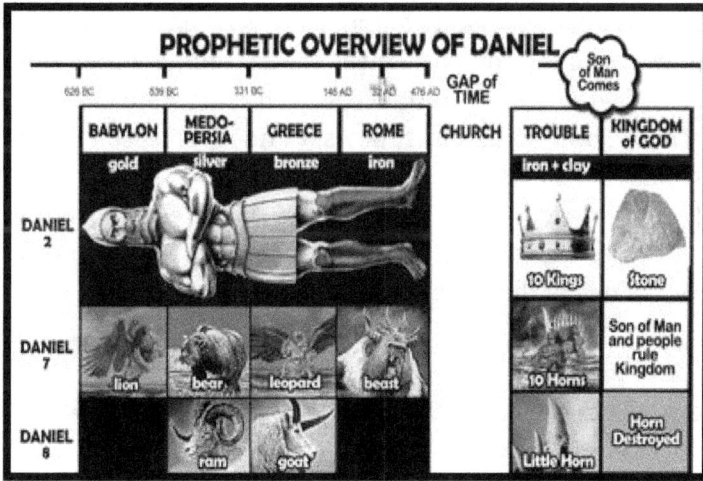

Note: For a full color image, go to BruceBMiller.com.

The ram and the goat

If we're not careful, we can start reading Daniel like a history book. Remember, these visions were prophetic! Everything Daniel envisioned was future to him. We know the ram represents Medo-Persia. According to a fourth century writer, when the Persian ruler marched before his army, he carried a gold head that looked like a ram.[28] One of the ram's horns was larger than another because Persia, although smaller at the start, grew to be the dominant of the two powers.

Although the ram was powerful, suddenly a goat with a prominent horn between its eyes shattered the ram in great rage as it charged at high speed. The goat is Greece led by Alexander the Great, the prominent horn. Alexander was educated under Aristotle and became one of the great military strategists of history. He was only 20 years old when he succeeded his dad as king. With about 35,000 troops, Alexander crossed the Hellespont and conquered the entire Medo-Persian Empire in a short three years. He died on June 13, 323 BC, at a mere 32 years of age. After his death, his kingdom was divided among four generals roughly according to the four directions of the compass; these are the four horns growing up toward the four winds. Cassander received "Macedonia and Greece; Lysimachus, Thrace and much of Asia Minor; Seleucus, Syria and vast regions to the east; and Ptolemy, Egypt."[29]

The description of the ram and the goat "are simply a prelude to the focus of the passage, which centers on a small horn that grows out of one of the four."[30]

The horn will destroy God's people

Who is this horn? Unlike the ram and goat, identifying the horn is not so clear. Let's talk about interpretation. Often an event or symbol in the Old Testament finds fuller meaning or fulfillment in the New Testament. For instance, the lamb's blood on the doors at Passover in Egypt saved the Jews from the angel of death killing the firstborn. That blood represents the blood of Jesus, the Lamb of God, poured over the cross, which provides salvation from eternal death for all humanity when we receive his gift in faith. When the Israelites wandered in the desert, God provided them with water and manna to sustain their lives. Later we learn that Jesus is the water of life (John 4:14) and the bread of life (John 6:35, 48, 51).

Sometimes prophecies will have a partial near fulfillment and a later complete fulfillment. For instance, God promised Israel a righteous king and he provided David and Solomon as kings over

Israel, but they are only small examples of the King of Kings to come, Jesus Christ, who will rule over the entire world.

The horn refers partially to a ruler named Antiochus IV, the eighth ruler of the Seleucid Empire, one of the four divisions of Greece. He ruled for about nine years from 175 to 164 BC and did horrible things to the Jews. However, Antiochus IV prefigures a much more evil ruler to come, the Antichrist. Through history there have been many antichrist figures who give us a terrible pattern of what the ultimate Antichrist will be like.

Some scholars think Daniel was only referring to Antiochus IV; others think that he was referring to both Antiochus and the Antichrist but exactly how is debated. Is the Antichrist described directly or only Antiochus who then functions as an historical type of the Antichrist to come? My view is that Antiochus is referenced in 8:9 as the one who comes from one of the four horns, but that most of the description in the vision and its interpretation directly depicts the future Antichrist. I base that view on the exaggerated language such as that the horn grew until it reached the host of heaven and secondly, on the time references such as that the vision concerns the time of the end, the distant future.

Historically we know about Antiochus IV, also called Antiochus Epiphanes, from 1 and 2 Maccabees (books contained in the Apocrypha) which describe the persecution of the Jews under Antiochus and the Jews' astonishing revolt against him led by Judas Maccabeus and celebrated in the Jewish festival of Hanukkah every December. Hanukkah celebrates the rededication of the temple by the Maccabees. Antiochus assassinated the high priest and slaughtered about 80,000 people including children. He erected an altar to Zeus in the Jewish temple area, desecrating it by offering pigs as sacrifices on it. He burned copies of the Torah scrolls. I will not give detail, but he grossly tortured people.

All of this anticipates the ultimate Antichrist who will do these things and worse. Let's look at Antichrist's character. The horn is described as arrogant; he considers himself superior setting himself up to be as great as the commander of the Lord's army. He is a liar who throws truth to the ground. He is a deceiver, a master of intrigue, which means he is good at twisting truth. He will make deceit prosper. And he becomes very strong but not by his own power implying his connection to black arts, the demonic world.

We all deal with people who to a lesser degree exhibit antichrist-like behavior: arrogance, lying, deception and dark supernatural interests. Frankly, we too can be tempted to live this way; to see that a way to power and success is through arrogance and deception. We must resist the ways of this world and instead embrace the way of Jesus in humility and truth.

This horn will take away religious practices such as the daily sacrifice and cause astounding devastation destroying many of God's people. Finally he will take his stand against the Prince of princes. Then we read the climactic line:

> *Yet he will be destroyed, but not by human power* (Daniel 8:25b).

The Big God will destroy the horn

Here's the deal. God and evil are not equal. Good and evil are not equal powers and we do not have to worry over who will win in the end. God wins. The Big God will destroy the horn and all evil once and for all. The book of Revelation gives us a sneak peek into John's vision:

> *I saw heaven standing open and there before me was a white horse, whose rider is called Faithful and True. With justice he judges and wages war. His eyes are like blazing fire, and on his head are many crowns. He has a name written on him that no one knows but he himself. He is dressed in a robe dipped in blood, and his name is the Word of God. The armies*

*of heaven were following him, riding on white horses
and dressed in fine linen, white and clean. Coming out
of his mouth is a sharp sword with which to strike
down the nations. "He will rule them with an iron
scepter." He treads the winepress of the fury of the
wrath of God Almighty. On his robe and on his thigh
he has this name written:*
KING OF KINGS AND LORD OF LORDS
(Revelation 19:11–16).

The Big God wins. The stone crushes the statue: the Son of Man will rule over an eternal kingdom. The Ancient of Days will throw the beasts into the lake of fire. And we will rule with the King of Kings forever.

God defeats evil

Notice how Daniel responded. He was exhausted and appalled. He did not understand all that he saw, but after he rested, he got up and went about the king's business. That's what we are to do. The point is not to understand all the details, but rather to confidently serve God in the face of terrible evil because while God allows evil to have its day, in the end he will destroy it. The Bible is realistic. Terrible evil is perpetrated by evil dictators and it is going to get worse. Another dictator is coming who will be the worst of all. But Daniel 8 teaches us that even though powerful evil people talk big and cause great suffering; in the end, they will be defeated. Daniel 8 builds our faith and hope. History is not out of control. Life is not out of control. God is in control.

The reason Musa Asake can live with faith in Nigeria in the face of the brutality of the Boko Haram is because he knows The Big God wins and we win with him. Whatever suffering we experience here is short term. It's what we tell our kids when they scrape their elbow. It's going to hurt for a little while, but you will feel better soon. In hard times, it helps to know how it all ends. You will feel better soon. One key insight helps us prevail in difficult times: while evil appears to be winning, God will defeat it.

You can confidently serve God in the face of terrible evil because while God allows evil to have its day, in the end he will destroy it. While evil rules today, God will end it one day.

To help us solidify the truth of Daniel in our hearts and minds, I have written a Daniel Declaration. You could call it a Daniel creed. This is a declaration you can memorize. You could say it each morning while you continue to read this book:

A Daniel Declaration

> *Praise God forever and ever.*
> *For he is the living God and endures forever.*
> *All rulers will worship him.*
> *His kingdom is everlasting.*
> *Wisdom and power are his.*
> *He gives wisdom.*
> *He rescues and he saves.*
> *He is the great and awesome Big God!*

For further study on chapter 8, see the Study Guide beginning on page 261.

9

Daniel's Prayer

Daniel 9:1–21

From time to time, we all need to get back on the right track. Daniel's prayer in chapter 9 shows us how to get back on the right track. Most of us would like to improve our prayer life. Daniel shows us how with a model prayer.

Pastor and author Tony Evans was preaching at a crusade in the University of South Carolina football stadium. Thousands had gathered for the evening session, but a serious thunderstorm was expected to hit the exact time the meeting was scheduled to start.

As the sky grew darker and darker, the threat of cancellation loomed. A group of preachers and other church leaders decided to gather for a prayer meeting. Evans noted that all the preachers prayed safe prayers—ones quite undemanding of God. Then, a woman named Linda spoke up asking if she could pray.

Linda's prayer went something like this: "Lord, thousands have gathered to hear the good news about your Son Jesus Christ.

You tell us in your Word, Lord, that you do not desire any to perish but all to repent and come to a saving knowledge of Jesus. It would be a shame on your name, Lord, for all these unbelievers to go home, without hearing the gospel when you control the weather. In the name of Jesus Christ, address this storm!"

The prayer meeting ended and everyone took their places under the dark, threatening sky. The crusade leader said, "We'll go as long as we can."

Evans says he and his wife watched as the rain clouds came up to the stadium and then split in two. The storm rained on both sides of the stadium and came back together on the other side. All of those gathered for the crusade stayed dry.

How did Linda get what the preachers didn't? She had the shameless audacity to make a big ask of our Big God. Daniel's prayer in chapter 9 is a "model prayer" that makes a big ask of our Big God.

God answers prayer

Daniel's spiritual awareness drove him to Scripture which then compelled him to pray, fostered his attitude and guided his choice of words. We can embody elements of Daniel's model prayer when we:

- ❖ Come before God with humility and intensity
- ❖ Praise the awesome God
- ❖ Confess our sins
- ❖ Ask The Big God for the sake of his glory
- ❖ Expect The Big God to answer

We can learn a great deal by studying Daniel's prayer and how he prayed to God. First he reminded God of what he had told Jeremiah which Daniel learned from the Scriptures:

Daniel 9:1–2

*In the first year of Darius son of Xerxes (a
Mede by descent), who was made ruler over the
Babylonian kingdom—²in the first year of his reign, I,
Daniel, understood from the Scriptures, according to
the word of the LORD given to Jeremiah the prophet,
that the desolation of Jerusalem would last seventy
years.*

Multiple sources date the first year of Darius as being 538 BC.
This was about 13 years after the vision in chapter 8, but right after
the events in chapter 5. These were exciting and scary days. In
chapter 5, we read how Babylon fell to the Medo-Persian Empire
who was then in charge.

Daniel's spiritual eyes were opened and his current life
situation drove him to God's Word for more insight. Daniel read the
prophet Jeremiah. Notice especially these two verses:

This whole country [Judah] *will become a
desolate wasteland, and these nations* [Israel] *will
serve the king of Babylon seventy years*
(Jeremiah 25:11).

*When seventy years are completed for Babylon,
I will come to you and fulfill my good promise to
bring you back to this place*
(Jeremiah 29:10b).

Jeremiah spoke this prophecy the year Daniel was taken
captive to Babylon in 605 BC. He was in captivity for 67 years. He
realized that his people were only a few short years away from
possibly returning to Jerusalem.

Picture Daniel searching the Scriptures for more truth and
finding passages such as Leviticus 26:40a–42, where God says,
after Israel violates the covenant and has been taken into captivity:

*But if they will confess their sins and the sins of
their ancestors . . . their . . . hearts are humbled . . . I
will remember my . . . covenant with Abraham, and I
will remember the land.*

The return from exile wasn't an automatic; the Law of Moses stipulated that any return would be done in response to the people's confession of sins and repentant hearts. What Daniel found in Scripture not only caused him to pray biblically but it also fostered his attitude.

Come before God with humility and intensity

Daniel was a humble man and he entered God's presence with humility and earnestness as he pleaded with the Lord.

Daniel 9:3

*So I turned to the Lord God and pleaded with
him in prayer and petition, in fasting, and in
sackcloth and ashes.*

Daniel addressed God as "the Lord," *ădōnāy*. It's the capital "L" "Lord" in our English Bibles identifying God as the owner and ruler of the universe. We have a Big God who's not only able to hear Daniel's prayer, but he has the power to direct the affairs of world history in order to answer his prayer.

The phrase, "I turned to," meant Daniel determined to look to God in prayer, until the Lord gave him an answer. The word "pleaded" means "to wrestle." This is earnestness. In Mixed Martial Arts language, there's no "tapping out" of this prayer.

"Fasting" shows that his spiritual concerns were more important than his physical comfort. "Sackcloth" was a symbol of mourning. "Ashes" symbolized repentance. They were outward signs of inner humility. Fasting, sackcloth and ashes aren't in vogue in our day, but repentance and humility never go out of style.

What did you do when you heard of the bombing at the Boston Marathon? I'd just come out of a meeting. When told, I stopped, shook my head, grimaced and shot up a "hope everyone's OK" silent prayer, then went about my business. That is not how the families of the runners prayed. They prayed with earnest passion. Daniel prayed that kind of prayer, and he did not hesitate to confess his sins to the Lord.

Daniel 9:4a

I prayed to the LORD my God and confessed.

"Prayed" is emphatic in the Hebrew, suggesting the extreme intensity of the prayer. "LORD" is in all caps in English, which translates the Hebrew divine name "Yahweh," the name by which God introduced himself to Israel at Mount Sinai when he gave them the Ten Commandments and entered into a covenant with them. By addressing God as Yahweh, Daniel reminded God of his covenant promises to Israel, promises he was about to ask him to keep.

Daniel shows us that we should come into the presence of the Lord with an earnestness that storms the gates of heaven and a humility that realizes that he is sovereign and we are not. It was the Word of God that fostered Daniel's attitude, and then it formed the contents of Daniel's prayer.

Praise the awesome God

Daniel next showed that he knew God is a great, awesome and majestic God by expressing his praise to him.

Daniel 9:4b

Lord, the great and awesome God, who keeps
his covenant of love with those who love him and
keep his commandments.

"Awesome" comes from a Hebrew root that in this case means "one who inspires fear." God's greatness and power produce "awe and wonder." "Covenant of love" is literally "the covenant and the love." It's significant that Daniel places these two words next to each other. They refer to a particular "covenant" and a particular kind of "love."

Since the point of Daniel's prayer was that the Jews be returned to their homeland, the Abrahamic covenant was probably in his view. In it, God specifically promised Abraham a land and national existence for his descendants, Israel. The "love" is that loyal love of God by which he faithfully keeps his promises to his people. But first things first—Daniel next confessed sin.

Confess our sins

Daniel continues his prayer by confessing specific sins of his people to God. Even though God already knows our sins, he wants us to acknowledge our specific sins before him.

Daniel 9:5–6

We have sinned and done wrong. We have been
wicked and have rebelled; we have turned away from
your commands and laws. ⁶ We have not listened to
your servants the prophets, who spoke in your name
to our kings, our princes and our ancestors, and to all
the people of the land.

Notice the plural personal pronoun "we." Daniel confessed not just his own sin but also the sin of his people. Rarely do most of us consider our complicity in the sins of our group or nation. Four different aspects of Israel's sin are set forth in 9:5–6. In the Hebrew, each one carries a certain nuance.

1. "Sinned" means Israel had "missed God's mark" of holy living and had "fallen short" of God's design to be a holy people.

2. "Done wrong" depicts something "twisted or perverted." Israel had veered from the straight and narrow and "made its path crooked."

3. "Be wicked" is one who is guilty of crimes. Their crime was rebellion against God.

4. "We have turned away" describes their rebellion, as turning from the covenant, refusing to obey God's commands and laws.

Yet God was gracious! He sent his prophets, from kings to common people, to warn the nation to repent. None of them, however, responded or acknowledged guilt.

Psychiatrist Scott Peck who often worked with convicted prisoners finally decided, "The central defect of evil is not the sin but the refusal to acknowledge it." We're much better at excusing our sins than we are at confessing them. We're quick to point out other peoples' sins but we have a hard time admitting our own. We live in a "no-fault" culture where you can get "no-fault" insurance, and a "no-fault" divorce. The mantra of our day is, "Hey, it's not my fault."

Ever had this conversation at home with your kids? Stop arguing, stop making excuses and stop blaming each other; just raise your hand, say, "I did it," and take responsibility for your own actions! Proverbs 28:13 says:

> *Whoever conceals their sins does not prosper,*
> *but the one who confesses and renounces them finds*
> *mercy.*

Let's keep following Daniel's confessions of sins. He moves beyond himself to the sins of his people in contrast to the righteousness of God. He does not hold back. Notice his vivid language of being covered with shame and rebellion.

Daniel 9:7–10

> *Lord, you are righteous, but this day we are*
> *covered with shame—the people of Judah and the*
> *inhabitants of Jerusalem and all Israel, both near and*
> *far, in all the countries where you have scattered us*
> *because of our unfaithfulness to you. ⁸We and our*
> *kings, our princes and our ancestors are covered with*
> *shame, LORD, because we have sinned against you.*
> *The Lord our God is merciful and forgiving, even*
> *though we have rebelled against him; ¹⁰we have not*
> *obeyed the LORD our God or kept the laws he gave us*
> *through his servants the prophets.*

The contrast here is emphatic, "Lord, *you* are righteous, but this day *we* are covered with shame" (9:7a) [emphasis added]. What was their shame? Foreign armies had overrun Israel, Jerusalem was destroyed and their holy temple was desecrated and burned. But it was their own sins that had brought about these disasters. Having the law and the prophets, they had no excuse.

Even though Israel rebelled against God, there was yet hope because the sovereign Lord is "merciful" and "forgiving." God doesn't quickly punish his people and he always stands ready to bless them when they turn to him in obedience. His discipline is always just. As Daniel continues his confession of sins, he affirms God's just judgment based on his Word. Even though God has brought discipline, yet the nation has not repented and returned to God.

Daniel 9:11–14

> *All Israel has transgressed your law and turned away, refusing to obey you.*
> *Therefore the curses and sworn judgments written in the Law of Moses, the servant of God, have been poured out on us, because we have sinned against you. [12]You have fulfilled the words spoken against us and against our rulers by bringing on us great disaster. Under the whole heaven nothing has ever been done like what has been done to Jerusalem. [13]Just as it is written in the Law of Moses, all this disaster has come on us, yet we have not sought the favor of the LORD our God by turning from our sins and giving attention to your truth. [14]The LORD did not hesitate to bring the disaster on us, for the LORD our God is righteous in everything he does; yet we have not obeyed him.*

Nine centuries earlier, Moses revealed the principle by which God would deal with his covenant people: Obedience would bring incredible blessings and disobedience would bring devastating curses.

Both the "curses" and "sworn judgments" are singular and definite in the Hebrew, indicating that a particular curse was in view, and a particular "sworn judgment" was intended. The "curses" are painstakingly detailed in Leviticus 26:14–39 and Deuteronomy 28:15–68 as the just response by God for violating the covenant.

Daniel grieved that even though this great disaster had come upon Israel, "just as it is written" (9:13a), the nation still did not repent. Repentance has two aspects. The first is where you admit what you said or did was wrong. The second aspect is where you believe it enough to stop doing it.

Repentance is used in two different ways in Scripture. The first way concerns our salvation. When Jesus said, "The kingdom of God has come near. Repent and believe the good news!" (Mark 1:15b), he meant stop rejecting the love of God toward you; stop rejecting his offer of forgiveness. Admit you've sinned and that you need a Savior. Then put your faith in Christ to begin a new relationship with God.

God forgives

The second way repentance is used comes after we've crossed the line of faith once we're saved. What happens if you sin against your spouse, your boss or neighbor, but never apologize or try to fix the issue? It negatively impacts your ongoing relationship.

Same with God! In repentance, as a believer, we acknowledge our sin; we agree with God about it. It's raising our hands and taking responsibility for our sin then changing our behavior. God calls us to repent of our sins to restore our loving relationship with him and to avoid his discipline.

From affirming God's just discipline, Daniel asked The Big God to act for the sake of his own glory.

Ask The Big God for the sake of his glory
Daniel 9:15–16

Now, Lord our God, who brought your people out of Egypt with a mighty hand and who made for yourself a name that endures to this day, we have sinned, we have done wrong. 16Lord, in keeping with all your righteous acts, turn away your anger and your wrath from Jerusalem, your city, your holy hill. Our sins and the iniquities of our ancestors have made Jerusalem and your people an object of scorn to all those around us.

God delivered Israel from Egypt in order to fulfill his covenant promises to Abraham and to establish his "name" among the nations. In spite of Israel's sin, Daniel was pleading with God to remember his promises and re-establish the nation again. He asked God to act, for the sake of his own name, because Jerusalem is his "city" and his "holy hill."

Daniel 9:17–18

Now, our God, hear the prayers and petitions of your servant. For your sake, Lord, look with favor on your desolate sanctuary. [18]Give ear, our God, and hear; open your eyes and see the desolation of the city that bears your Name. We do not make requests of you because we are righteous, but because of your great mercy.

- ❖ Daniel appealed for *mercy* because the people bore God's own name.
- ❖ Daniel appealed for the *restoration* of Jerusalem, because it is God's own city.
- ❖ Daniel longed for the *rebuilding* of the temple, because it is God's own sanctuary.

The prayer reached a passionate crescendo as Daniel beseeched the Lord three times in quick succession to: "listen," "forgive," "hear," and "act," emphasizing God's sovereign power and ability to answer this prayer.

Daniel 9:19

Lord, listen! Lord, forgive! Lord, hear and act! For your sake, my God, do not delay, because your city and your people bear your Name.

Daniel felt God should answer because God's own reputation was at stake. Each day that Jerusalem lay in ruins and the Jewish people were in exile brought more shame to God's name. The cry of Daniel's heart was: Save your people, Lord, "for your sake." In faith, he expected God to answer.

Expect The Big God to answer

Daniel 9:20–21

> *While I was speaking and praying, confessing my sin and the sin of my people Israel and making my request to the LORD my God for his holy hill—²¹while I was still in prayer, Gabriel, the man I had seen in the earlier vision, came to me in swift flight about the time of the evening sacrifice.*

FedEx and UPS have nothing on the DPS, Divine Prayer Service. Light travels at over 186,000 miles per second. The prayers we pray and the answers to our prayers go even faster. Isaiah 65:24 gives an amazing promise: "Before they call I will answer; while they are still speaking I will hear." God doesn't have voicemail. We're not put on hold and told all calls will be answered in the order received.

When you pray, realize that God hears, forgives and form-ulates an answer immediately. God loves you! Your prayers are important to him. He hears and answers them before you even finish! Let's pray like Daniel based on God's Word, with humility and intensity, praising the awesome God, confessing sins with a repentant heart and making big asks all for his glory, expecting The Big God to answer.

The Big God has given us access to his throne room, directly and immediately, and promised us that he will reply. Take some time to pray to The Big God in line with Daniel's model.

> For further study on chapter 9, see the Study Guide beginning on page 273.

10

The Seventy Sevens

Daniel 9:22–27

Daniel's prophecy of "seventy 'sevens'" is a story of good news/bad news! It's neither a vision nor a dream. There are no strange animals or statues. It's a direct message from God delivered by the angel Gabriel to answer Daniel's prayer.

The second kingdom, Medo-Persia, had just defeated the first kingdom, Babylon, in fulfillment of Daniel's vision in chapter 2. This drove Daniel to God's Word. There he read that Jeremiah had prophesied the Babylonian captivity would be 70 years long. Daniel had already been in captivity 67 years, so the end of exile was in sight.

Daniel further realized from Scripture that a return from captivity would only come after confession of sins and repentance by Israel, so he prayed on behalf of the nation. The moment Daniel started praying, the heavens were set in motion and The Big God sent his messenger Gabriel with the answer.

Gabriel's message was, Daniel, I have good news, and I have bad news. The good news is that your prayer will be answered. But there's bad news! Israel must still endure the full extent of her punishment for violating the covenant.

The good news is Jerusalem and the temple will be restored and the Messiah will soon come. But the bad news is that the Messiah will be executed in that city!

But the best news of all is that when the Messiah dies, he will be the final sacrifice for the forgiveness of sins. But the bad news is that many will reject his atoning sacrifice. As a result, the temple and Jerusalem will be destroyed once more. Good news/bad news. That's what we'll find in Daniel 9:22–27. This text reads like a play, the unfolding of a great drama.

Prelude to the divine prophetic revelation

Daniel 9:22–27

He instructed me and said to me, "Daniel, I have now come to give you insight and understanding. 23As soon as you began to pray, a word went out, which I have come to tell you, for you are highly esteemed. Therefore, consider the word and understand the vision:

24"Seventy 'sevens' are decreed for your people and your holy city to finish transgression, to put an end to sin, to atone for wickedness, to bring in everlasting righteousness, to seal up vision and prophecy and to anoint the Most Holy Place.

25"Know and understand this: From the time the word goes out to restore and rebuild Jerusalem until the Anointed One, the ruler, comes, there will be seven 'sevens,' and sixty-two 'sevens.' It will be rebuilt with streets and a trench, but in times of trouble. 26After the sixty-two 'sevens,' the Anointed One will be put to death and will have nothing. The people of the ruler who will come will destroy the city and the

sanctuary. The end will come like a flood: War will
continue until the end, and desolations have been
decreed. *27He will confirm a covenant with many for*
one 'seven.' In the middle of the 'seven' he will put an
end to sacrifice and offering. And at the temple he
will set up an abomination that causes desolation,
until the end that is decreed is poured out on him."

Daniel's passionate prayer and humble spirit had touched the heart of God. So God sent Gabriel in person. What he brought was a prophetic revelation from God, not a vision like in chapters 7 and 8.

This is the answer to Daniel's prayer earlier in chapter 9. Let's break it down into digestible parts.

Seventy "sevens"

"Sevens" refers to periods of seven without specifying what the units are. It's the context that determines what the "sevens" are. In this context, the period of time = 490 years.

How do we get that? We saw in our last chapter that Daniel was reading Jeremiah's prophecy in chapters 25 and 29 and found that the exile would last 70 years; and it did. But Daniel missed something significant from the Law of Moses as it related to their ongoing violation of the covenant.

Four times in Leviticus 26 God says something striking. In 9:18b (ESV), "I will discipline you again sevenfold for your sins," in 9:21 (ESV), "I will continue striking you, sevenfold for your sins," then again in 9:24 and 9:28 he repeats a sevenfold penalty for violating the covenant. In other words, the full penalty for their covenant violations is that the 70 years of exile would be multiplied sevenfold, thus 70 years x 7 = 490 years of additional punishment.

God takes sin seriously and he poured out every ounce of discipline on the nation of Israel for their rebellion. As the prophet Nahum affirms,

> *The LORD is slow to anger but great in power:*
> *the LORD will not leave the guilty unpunished*
> (Nahum 1:3a).

You may wonder how this text connects to your daily life. We see the same powerful truth in the New Testament where Paul affirms,

> *Do not be deceived: God cannot be mocked. A*
> *man reaps what he sows. Whoever sows to please*
> *their flesh, from the flesh will reap destruction:*
> *whoever sows to please the Spirit, from the Spirit will*
> *reap eternal life* (Galatians 6:7–8).

Either we confess our sins and repent, or we face the consequences of our actions.

Gabriel said, "Seventy 'sevens' are decreed." The verb "decreed" means to "cut off." God had "snipped off" 490 years from the remainder of world history for a specific purpose. But for who? "Seventy 'sevens' are decreed" for your people. The people = God's chosen people, Israel. Many of us are not Israelites. The entire Bible is "for us" as believers, but not all of the Bible is addressed "to us."

Daniel prayed on behalf of his people Israel. God answered that prayer as it relates to his people the Jews. If the people are the Jews, then the place = Jerusalem, the Holy City. The prophet Ezekiel wrote, "This is Jerusalem, which I have set in the center of the nations, with countries all around her" (Ezekiel 5:5b). Jerusalem will be the capital city of the world one day. God calls it his "holy hill" in Psalm 2:6 (ESV). The 35 acres that make up the Temple Mount is the most disputed tract of land on the planet! To Muslims, it is one of their most holy places where the Dome of the Rock now sits.

The Temple Mount was where Abraham was willing to offer up his son, Isaac, to God: it's where Jesus offered himself as the Lamb of God on the cross, and it's where the third Jewish temple will be built. Jerusalem will be center stage at the end of this age when Christ returns. So we have the time, the people and the place.

The purpose—usher in the kingdom of God

The Big God is going to do six big things during this period of the "seventy 'sevens'... to finish transgression, to put an end to sin, to atone for wickedness, to bring in everlasting righteousness, to seal up vision and prophecy and to anoint the Most Holy Place" (Daniel 9:24). These six things include what Jesus did on the cross, and also the total scope of God's plan in the future. The "seventy 'sevens'" then take us up to the very end of the world as we know it. What are the two most basic problems of humanity? No, it's not taxes and your mother-in-law. Of all the problems of humanity, the two most basic are sin and death.

Every other problem fades in comparison. It doesn't matter who you are or where you live, sin and death must be dealt with. God reveals his plan of redemption to solve those two problems in six steps.

1. *To finish transgression*
    God will put an end to Israel's rebellion against their covenant. Israel is still in rebellion today, but that will change when Jesus returns.

2. *To put an end to sin*
    Jesus' work on the cross broke the power of sin in believers' lives, but this prophecy cannot be completely fulfilled until Christ personally returns to earth.

3. *To atone for wickedness*
    In the Old Testament sacrificial system, blood was sprinkled over the altar, depicting the people's sin was forgiven because

it was covered by the blood. Paul said in Romans, "God presented Christ as a sacrifice of atonement, through the shedding of his blood—to be received by faith" (Romans 3:25a). But Israel hasn't yet turned in faith to Christ. This won't happen until his second coming.

4. *To bring in everlasting righteousness*
   At the end of the "seventy 'sevens'" God will bring in an age of righteousness. This is the kingdom of God.

5. *To seal up vision and prophecy*
   All of God's covenant promises to Israel will be fully realized in the final kingdom. Until then, prophecies are unsealed.

6. *To anoint the Most Holy Place*
   This may refer to the dedication of the Most Holy place in the future temple described in Ezekiel 41–46. Or it may refer to the Holy One, Christ. If so, this would be the enthronement of Jesus as King of Kings and Lord of Lords in the kingdom.

These six things anticipate the establishment of Israel's promised kingdom under the authority of her promised King which will happen at the end of the decreed "seventy 'sevens.'"

* We know how long: 490 years
* We know for whom: Israel
* We know where: Jerusalem
* We know why: to bring in the kingdom of God

Now let's look at how. Gabriel detailed the program of God by explaining the divisions of "seventy 'sevens.'" Keeping with the theme of God's unfolding drama, we're going to look at God's program in six acts.

Act 1. The commencement of the clock

Daniel 9:25b

> *From the time the word goes out to restore and rebuild Jerusalem.*

The countdown clock started with the decree to rebuild Jerusalem. We read in Nehemiah 2:1 that Artaxerxes, a Persian king, issued this decree specifically to allow the Jews to rebuild the city of Jerusalem in the month Nisan in the twentieth year of his reign. Historians tell us this was spring of 444 BC. Ezra 4 says it was March of that year. So the clock on the "seventy 'sevens'" begins in March of 444 BC.

Act 2. The coming of the Christ

Daniel 9:25c

> *Until the Anointed One, the ruler, comes, there will be seven "sevens," and sixty-two "sevens." It* [Jerusalem] *will be rebuilt with streets and a trench, but in times of trouble.*

The "seventy 'sevens'" are divided into three groups: "seven 'sevens'" and "sixty-two 'sevens'" which then leaves one final "seven." A total of sixty-nine "sevens" would pass and then a significant event would take place, the "Anointed One, the ruler" would come.

"Anointed One" in Hebrew is "Messiah," a term that could designate kings, priests or prophets. Dozens of Old Testament and New Testament passages indicate Jesus fulfills all three roles—prophet, priest and king. Christ is the Greek translation of Messiah.

Daniel had just been told how to calculate exactly when the Messiah would come. The first period of "seventy 'sevens'" = 490 years, and refers to the rebuilding of Jerusalem permitted by Artaxerxes' decree. The Hebrew word "streets" has been found in the Dead Sea Copper Scrolls with the meaning "conduit," which would refer to the city's water system. "Trench" comes from a root word meaning "to cut." Jerusalem had such a trench cut into the rock outside the city walls in order to increase the exterior wall height for defense purposes.

The book of Nehemiah records that the city wall project took only 52 days and was done under extreme duress. The men worked with a weapon in one hand and a tool in the other.

Immediately following the "seven 'sevens'" were another set of "sixty-two 'sevens'" which ran consecutively with no gap in-between them. These sixty-nine "sevens" would end when the "Anointed One" comes. The New Testament calls this day the triumphal entry of Christ, which happened just days before he was crucified. Why this day?

In his triumphal entry, Jesus officially presented himself to the nation of Israel as the Messiah in fulfillment of Zechariah 9:9:

> *Rejoice greatly, Daughter Zion!*
> *Shout, Daughter Jerusalem!*
> *See, your king comes to you,*
> *   righteous and victorious,*
> *lowly and riding on a donkey,*
> *   on a colt, the foal of a donkey.*

You may recall Jesus sent his disciples to a certain man to secure this very donkey. Then while he entered Jerusalem on this donkey's back, Jesus said, "If you, even you, had only known on this day what would bring you peace—but now it is hidden from your eyes . . . because you did not recognize the time of God's coming to you" (Luke 19:42b, 44b). Israel had no excuse for not knowing this day. This day had been spelled out in their Scripture by Daniel over 500 years earlier!

I've placed the exact calculations in an endnote for all you math enthusiasts.[31] Artaxerxes' decree was issued on March 5, 444 BC, and the triumphal entry fell on March 30, AD 33. This is amazing! Why didn't someone back then just read this prophecy and calculate the general timeframe when the Messiah would come?

They did! In Matthew 2, we read of the wise men from the East who came to Jerusalem seeking the one born King of the Jews. We sing about them in our Christmas carols. These Magi were from Persia where Daniel lived. They read his prophecy and were able to understand the timing and so they traveled to Jerusalem following his star to worship Jesus at his birth. If the Magi figured out his birth, Israel should have figured out his coming.

Gabriel said two big events would occur after the sixty-nine "sevens" were completed.

Act 3. The crucifixion on the cross

Daniel 9:26a

After the sixty-two "sevens," the Anointed One will be put to death and will have nothing.

Gabriel used the Hebrew word for executing the death penalty on a criminal. Here we are reminded of Isaiah's prophecy in 53:8b that the suffering servant of God would be "cut off from the land of the living; for the transgression of my [his] people he was punished." And he would "have nothing" in the sense that Israel had rejected him and the kingdom he came to receive couldn't be instituted at that time. The second major event that would take place is revealed in Act 4.

Act 4. The collapse of the city

Daniel 9:26b

*The people of the ruler who will come will
destroy the city and the sanctuary.*

When Daniel received this prophecy, Jerusalem hadn't yet been rebuilt. So in this verse, Gabriel predicted that after the Messiah is cut off, some people will come and destroy the rebuilt city and sanctuary, again.

We know from history that in AD 70, Emperor Titus led the Roman legions against Jerusalem and utterly destroyed both the city and the temple. Josephus, the historian, who was an eyewitness, recorded this as one of the most horrible sieges in all of history. So horrible in fact any description of it would be rated NC-17 so I'll forgo. But that invasion, gruesome as it was, didn't end the nation's sufferings, for Gabriel said, "The end will come like a flood: War will continue until the end, and desolations have been decreed" (Daniel 9:26c).

Act 5. The calling of the church

The sixty-nine "sevens" ended on the day of Christ's triumphal entry. We determined earlier that the seventieth "seven" ends with Christ's return, the second coming. So there must be an interval in-between the sixty-ninth and seventieth "sevens." We've just seen two events that happened within the interval.

The Anointed One was cut off, and Jerusalem was destroyed, after the sixty-ninth "seven" but before the start of the seventieth "seven." Why this strange gap? Because Daniel's prayer and this divine revelation in answer to it has to do with Israel, the Jewish temple and the city of Jerusalem. But the period between the sixty-ninth and seventieth "seven" has to do with the church, the body of Christ. God's prophetic countdown clock for Israel's 490 years was put on hold at the triumphal entry. God pressed pause! But another clock started ticking and it's ticking away right now. It's the church clock.

Ten times in his letters, the apostle Paul calls this the "mystery of God." Colossians 1 says this "mystery" has been "kept hidden for ages and generations but is now disclosed to the saints." What is the mystery? Paul said:

> I do not want you to be ignorant of this
> mystery, brothers and sisters, so that you may not be
> conceited: Israel has experienced a hardening in part
> until the full number of the Gentiles has come in
> (Romans 11:25).

God called Israel to be a blessing to the entire world and the vessel through which the message of the kingdom of God would go out, calling all people to salvation through faith in the Messiah. But Israel rejected their Messiah and their calling, so Jesus said, "The kingdom of God will be taken away from you and given to a people who will produce its fruit" (Matthew 21:43b). The church is now "the people" charged with producing the fruit of the kingdom. This is our age; this is our purpose; this is our time; this is why we're here; it's our responsibility to produce the fruit of the kingdom.

That means it's our time to get busy serving our Lord and Master, I'm talking about serving Jesus Christ our Lord as:

❖ Emissaries of the Savior in our workplaces
❖ Ambassadors of the King with our family and friends
❖ Missionaries of the living God in our communities and world

I'm talking about declaring the gospel of Jesus Christ! The gospel of Jesus Christ is that Messiah has come. He's made a way for us to be reconciled to God. He's paid the penalty for sin. He offers us forgiveness, eternal life and all the blessings of the coming kingdom of God through faith in him now.

But we need to understand something! The church clock will stop ticking one day. It will happen when "the full number of Gentiles has come in" (Romans 11:25b). Boom! That's it. And it could literally happen today.

There's not a single event on God's prophetic calendar that prevents this from happening today. We could turn on the news and learn about events that initiate the final seventieth "seven." At that precise moment, the church clock stops. But the other clock, the one put on pause after sixty-nine "sevens" will start ticking again. What will happen when Israel's clock starts again? The answer comes in Act 6.

Act 6. The crushing of the Antichrist

Daniel 9:27

> *He will confirm a covenant with many for one*
> *"seven." In the middle of the "seven" he will put an*
> *end to sacrifice and offering. And at the temple he*
> *will set up an abomination that causes desolation,*
> *until the end that is decreed is poured out on him.*

It's a covenant that starts the countdown clock on Israel's seventieth "seven." This final "seven" coincides with the tribulation period of Revelation 6–19. Who is the "he" in 9:27?

❖ The "he" is the ruler "who will come"
❖ He is the "little horn" in Daniel 7 and 8
❖ He is the "beast" of Revelation 13
❖ He is the "man of sin" of 2 Thessalonians 2
❖ He is the Antichrist

Gabriel says he'll confirm a covenant. There's some ambiguity in the Hebrew as to whether he forces an agreement through superior strength, or does he swoop in to save a faltering covenant making it strong again, thus appearing to be the Messiah, the Prince of Peace.

Just imagine with me for a moment, a ten-nation alliance forms a peace agreement with Israel. By the way, this agreement could be floating around as a proposal right now. But it begins to fall apart due to three nations' leaders waffling. Then some world leader comes along and supplants those three faltering leaders, ala Daniel 7, and he confirms the agreement for seven years, making it even stronger.

What if he convinced the Arab world to allow Israel access to the Temple Mount so they could rebuild their temple? That man would receive the Nobel Peace Prize and would be *Time Magazine* "Man of the Year." This "ruler who is to come" will be that persuasive and effective. But then in the middle of that seven-year period, his true devilish nature will be revealed. He will break the agreement and set up something that will be an abomination which causes desolation.

Second Thessalonians 2:4 says he will claim to be God and demand to be worshiped. The Jews will refuse, which will unleash the Antichrist's wrath upon them for the last half of the final "seven," called the great tribulation. It will be the greatest outpouring of persecution the world has ever known. It will be an unparalleled time of evil in world history.

However, the Antichrist's wickedness will last only "until the end that is decreed is poured out on him" (Daniel 9:27b). "Poured out" picturesquely describes the flood of judgment that will overtake him. The judgment is that Christ returns and this Antichrist is thrown alive into the lake of fire.

The six big things of 9:24 will all then be completely fulfilled by our Big God as Christ ushers in the kingdom of God. God has a timetable in world history and he is working carefully according to that plan. He's unfolding his timetable and one day Jesus Christ will come again and all who are in rebellion against him and his kingdom will be judged.

The good news is that today is a day of God's mercy. It's a day of salvation. But it is not an endless day. The time for turning to Jesus in faith and obedience is limited. The church clock could literally end today. And although God works according to his **God is merciful** own timetable, he nevertheless also works through people. God expects his people, the church, to produce the fruit of the kingdom by sharing the gospel of the Messiah, the message of his kingdom.

For further study on chapter 10, see the Study Guide beginning on page 285.

11

Angels and Demons

Daniel 10:1–11:1

People are confused about angels and demons because most of our information comes from popular culture in books, movies and TV shows such as Dan Brown's best-seller *Angels and Demons,* which was later turned into a movie by the same title. Most of us can do the motions that the crowd did toward the end of *Angels in the Outfield.*

What do you really know about angels and demons? Are they real? Do they have any impact in our world today? What if you could have a better understanding of the unseen world? Sadly, even by Christians, there is so much kooky, weird teaching on this topic. Daniel 10 gives us solid insight. In this chapter, may God open our eyes to see what we do know and warn us against speculating on what we don't know. For instance, do our prayers have any impact on the unseen world?

It's common to hear someone say life is a battle. From moms with little kids on the playground, to executives in the corporate world, to drivers in traffic, it's a war out there. The Bible also describes this life as a war. What do we mean when we use war metaphors to describe our daily lives? Life is hard. On the simplest level, we feel like we have to fight just to get through corporate voicemail to get help. We have to fight to get our insurance company to pay for our obvious medical needs. We do battle with our kids and spouses. Business is a war zone where espionage, sabotage and sneak attacks are normal. We even battle with ourselves: we battle losing weight, we battle a quick temper and we battle addictions.

Sometimes the sick evil around us makes us wonder about the demonic. When a local chiropractor is convicted of sexually abusing teenage patients and a man who lives blocks from your church building kills his wife and then jumps off a bridge to his death, you rightly wonder what role supernatural evil plays in our world.

No wonder we feel weak, exhausted, and at times, terrified when it seems like we are losing the battle. We will see in our text that Daniel himself felt weak, anguished and terrified. He was deathly pale and even fainted. He knew what it felt like to face life's battles and get overwhelmed in the war. But what if you could find peace and get strength for the battle? In the end, Daniel was strengthened. Six times in the next few verses we will read about being strong. Here's my big question for us: How can we prepare for the war? We need to have more peace, insight and strength for life's battles.

For us to get there, we must first understand the war. We need to open our eyes to what is really going on in the unseen world. The great war is more than human; it is cosmic. Daniel 10 pulls back the curtain on the unseen world giving us fresh understanding of the vast war that we are involved in whether we realize it or not.

Daniel was about 85 years old when he saw the final vision. He gives us the exact time and place where he saw the vision. Read right through the entire chapter, watching closely to identify the angels and demons. Before you read, ask the Spirit to help you understand his Word.

Daniel 10:1–11:1

In the third year of Cyrus king of Persia, a revelation was given to Daniel (who was called Belteshazzar). Its message was true and it concerned a great war. The understanding of the message came to him in a vision.

²At that time I, Daniel, mourned for three weeks. ³I ate no choice food; no meat or wine touched my lips; and I used no lotions at all until the three weeks were over.

⁴On the twenty-fourth day of the first month, as I was standing on the bank of the great river, the Tigris, ⁵I looked up and there before me was a man dressed in linen, with a belt of fine gold from Uphaz around his waist. ⁶His body was like topaz, his face like lightning, his eyes like flaming torches, his arms and legs like the gleam of burnished bronze, and his voice like the sound of a multitude.

⁷I, Daniel, was the only one who saw the vision; those who were with me did not see it, but such terror overwhelmed them that they fled and hid themselves. ⁸So I was left alone, gazing at this great vision; I had no strength left, my face turned deathly pale and I was helpless. ⁹Then I heard him speaking, and as I listened to him, I fell into a deep sleep, my face to the ground.

¹⁰A hand touched me and set me trembling on my hands and knees. ¹¹He said, "Daniel, you who are highly esteemed, consider carefully the words I am about to speak to you, and stand up, for I have now been sent to you." And when he said this to me, I stood up trembling.

¹²Then he continued, "Do not be afraid, Daniel. Since the first day that you set your mind to gain understanding and to humble yourself before your God, your words were heard, and I have come in response to them. ¹³But the prince of the Persian kingdom resisted me twenty-one days. Then Michael, one of the chief princes, came to help me, because I was detained there with the king of Persia. ¹⁴Now I have come to explain to you what will happen to your people in the future, for the vision concerns a time yet to come."

¹⁵While he was saying this to me, I bowed with my face toward the ground and was speechless. ¹⁶Then one who looked like a man touched my lips, and I opened my mouth and began to speak. I said to the one standing before me, "I am overcome with anguish because of the vision, my lord, and I feel very weak. ¹⁷How can I, your servant, talk with you, my lord? My strength is gone and I can hardly breathe."

¹⁸Again the one who looked like a man touched me and gave me strength. ¹⁹"Do not be afraid, you who are highly esteemed," he said. "Peace! Be strong now; be strong."

When he spoke to me, I was strengthened and said, "Speak, my lord, since you have given me strength."

²⁰So he said, "Do you know why I have come to you? Soon I will return to fight against the prince of Persia, and when I go, the prince of Greece will come; ²¹but first I will tell you what is written in the Book of Truth. (No one supports me against them except Michael, your prince. ¹¹:¹And in the first year of Darius the Mede, I took my stand to support and protect him.)

Daniel was overwhelmed. Let's go back and walk through what happened in chapter 10 in chronological order. It was the third year of Cyrus, also called Darius, who was the human king of Persia. Daniel was given a message concerning a great war, but we never hear the message in this chapter. Rather chapter 10 is the story behind the vision. We will see the vision when we enter the last two chapters of the book.

First Daniel mourned for three weeks during a partial fast where he denied himself "choice foods," meat, wine and lotions. We know from 10:12 that during this time, he was setting his mind to gain understanding and he was humbling himself before God.

At the end of three weeks on the twenty-fourth day of the first month on the banks of the Tigris River, Daniel saw an amazing man dressed in linen with a belt of fine gold, a body like topaz, a face like lightning and arms and legs like gleaming bronze with a voice like the sound of a huge crowd. Daniel was the only one who saw the vision, but those with him were so overwhelmed with terror they ran and hid. Daniel felt helpless, turned deathly pale and fainted in a deep sleep. It's possible the man in Daniel's vision was a pre-incarnate appearance of Jesus.

A hand touched him. A new figure entered the story and got him up as he was trembling. This is the first of three times that an angelic being physically touched Daniel and brought him assurance. The angel called Daniel "highly esteemed," which means "one in whom God takes delight."[32] You might remember that Mary, the mother of Jesus, was also called highly favored by an angel. The angel said this again in 10:19. Can you imagine an angel calling you "highly esteemed?" Daniel was an amazing guy. We would do well to follow his example.

The angel told Daniel not to be afraid and then opened the curtain on the unseen world. He revealed that he started coming in to answer Daniel's prayer three weeks ago but he was detained by someone called the "prince of Persia" who resisted him until another individual named Michael, one of the chief princes, came to help him. We will dig into this later. For now, we just want to get an overview of the basic flow of events. The angel said he would explain what's going to happen in the future.

For the second time, Daniel's face hit the ground as he bowed down, speechless. For the second time, the angel touched Daniel. Daniel said he was overcome with anguish and very weak; he could hardly breathe. Then in 10:18 for a third time, the angel touched him, giving him strength, encouraging him not to be afraid, reminding him that he was highly esteemed. He encouraged him to be at peace and be strong.

In the final scene of the chapter, the angel said he would soon return to fight the prince of Persia and then the prince of Greece would come, but first he would tell Daniel what was in the Book of Truth. The section ends with the note that no one supported this angel except "Michael, your prince" (10:21b), and this angel supported and protected Michael two years earlier.

This is some wild stuff. The chapter reads like a modern-day novel about the supernatural, except that this is true. So let's unpack what Daniel called in 10:1, "the great war." After we get some understanding of the war, specifically how angels and demons are involved, then we will consider how we can prepare for the war.

The great war

The Hebrew word for "war" in 10:1 describes a military conflict. But, as the chapter makes clear, this war is more than human. Since this is a topic on which some people tend to go to weird extremes seeing demons everywhere, it is easy to swing the pendulum the other way and dismiss angels and demons as unreal. But that is as big a mistake as is the other. We must neither obsess over angels and demons nor dismiss them as fake. Instead, we want to see sober biblical truth. Let's avoid the temptation to speculate beyond the limited information the Bible gives us, but let's learn what the

Bible teaches us about the unseen world. Obviously, there is a lot going on that we don't see and often don't think about.

Let's look at what God has revealed to us about the unseen world in Daniel 10 by identifying some of the characters in the chapter. First, the man figure who appears to Daniel in 10:5 appears to be a vision of the pre-incarnate Christ. However, is this the same person who touched Daniel in 10:10? Here's the problem. This individual said he was detained for 21 days by the prince of Persia. It seems highly unlikely that Christ would need an angel to help him. In 10:11, this new unnamed figure says he has "*now* been sent." So it appears that the pre-incarnate Christ appeared and then sent an angel to bring Daniel the message.

From the text, we know that the prince of the Persian kingdom who resisted the unnamed angel has some relation to the kingdom of Persia. He has the rank of prince. He is powerful enough to resist an angel for 21 days. Therefore, when you bring the rest of biblical truth to bear, this prince of Persia is a fallen angel, a demon. He appears to have been assigned to Persia for a long period of time since this unnamed angel would return to fight him according to 10:20. He is paralleled by another figure called the prince of Greece. So we can assume some demons and angels are assigned to influence specific nations.

Angels obviously have rank since we are introduced to another angelic figure named Michael who carries the rank of chief prince. He is called "your prince" in 10:21, so Michael is assigned to the Jewish people. Angels coordinate efforts to fight demons. We see this when Michael came to help this unnamed angel and he supported and protected Michael.

We are not told why the demonic prince of Persia detained the angel that was coming to bring the message to Daniel. We do know that Persia ruled the world at that time including the land of Israel. We also know that the 70 years of captivity were finished, so Cyrus was helping the Jews return to their land and rebuild the walls of Jerusalem and the temple against serious opposition. You can read more about this in Nehemiah, Ezra and Esther where there was a Hitler-like plot to exterminate the Jews.

We learn several things about angels and demons from Daniel 10. First, angels and demons are real, have ranks, names and coordinate their activity. They are not made up fantasies. Second, angels and demons specifically influence governments and their leaders. Third, there is an unseen war going on where angels and demons are fighting each other. Fourth, our prayers impact the unseen world and answers to our prayers can be delayed by demons.

Let me address a topic you might encounter from this chapter. Some Christians teach the concept of territorial spirits. They believe territories such as the United States, Los Angeles or neighborhoods such as the Bronx have specific territorial demons assigned to them. They advocate spiritual mapping of these demons and praying against them. This is speculation beyond what Daniel teaches. Clearly there is a relationship between certain demons and specific geo-political entities. However, nowhere does the Bible instruct us to map demons or to engage territorial spirits. Rather, we are told to pray for governmental leaders with a fresh understanding of what they face.

From the rest of the Bible, we know that at the center of this cosmic war is Yahweh, the divine warrior. God fights on his people's behalf to give them the victory.[33] Daniel has been teaching us that The Big God rules. He is in charge of world affairs now and into the future. While he can, of course, override the united forces of hell or any human king, no matter how powerful, God allows demons and humans to make their own choices, but only for a limited time. We know how the war ends. We know who wins.

But today we fight battles. So how can we prepare to fight well in this great cosmic war that we are in? Today physical workout apps are popular. If you follow the plan, you can go from couch to 5K in a matter of weeks. We are involved in something so much bigger and more serious than physical fitness. But by way of analogy, what could you do to transform from spiritual couch potato to godly warrior?

The Bible describes life as a war. You need to be prepared to fight. Are you willing to work as hard for spiritual fitness as you do for physical fitness? You can prepare for the great war in three intentional ways:

1. Seek spiritual understanding
2. Humble yourself before The Big God
3. Study God's book

Daniel exemplified these ways to prepare for the war. We will do well to follow the example of the man "highly esteemed."

1. Seek spiritual understanding

Remember what Daniel did. He took three weeks to gain understanding of spiritual realities. He was a busy man with important responsibilities in the Babylonian Empire, but he took three weeks off to seek God. In fact, he left his home and his office to go to an area by the Tigris River. There were people with him, so maybe he and some friends took a spiritual retreat together to seek spiritual understanding.

In June each year, I take a three to four-day spiritual retreat alone with God, during which I often fast to seek spiritual understanding. Over the last decade, these have been some of the most significant days in my year. On our Christ Fellowship staff, we require each full-time person to take a quarterly day with God for spiritual strength.

What about you? Have you ever taken a vacation day just to seek God? Have you ever dedicated an entire Sunday to seek God? Have you ever left your home and office to get alone for several hours to seek spiritual understanding? Try it. It's worth it.

Daniel 10:12 says Daniel set his mind to gain understanding. To set your mind means to exercise your willpower to an intentional end. You will not spend extended time with God unless you are very intentional and determined. Even though it is required and paid for, our team finds it challenging to take their quarterly day with God. The author of Proverbs says if you will, "call out for insight and cry aloud for understanding, and if you look for it as for silver and search for it as for hidden treasure" (Proverbs 2:3b–4), then you will find spiritual understanding. Daniel didn't sit back and wait for understanding. He sought it with all his might. His seeking was done by humbling himself before God.

2. Humble yourself before The Big God

Pride is an anti-God state of mind. God opposes the proud but gives grace to the humble. So if we really want to seek God and be godly warriors, we will humble ourselves. We humble ourselves by becoming increasingly aware of God's holiness and our sin; of God's bigness and our humanity. Often in Scripture, fasting is connected with humbling ourselves before God.

Daniel did a partial fast for three weeks. He did not eat meat or drink wine. In addition, he did not eat "choice" food. I think he essentially fasted from chocolate; maybe no desserts or chips—those are choice foods! He limited himself to a basic diet; something like rice and beans. The point is to increase focus on seeking God. In the process of finding a new worship pastor for Christ Fellowship, I did a 40-day partial fast to seek God's guidance. I will tell you that one of my choice foods is bread, along with chips and salsa, which I did without for 40 days. As a result of the fast, I felt increased confidence in our decision.

Daniel also did not use lotion, which was common to use in a hot, dry climate. That would be like ladies not wearing make-up or guys not shaving for three weeks.

The decision to fast communicates your seriousness about humbling yourself to prepare to be a warrior for God. Having three sons in the military, I can guarantee you that during their early training, they endured rigorous discipline to prepare to serve our country. We are preparing to serve our God. We need some rigorous discipline. The cosmic war is going on today and we have a role to play in it. We are in it whether we like it or not. There are ways we can prepare. We can seek spiritual understanding, humble ourselves before The Big God and study God's book.

3. Study God's book

Take a look at 10:11 where the angel told Daniel to "consider carefully the words I am about to speak to you." To "consider carefully" means to be mentally alert. The angel said he would tell Daniel what is written in the Book of Truth. We are not told exactly what that book is. It may refer to the Bible, or to a book of what God will do in the future.

But for us today, the implication is that we should consider carefully the written revelation of God in the Bible, which is God's Book of Truth for us today. Each of us is in a different place along the path to knowing God. Let's start near the beginning and move up the path of knowing the Scriptures.

Do you have a Bible in a modern translation? Do you have a study Bible? Do you read the Bible on a daily basis? Do you have a Bible app on your smart device? Have you accessed Bible study websites? Have you read the entire Bible? Have you memorized any verses in the Bible? Have you gone beyond reading the Bible to studying the Bible? As a comparison, have you studied the Bible as hard as you have studied anything else in your life: engineering, sales, finance, whatever you are interested in? Have you gone to a seminar or conference about the Bible? You get the point.

Daniel did not just close his eyes and hope God's truth entered his mind; he studied it carefully. Today we have so many wonderful tools and resources available. Get into training. Prepare yourself to be a godly warrior by studying God's book.

This life is hard. It is appropriate to call it a battle, a war. It often feels that way, and yet rarely do we consider the unseen dimensions of the war. This is a great cosmic war in which we are part. As Daniel did, at times we feel weak and terrified. But we can find God's peace and strength by following Daniel's model.

Today, the battle is not fought with physical weapons, but spiritual ones. The apostle Paul says in Ephesians:

> *Finally, be strong in the Lord and in his mighty power. Put on the full armor of God, so that you can take your stand against the devil's schemes. For our struggle is not against flesh and blood, but against the rulers, against the authorities, against the powers of this dark world and against the spiritual forces of evil in the heavenly realms* (Ephesians 6:10–12).

Our weapons are prayer, bold faith and deep love. The irony of the gospel is that the battle is won, not through killing, but rather by dying. Jesus, the divine warrior, won his victory by dying on the cross. While we are in a tremendous war, the outcome is sure. The victory was secured on the cross and in the empty tomb. Today we join the winning side by placing our faith in Jesus Christ. If you have not done so, I urge to trust in Jesus or perhaps you need to renew your commitment to Christ. Once we are following Jesus, then we can start helping other people find and follow Christ.

We should not underestimate or ignore our enemy. Neither should we fixate on angels and demons. Rather, Daniel calls us to prepare for the great war by seeking spiritual understanding, humbling ourselves before The Big God and studying God's Word.

When we take time, as Daniel did, to seriously seek God, we will find God's peace, insight and strength. God strengthened Daniel when he felt so weak.

We are called to be warriors in a world at war so we need to be prepared. Prayer is our great communication channel with the commander in chief. In answer to prayer, sometimes God sends angels to help us. When we share the gospel, we are participating in the mission of God. When we help others, we are carrying out missions for our Big God. Be aware of the cosmic war and remember how it will all end. The Big God wins.

As a direct application of this text, I believe it would be appropriate to pray for leaders in our church and in our country. They face demonic attacks. Based on Daniel 10, we know that angels and demons fight over geo-political entities. Not only do our governmental leaders have to deal with the economy and everything else we can see, but they also face unseen influences of which they might not even be aware. In his first letter to Timothy, Paul wrote these instructions:

> *I urge, then, first of all, that petitions, prayers, intercession and thanksgiving be made for all people—for kings and all those in authority, that we may live peaceful and quiet lives in all godliness and holiness. This is good, and pleases God our Savior, who wants all people to be saved and to come to a knowledge of the truth. For there is one God and one mediator between God and mankind, the man Christ Jesus, who gave himself as a ransom for all people* (1 Timothy 2:1–6a).

Please take a moment right now to pray for your church leaders and your political leaders.

For further study on chapter 11, see the Study Guide beginning on page 295.

12

The Big God Wins

Daniel 11–12

In the finale to the book of Daniel, God opens our eyes to see that he is bigger than all our chaos, bigger than all the uncertainty of the future. Even though the present and the future may appear to be out of control, The Big God is in charge and will win in the end.

Most of us want to know what will happen in the end times. Who is the Antichrist? Are we going to suffer through a great tribulation? When is it all going to happen? What if we could know? I believe it would change how we live our daily lives. Practically, today, how should we live in light of biblical prophecy? How can we live these days well in light of what is happening and what is coming? Daniel tells us how.

Daniel's final vision in the last two chapters, 11 and 12, comes in answer to Daniel's prayer in chapter 9, even though the answer was delayed because of the battles between angels and demons that we saw in chapter 10.

151

Daniel 11:2–12

"Now then, I tell you the truth: Three more kings will arise in Persia, and then a fourth, who will be far richer than all the others. When he has gained power by his wealth, he will stir up everyone against the kingdom of Greece. ³Then a mighty king will arise, who will rule with great power and do as he pleases. ⁴After he has arisen, his empire will be broken up and parceled out toward the four winds of heaven. It will not go to his descendants, nor will it have the power he exercised, because his empire will be uprooted and given to others.

⁵"The king of the South will become strong, but one of his commanders will become even stronger than he and will rule his own kingdom with great power. ⁶After some years, they will become allies. The daughter of the king of the South will go to the king of the North to make an alliance, but she will not retain her power, and he and his power will not last. In those days she will be betrayed, together with her royal escort and her father and the one who supported her.

⁷"One from her family line will arise to take her place. He will attack the forces of the king of the North and enter his fortress; he will fight against them and be victorious. ⁸He will also seize their gods, their metal images and their valuable articles of silver and gold and carry them off to Egypt. For some years he will leave the king of the North alone. ⁹Then the king of the North will invade the realm of the king of the South but will retreat to his own country. ¹⁰His sons will prepare for war and assemble a great army, which will sweep on like an irresistible flood and carry the battle as far as his fortress.

¹¹"Then the king of the South will march out in a rage and fight against the king of the North, who will raise a large army, but it will be defeated.

¹²When the army is carried off, the king of the South will be filled with pride and will slaughter many thousands, yet he will not remain triumphant. ¹³For the king of the North will muster another army, larger than the first; and after several years, he will advance with a huge army fully equipped.

¹⁴"In those times many will rise against the king of the South. Those who are violent among your own people will rebel in fulfillment of the vision, but without success. ¹⁵Then the king of the North will come and build up siege ramps and will capture a fortified city. The forces of the South will be powerless to resist; even their best troops will not have the strength to stand. ¹⁶The invader will do as he pleases; no one will be able to stand against him. He will establish himself in the Beautiful Land and will have the power to destroy it. ¹⁷He will determine to come with the might of his entire kingdom and will make an alliance with the king of the South. And he will give him a daughter in marriage in order to overthrow the kingdom, but his plans will not succeed or help him. ¹⁸Then he will turn his attention to the coastlands and will take many of them, but a commander will put an end to his insolence and will turn his insolence back on him. ¹⁹After this, he will turn back toward the fortresses of his own country but will stumble and fall, to be seen no more.

²⁰"His successor will send out a tax collector to maintain the royal splendor. In a few years, however, he will be destroyed, yet not in anger or in battle.

²¹"He will be succeeded by a contemptible person who has not been given the honor of royalty. He will invade the kingdom when its people feel secure, and he will seize it through intrigue. ²²Then an overwhelming army will be swept away before him; both it and a prince of the covenant will be destroyed. ²³After coming to an agreement with him, he will act deceitfully, and with only a few people he will rise to power. ²⁴*When the richest provinces feel secure, he will invade them and will achieve what neither his fathers nor his forefathers did. He will distribute plunder, loot and wealth among his followers. He will plot the overthrow of fortresses— but only for a time.*

²⁵*"With a large army he will stir up his strength and courage against the king of the South. The king of the South will wage war with a large and very powerful army, but he will not be able to stand because of the plots devised against him. ²⁶Those who eat from the king's provisions will try to destroy him; his army will be swept away, and many will fall in battle. ²⁷The two kings, with their hearts bent on evil, will sit at the same table and lie to each other, but to no avail, because an end will still come at the appointed time. ²⁸The king of the North will return to his own country with great wealth, but his heart will be set against the holy covenant. He will take action against it and then return to his own country.*

²⁹*"At the appointed time he will invade the South again, but this time the outcome will be different from what it was before. ³⁰Ships of the western coastlands will oppose him, and he will lose heart. Then he will turn back and vent his fury against the holy covenant. He will return and show favor to those who forsake the holy covenant.*

³¹*"His armed forces will rise up to desecrate the temple fortress and will abolish the daily sacrifice. Then they will set up the abomination that causes desolation. ³²With flattery he will corrupt those who have violated the covenant, but the people who know their God will firmly resist him.*

³³*"Those who are wise will instruct many, though for a time they will fall by the sword or be burned or captured or plundered. ³⁴When they fall, they will receive a little help, and many who are not sincere will join them. ³⁵Some of the wise will*

*stumble, so that they may be refined, purified and
made spotless until the time of the end, for it will still
come at the appointed time.*

³⁶*"The king will do as he pleases. He will exalt
and magnify himself above every god and will say
unheard-of things against the God of gods. He will be
successful until the time of wrath is completed, for
what has been determined must take place.* ³⁷*He will
show no regard for the gods of his ancestors or for
the one desired by women, nor will he regard any
god, but will exalt himself above them all.* ³⁸*Instead of
them, he will honor a god of fortresses; a god
unknown to his ancestors he will honor with gold and
silver, with precious stones and costly gifts.* ³⁹*He will
attack the mightiest fortresses with the help of a
foreign god and will greatly honor those who
acknowledge him. He will make them rulers over
many people and will distribute the land at a price.*

⁴⁰*"At the time of the end the king of the South
will engage him in battle, and the king of the North
will storm out against him with chariots and cavalry
and a great fleet of ships. He will invade many
countries and sweep through them like a flood.* ⁴¹*He
will also invade the Beautiful Land. Many countries
will fall, but Edom, Moab and the leaders of Ammon
will be delivered from his hand.* ⁴²*He will extend his
power over many countries; Egypt will not escape.*
⁴³*He will gain control of the treasures of gold and
silver and all the riches of Egypt, with the Libyans
and Cushites in submission.* ⁴⁴*But reports from the
east and the north will alarm him, and he will set out
in a great rage to destroy and annihilate many.* ⁴⁵*He
will pitch his royal tents between the seas at the
beautiful holy mountain. Yet he will come to his end,
and no one will help him.*

¹²:¹*"At that time Michael, the great prince who
protects your people, will arise. There will be a time*

155

of distress such as has not happened from the beginning of nations until then. But at that time your people—everyone whose name is found written in the book—will be delivered. ²Multitudes who sleep in the dust of the earth will awake: some to everlasting life, others to shame and everlasting contempt. ³Those who are wise will shine like the brightness of the heavens, and those who lead many to righteousness, like the stars for ever and ever. ⁴But you, Daniel, roll up and seal the words of the scroll until the time of the end. Many will go here and there to increase knowledge."

⁵Then I, Daniel, looked, and there before me stood two others, one on this bank of the river and one on the opposite bank. ⁶One of them said to the man clothed in linen, who was above the waters of the river, "How long will it be before these astonishing things are fulfilled?"

⁷The man clothed in linen, who was above the waters of the river, lifted his right hand and his left hand toward heaven, and I heard him swear by him who lives forever, saying, "It will be for a time, times and half a time. When the power of the holy people has been finally broken, all these things will be completed."

⁸I heard, but I did not understand. So I asked, "My lord, what will the outcome of all this be?"

⁹He replied, "Go your way, Daniel, because the words are rolled up and sealed until the time of the end. ¹⁰ any will be purified, made spotless and refined, but the wicked will continue to be wicked. None of the wicked will understand, but those who are wise will understand.

¹¹"From the time that the daily sacrifice is abolished and the abomination that causes desolation is set up, there will be 1,290 days. ¹²Blessed is the one who waits for and reaches the end of the 1,335 days.

> [13]"As for you, go your way till the end. You will rest, and then at the end of the days you will rise to receive your allotted inheritance."

The details of the final vision are so specific and so amazingly accurate that it has astounded historical scholars. Any reputable historian of the last few centuries before Christ will give you the names and military campaigns that correspond exactly with what Daniel records in chapter 11. Those who doubt the Bible insist that chapter 11 must have been written after the events happened because the vision is so accurate, down to specific details, but the evidence shows that Daniel was written before the events happened. The Bible is true and God has revealed what will happen in the future.

Unlike some of Daniel's previous visions, this one is more verbal than symbolic. There are no wild beasts. Even still, some of it remains mysterious. Before we jump into the individual pieces, I want to show you the picture on the back of the puzzle box. The chart below puts together all of Daniel's visions.

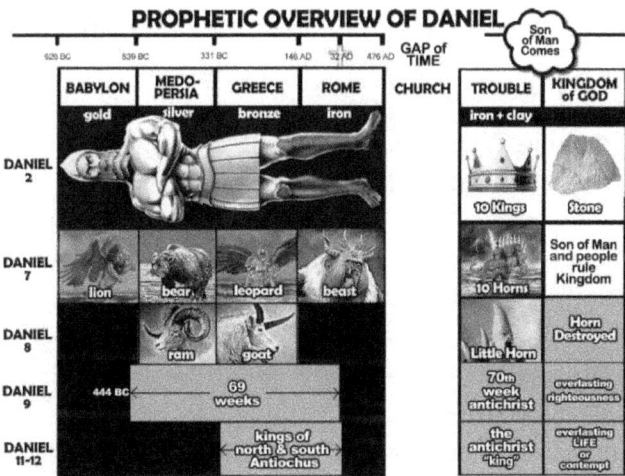

PROPHETIC OVERVIEW OF DANIEL

Son of Man Comes

	626 BC	539 BC	331 BC	146 AD	32 AD	476 AD	GAP of TIME		
	BABYLON	MEDO-PERSIA	GREECE	ROME			CHURCH	TROUBLE	KINGDOM of GOD
	gold	silver	bronze	iron				iron + clay	
DANIEL 2								10 Kings	Stone
DANIEL 7	lion	bear	leopard	beast				10 Horns	Son of Man and people rule Kingdom
DANIEL 8		ram	goat					Little Horn	Horn Destroyed
DANIEL 9	444 BC		69 weeks					70th week antichrist	everlasting righteousness
DANIEL 11-12			kings of north & south Antiochus					the antichrist "king"	everlasting LIFE or contempt

Note: For a full color image, go to BruceBMiller.com.

In chapter 2, Daniel interpreted the giant metal statue predicting four empires: the gold, Babylon; silver, Medo-Persia; the bronze, Greece; and the iron, Rome. Then the toes are mixed iron and clay, a future evil kingdom. Finally a stone not cut by human hands will smash the statue and expand to be an everlasting kingdom that covers the earth. In chapter 7, the beasts parallel the four kingdoms with the lion, bear, leopard and fourth terrible beast. Then ten horns arise matching the ten toes of the statue. But now out of the beast comes a little horn who is the Antichrist. After time, times and half a time, the Son of Man comes from the clouds.

Daniel 7:14

He was given authority, glory and sovereign power; all nations and peoples of every language worshiped him. His dominion is an everlasting dominion that will not pass away, and his kingdom is one that will never be destroyed.

In chapter 8, Daniel focused on the ram who is Medo-Persia and the goat with four horns, which is Greece, and the four generals of Alexander the Great. But then he saw one horn that represents both Antiochus and the future Antichrist who "will be destroyed, but not by human power" (8:25b).

In chapter 9, we learned about the sixty-nine "sevens" that take us to the first coming of Jesus Christ the Messiah. Then in the seventieth "seven," the Antichrist will come who will cut off sacrifices and put up the abomination of desolation until his decree ends.

In chapter 11, we will be reminded about Persia and Greece and learn much more about the kings following Alexander, especially Antiochus Epiphanes who foreshadows the Antichrist, who will be called "the king" and create havoc in the time of the end, waging war and abusing the Jews until his end comes suddenly.

We are going to work through the text, pausing to give interpretation along the way and skipping some parts to highlight other parts. Chapter 11 surveys some of the same history that was covered in chapters 2, 7 and 8 with Persia and Greece. Then it focuses on two of the generals who followed Alexander the Great. But the real emphasis is on Antiochus and the Antichrist, the former foreshadowing the latter.

Daniel 11:2

Now then, I tell you the truth: Three more kings will arise in Persia, and then a fourth, who will be far richer than all the others. When he has gained power by his wealth, he will stir up everyone against the kingdom of Greece.

The fourth wealthy king of Persia is Xerxes who invaded Greece, which made them really angry, driving the mighty Alexander to invade Persia.

Daniel 11:3–4

Then a mighty king will arise, who will rule with great power and do as he pleases. ⁴After he has arisen, his empire will be broken up and parceled out toward the four winds of heaven. It will not go to his descendants, nor will it have the power he exercised, because his empire will be uprooted and given to others.

Alexander the Great of Greece rapidly conquered Persia, but then died early at the age of 32. As the vision predicted, none of his descendants took over. He only had three: a half-brother, Philip, who was mentally handicapped; a son, Alexander, and an illegitimate son, Hercules.[34] All three were murdered in a two-year period. Then as we learned from earlier visions, Alexander's kingdom was divided up among four generals along the four points of the compass, the four winds of heaven. But as the vision said, none of them had anything like the power of Greece.

At this point in the vision, in 11:5–20, the angel focused on two of the divisions: "The Syrian division, lying just north of Palestine, over which the Seleucid line of kings would rule; and the Egyptian division, lying just south."[35] These were important because they fought over control of Palestine where Israel was located. Secondly, they were important because Antiochus, the "little horn" of chapter 8, came from the Seleucids in Syria and he waged war against the Ptolemies in Egypt. It is in this section that we see some of the most incredible historical detail. You can discover this detail in standard histories of the period.

Antiochus foreshadows the future Antichrist. See the following verse where Antiochus is introduced as a "contemptible person."

Daniel 11:21

He will be succeeded by a contemptible person who has not been given the honor of royalty. He will invade the kingdom when its people feel secure, and he will seize it through intrigue.

He called himself "Epiphanes" meaning "the revealed one," but others gave him the nickname "Epimanes" meaning "madman." He was an evil, lying ruler who hated the Jews; the Hitler of his day as you can see from scanning the next verses. He acted deceitfully, rose to power and gave wealth to his cronies, but only for a time. God brought him to an abrupt end in 164 BC after a reign of only 12 years.

Notice in 11:30 that he would "vent his fury against the holy covenant." This phrase, "holy covenant," refers to Jewish religion. We know that Antiochus declared Jewish ceremonies illegal and

160

burned copies of the Torah. According to 11:31, he would abolish the daily sacrifice and set up an abomination of desolation. Historically, we know he set up an altar to Zeus in the Jewish temple and sacrificed pigs on it.

Daniel 11:32–35

> With flattery he will corrupt those who have violated the covenant, but the people who know their God will firmly resist him.
> 33 Those who are wise will instruct many, though for a time they will fall by the sword or be burned or captured or plundered. 34 When they fall, they will receive a little help, and many who are not sincere will join them. 35 Some of the wise will stumble, so that they may be refined, purified and made spotless until the time of the end, for it will still come at the appointed time.

Here we get some insight into how we should live. People who know their God resist evil. We will come back to this later, but clearly our call is to know God and resist evil. He references "the wise" who instruct many, but for a time are seriously persecuted. The wise may stumble, but in the process are being refined for the time of the end. We are to be the wise today.

The reference to the time of the end hints at a shift from the historical Antiochus to the future Antichrist. Starting in 11:36, we see exaggerated language that cannot describe Antiochus, but must describe someone even more evil. For instance, Antiochus was not a king, but the Antichrist will be. This Antichrist is the ruler to come mentioned in chapter 9. He is the "little horn" of Daniel 7.

Daniel 11:36, 45

The king will do as he pleases. He will exalt and magnify himself above every god and will say unheard-of things against the God of gods. He will be successful until the time of wrath is completed, for what has been determined must take place. . . . ⁴⁵He will pitch his royal tents between the seas at the beautiful holy mountain. Yet he will come to his end, and no one will help him.

The Antichrist will be the worst example of arrogance and blasphemy who ever walked the earth. He will be full of himself. Sadly, this antichrist pattern is common in humanity. A smart, skilled, proud person gets power and then arrogantly uses his power ruthlessly to smash anyone who opposes him. Self-exaltation goes all the way back to Eden and Babel. We must always be on guard against anti-God, poisonous pride. But just like with Antiochus, the Antichrist's end will come suddenly.

Chapter 12 continues chapter 11 without a break in subject matter.

Daniel 12:1a

At that time Michael, the great prince who protects your people, will arise.

Remember from chapter 10, that Michael is the angelic chief prince who watches over the Jewish people. This great war in which we are involved today is not merely human, but cosmic, involving angels and demons as well. The text continues.

Daniel 12:1b

There will be a time of distress such as has not happened from the beginning of nations until then.

*But at that time your people—everyone whose name
is found written in the book—will be delivered.*

Toward the end of history as we know it will come a brief time of severe distress often called the great tribulation. At that time, everyone whose name is found written in the Book of Life will be delivered. The image is that of an ancient city census list. Here's the important question for each of us: Is your name in the Book?

The next two verses are among the most theologically significant in Daniel. Read 12:2 carefully.

Daniel 12:2

*Multitudes who sleep in the dust of the earth
will awake: some to everlasting life, others to shame
and everlasting contempt.*

Sleep is a figure of speech for death. We will all awake from the sleep of death. We will all be raised from the dead. This is the first use of the phrase "everlasting life" in the Bible. We will all exist forever. There are only two destinies: everlasting life and everlasting contempt. The word "contempt" means something abhorrent.

When we put this passage in the overall context of the Bible, we realize he is talking about hell and heaven, about eternal death or eternal life. Every human will either awake to everlasting life or to everlasting contempt and shame. Those who have not embraced salvation in the Messiah, Jesus Christ, will not have their names written in the Book of Life. They will be ashamed before the Lord on judgment day and go to everlasting contempt.

In contrast, those whose names are in the Book will experience everlasting life.

Daniel 12:3

*Those who are wise will shine like the
brightness of the heavens, and those who lead many
to righteousness, like the stars for ever and ever.*

"Just as stars display their beauty and glory in the sky, a bright . . . future and a great reward . . . awaits those" who are wise.[36] Notice what the wise do: lead many to righteousness, and it is Christ who is the righteous One.

Then the angel gave instruction to Daniel.

Daniel 12:4a

*But you, Daniel, roll up and seal the words of
the scroll until the time of the end.*

People living in the time of the end will be helped by Daniel's vision as it all starts to happen.

As chapter 12 continues, Daniel saw a vision of two angelic figures on the banks of the river and a figure like a man above the water. He asked how long and what the outcome would be. Here's the answer:

Daniel 12:9–10

*He replied, "Go your way, Daniel, because the
words are rolled up and sealed until the time of the
end. [10]Many will be purified, made spotless and
refined, but the wicked will continue to be wicked.
None of the wicked will understand, but those who
are wise will understand."*

Basically the angel told Daniel, "You are not going to understand it at this point, but go your way, faithfully serve God knowing many will be refined during hard times. Wicked people will continue to be wicked, not understanding that the end is coming. Wise people will understand." Some Christians desperately seek more prophetic details than God has given us. Our calling is not to figure out all the details and timing, but to obey God faithfully today, knowing the end is coming and when it does, The Big God wins.

Daniel 12:11-12

From the time that the daily sacrifice is abolished and the abomination that causes desolation is set up, there will be 1,290 days. [12]Blessed is the one who waits for and reaches the end of the 1,335 days.

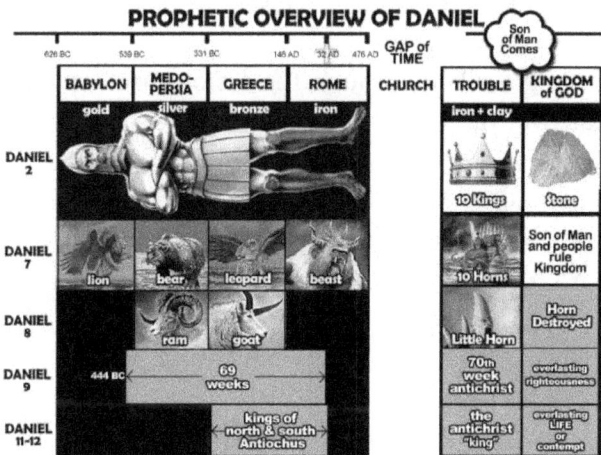

For a full color image, go to BruceBMiller.com.

Frankly, even the best scholars are unsure of exactly how to read the specific numbers, but they approximate three and a half years which correlates with time, times and half a time. Toward the end of history, a brief time of great distress will come led by the evil Antichrist. But then God will bring an end to him and all evil. The Big God will set up his kingdom.

Read the final words to Daniel in the great last verse of the book.

Daniel 12:13

As for you, go your way till the end. You will rest, and then at the end of the days you will rise to receive your allotted inheritance.

Your job is to go your way serving God. Then you will rest, meaning you will die, but then at the end of time as we know it, you will rise from the dead to your divine inheritance. Your eternal reward is coming. We can have confidence today to serve God in the face of suffering and evil because we know how it ends. The Big God wins and we win with him.

Now, having walked through the vision of chapters 11–12, let's ask and answer three questions:

1. How can we understand the end times?
2. How can we live wisely in these times before the end?
3. How can we win in the end?

1. How to understand the end times

Let's go back to the chart comparing Daniel's visions. You know what was revealed in chapters 2, 7, 8, 9 and 11. Finally in chapter 12, we learn that there will be a resurrection of all people. Each person will awake from death either to everlasting contempt or to everlasting life. Those who are wise, who have trusted in Jesus Christ, will shine like the stars, receiving their divine eternal inheritance. The Big God wins and we win with him. Wow! With a better understanding of the end times from Daniel, how are we to live wisely today? How can we be like the wise ones that Daniel described in chapters 11–12?

2. How to be wise in these times before the end

Several times in chapters 11 and 12 Daniel mentioned "the wise." Who are they and how can we follow their example? The wise are the heroes during the time of distress who honor God. As we approach the end, times will become more difficult so we will need courage and also wisdom. From these two chapters, we can see three characteristics of the wise.

a. The wise understand The Big God and eternity

In Daniel 11:32b, Daniel describes people "who know their God." In chapter 12, we hear that it is the wise who understand. What do they understand? I believe they understand eternity, the truths we have just covered about the resurrection of all people to everlasting death or everlasting life.

What do they know about The Big God? Let's review what we have learned about The Big God from the book of Daniel:

- ❖ Chapter 1   The Big God honors convictions
- ❖ Chapter 2   The Big God controls nations
- ❖ Chapter 3   The Big God delivers through the fire
- ❖ Chapter 4   The Big God humbles the proud
- ❖ Chapter 5   The Big God has the last word
- ❖ Chapter 6   The Big God tames lions
- ❖ Chapter 7   The Big God sends the Son of Man to rule the world
- ❖ Chapter 8   The Big God destroys evil in the end

Even though evil appears to be unchecked, The Big God is in charge and in the end, he wins. Wise people understand God and eternity.

b. The wise firmly resist evil

If you truly know God and see eternity, you will firmly resist evil. You will stand for righteousness and justice. Even in the dark period of Antiochus, there were true believers, wise people who firmly resisted evil. The ancient book 1 Maccabees 1:62–63 speaks of them: "Many in Israel stood firm and were resolved in their hearts not to eat unclean food. They chose to die rather than to be defiled by food or to profane the holy covenant; and they did die".[37]

Throughout history, godly men and women have risked their lives to resist evil. Think of those who joined the resistance movement against Hitler during World War II. Today in northern Nigeria, Christians such as Musa are standing against Boko Haram, the terrorist group killing Christians and burning churches. Today bold Christians are courageously standing against the global sex trade, especially the slavery of children.

What could we do to resist evil in our cities today, in our neighborhoods? How about in how we raise our kids? What about in what we put into our bodies or in what we allow our eyes to see?

Our call is to stand for the oppressed, the poor and the orphans. I love what Paul says at the end of 1 Corinthians after he has fully explained the truth of our future resurrection. He charges:

Therefore, my dear brothers and sisters, stand firm. Let nothing move you. Always give yourselves fully to the work of the Lord, because you know that your labor in the Lord is not in vain (1 Corinthians 15:58).

In these times before the end, the wise are characterized by understanding God and eternity, and by firmly resisting evil.

c.   The wise lead many to Christ

In chapter 11, Daniel says the wise "will instruct many" (33). In chapter 12, he says they "lead many to righteousness" (3). The picture is not of formal teaching in a classroom, but informal conversation in daily life. The wise help other people become wise by helping people understand The Big God and eternity.

Essentially Daniel was expressing our mission: to be people helping people find and follow Christ. In these hard times before the end, we are to be disciplining the nations, being witnesses to Jesus Christ. We are ambassadors of the King, announcing that the King has come and is returning. We are inviting people to join the winning side. This is how to be wise in these times: more and more come to understand God and eternity; firmly resist evil and lead many to Christ.

3.   How to win in the end

In the last verse of the book, the angel told Daniel that he was to go his way, rest, and at the end, he would rise and receive his allotted inheritance. In the end, Daniel won.

We only win in the end by joining the winning side. We only rise to everlasting life if our names are in the Book of Life. How can that happen? The New Testament is clear: if you believe in the Lord

Jesus Christ, you will be saved, and your name is written in the Book of Life. In John, Jesus referred to Daniel 12, when he said:

> *For God so loved the world that he gave his one and only Son, that whoever believes in him shall not perish but have **eternal life*** (John 3:16) [emphasis added].

Whoever believes in Jesus Christ will rise to everlasting life. Whoever does not trust in Jesus Christ will rise to suffer everlasting contempt, death and hell. I do not want anyone reading this book to be there. If you have never done so, I urge you to trust in Jesus Christ today. Make sure of your eternal destiny. Make sure you are on the winning side.

Then God will give you wisdom and strength to live for him in a difficult, evil world. In light of the coming increase in evil, you can be wise by understanding God and eternity; by firmly resisting evil; and by leading many to Christ; because even though for a time, evil people will create distress making us suffer (which will refine us), God will bring them to an end, and we will be delivered to everlasting life where we will shine like the brightest stars as we receive our eternal inheritance.

In the sixth century BC, it looked as if Babylon was in control. But it wasn't. In second-century Palestine, it looked as if Antiochus was in control, but he wasn't. In the first century of Paul, it looked as if Rome was in control, but it wasn't. Today, it may look as if Satan is in control, but he isn't. God is in charge, and because of that we can have boundless courage, peace and joy in the midst of our struggles.[38]

We know how it all ends. He is the great I AM. Today we can faithfully honor God in the face of any chaos because

God is the great I AM

we know The Big God wins and we win with him. Our God is an awesome God. He is The Big God!

For further study on chapter 12, see the Study Guide beginning on page 305.

170

Study Guide

1
God Honors Convictions
Study Guide

Daniel 1

✝ Pray

Prepare your heart and mind before engaging God's Word. Take a moment to pray about questions in your life and issues arising from the Scripture you are studying.

W Work the issue: *What's really at stake?*

The biblical author is usually addressing a question, issue or problem. At any given moment in our lives, we are facing difficulties, asking questions and trying to make decisions. Your study will be more transforming if you take time to consider what is at stake in the passage and what is currently at stake in your life to which the passage may speak.

Quickly scan the passage considering what underlying issues may be present. Reflecting on what the author might be addressing in his time, what about you today? What questions does this text raise in your own mind? What do you wonder about?

We are not the first people to look out at the world and long for rock-solid assurances in times of tension and distress. What matters is where we seek comfort and security. As those taken to Babylon in the first wave of Judean exiles, how could Daniel, Hananiah, Mishael and Azariah live as worshippers of the one true God while surrounded by a culture with competing values? Are you facing any situations parallel to what Daniel and his friends faced? What pressures do you face to conform to the culture in which you live? Daniel and his companions found themselves having to draw a line that they did not want to cross.

What's at stake? What is the central issue or issues being addressed? What is the biggest issue for you?

Write down the main issue(s):

▌**I** Investigate Scripture: *What does God say?*

Read the chapter slowly underlining what seems important to you. You will benefit from reading it several times. Mark key words. Notice who is speaking in each section. I encourage you to engage God in his Word. A good way to do that is to compare several English translations of the Bible. To easily compare various English translations, I recommend YouVersion as a good Bible reading app. In your study of Daniel, it will help you to compare the New International Version, English Standard Version, Holman Christian Standard Bible and the New Living Translation, especially for a line or verse that is hard to understand.

Daniel 1

In the third year of the reign of Jehoiakim king of Judah, Nebuchadnezzar king of Babylon came to Jerusalem and besieged it. ²And the Lord delivered Jehoiakim king of Judah into his hand, along with some of the articles from the temple of God. These he carried off to the temple of his god in Babylonia and put in the treasure house of his god.

³Then the king ordered Ashpenaz, chief of his court officials, to bring into the king's service some of the Israelites from the royal family and the nobility— ⁴young men without any physical defect, handsome, showing aptitude for every kind of learning, well informed, quick to understand, and qualified to serve in the king's palace. He was to teach them the language and literature of the Babylonians. ⁵The king assigned them a daily amount of food and wine from the king's table. They were to be trained for three years, and after that they were to enter the king's service.

⁶Among those who were chosen were some from Judah: Daniel, Hananiah, Mishael and Azariah. ⁷The chief official gave them new names: to Daniel, the name Belteshazzar; to Hananiah, Shadrach; to Mishael, Meshach; and to Azariah, Abednego.

⁸But Daniel resolved not to defile himself with the royal food and wine, and he asked the chief official for permission not to defile himself this way. ⁹Now God had caused the official to show favor and compassion to Daniel, ¹⁰but the official told Daniel, "I am afraid of my lord the king, who has assigned your food and drink. Why should he see you looking worse than the other young men your age? The king would then have my head because of you."

¹¹*Daniel then said to the guard whom the chief official had appointed over Daniel, Hananiah, Mishael and Azariah,* ¹²*"Please test your servants for ten days: Give us nothing but vegetables to eat and water to drink.* ¹³*Then compare our appearance with that of the young men who eat the royal food, and treat your servants in accordance with what you see."* ¹⁴*So he agreed to this and tested them for ten days.*

¹⁵*At the end of the ten days they looked healthier and better nourished than any of the young men who ate the royal food.* ¹⁶*So the guard took away their choice food and the wine they were to drink and gave them vegetables instead.*

¹⁷*To these four young men God gave knowledge and understanding of all kinds of literature and learning. And Daniel could understand visions and dreams of all kinds.*

¹⁸*At the end of the time set by the king to bring them into his service, the chief official presented them to Nebuchadnezzar.* ¹⁹*The king talked with them, and he found none equal to Daniel, Hananiah, Mishael and Azariah; so they entered the king's service.* ²⁰*In every matter of wisdom and understanding about which the king questioned them, he found them ten times better than all the magicians and enchanters in his whole kingdom.*

²¹*And Daniel remained there until the first year of King Cyrus.*

❖ Imagine that you are Daniel and his friends. Describe what you think it would be like to be taken to a foreign country and forced to assimilate into their culture.

❖ Scan the passage again for God's name. Where do you see his activity?

❖ According to 1:2, who was responsible for the defeat of Judah? What was carried off?

❖   What were the characteristics of the people brought into the king's service (1:4)? What was going to happen to them (1:5)?

❖   What did Daniel resolve not to do? What did he do in 1:8?

❖   What "test" did Daniel devise? What was the result?

❖ According to 1:17, who gave the young men "knowledge and understanding"?

❖ What impression did Nebuchadnezzar form of Daniel and his companions? Why?

⬛S **Seek counsel:** *What do wise people say?*

Review chapter 1 beginning on page 1 or watch a video presentation of this chapter. Access the QR (Quick Response) code that can be read by many smart devices using a scanning app. It allows you to immediately watch the video. If you do not have a QR code reader, you can access the same material at http://vimeo.com/74772470.
To the extent you have time and ability, read the relevant section from one of the recommended studies on page 325. Also check out the resources available on Bible.org.

D Develop your response: *What do I think?*

❖ What is the main point of the chapter? Take some time to think through and write down a one-sentence statement of the main point.

❖ From this biblical text, how is God answering your questions in the "Work the issue" section?

❖ What do you believe the Spirit of God is impressing on you to do in response to this chapter? This could be a change in your thoughts about God; an attitude to transform or an action to take. For instance, how will you resolve to hold to biblical convictions against pressures to conform to the world?

◉ Openly discuss: *What do we think?*

When you meet with your friend or group, walk through the following questions together but do not be limited by them. Prayerfully allow the Spirit of God to guide your conversation as you seek God together in his Word.

1. In our society, what pressures do Christians face to compromise their convictions or their loyalty to Jesus Christ? What pressures have you faced?

2. Have you ever before encountered the book of Daniel or stories from it? What has been your previous experience, if any?

3. In this chapter, you are asked to imagine China has taken over the USA. You are taken by boat to Beijing where you are put into a three-year program to learn Mandarin and Chinese customs in preparation for service in the Chinese government. What pressures do you imagine you would face? How would you stay loyal to Christ?

4. What actions do you see God take in Daniel 1? How did God show that he is bigger than any other force, person or power?

5. Walk through how Daniel handled the conversations with the chief official and the guard with wisdom and tact. How did Daniel show graciousness in his determination not to defile himself with the royal food and wine? How could you show similar tact with an authority in your life?

6. Why do you think Daniel and his friends agreed to learn the pagan curriculum but refused to eat the king's food and wine? How can we discern where in culture it is fine to join in and where we need to draw a line?

7. How can we follow Daniel's model today against the pressures to conform to this immoral, chaotic world? Do you have any situations in your life that are analogous to what Daniel and his friends faced? How could you approach the situation in a more Daniel-like way?

M Move to action: *What will I do?*

❖ As you are aware of the tension of living in "exile," how will you strive to maintain your Christian distinctiveness without isolating yourself?

In reflecting on your study of Daniel 1:1–21, how will you move to action? God calls us not just to know his Word, but also to obey it, to be transformed by it through his Spirit. How do you believe God wants to change you through this text? Write down what you will do differently. This could be a transformation in your mind, in your heart, in your actions or in a relationship with another person. For instance, consider how the Spirit has strengthened you by the reminder that God is bigger than the confusion in this world.

2

God Controls Nations
Study Guide

Daniel 2

✝ Pray

W Work the issue: *What's really at stake?*

Quickly scan the passage considering what underlying issues may be present. Reflecting on what the author might be addressing in his time, what about you today? What questions does this text raise?

Daniel is written about people in exile for people in exile. You need a Big God to thrive in exile. In Daniel 2, King Nebuchadnezzar got an introduction to Daniel's God and we will see once again that Yahweh is the one with the real power. Mightier than a king's decree and wiser than Babylon's most learned, God will again prove himself to be The Big God.

Most of us have had experience with someone whose expectations were hard to meet. Maybe you've even worked for an impossible boss—someone who demanded what no one, including you, could ever do. Are you facing any issues with your boss or an authority in your life that the book of Daniel might address?

What's at stake? What is the central issue or issues being addressed? What is the biggest issue for you?

Write down the main issue(s):

█ Investigate Scripture: *What does God say?*

Read the chapter slowly underlining what seems important to you. You will benefit from reading it several times. Mark key words. Look for the different kinds of chaos experienced by the furious king and his frustrated advisors. Put yourself in the shoes of each character in the account.

Daniel 2

In the second year of his reign,
Nebuchadnezzar had dreams; his mind was troubled
and he could not sleep. ²So the king summoned the
magicians, enchanters, sorcerers and astrologers to

*tell him what he had dreamed. When they came in
and stood before the king, ³he said to them, "I have
had a dream that troubles me and I want to know
what it means."*

*⁴Then the astrologers answered the king, "May
the king live forever! Tell your servants the dream,
and we will interpret it."*

*⁵The king replied to the astrologers, "This is
what I have firmly decided: If you do not tell me what
my dream was and interpret it, I will have you cut
into pieces and your houses turned into piles of
rubble. ⁶But if you tell me the dream and explain it,
you will receive from me gifts and rewards and great
honor. So tell me the dream and interpret it for me."*

*⁷Once more they replied, "Let the king tell his
servants the dream, and we will interpret it."*

*⁸Then the king answered, "I am certain that
you are trying to gain time, because you realize that
this is what I have firmly decided: ⁹If you do not tell
me the dream, there is only one penalty for you. You
have conspired to tell me misleading and wicked
things, hoping the situation will change. So then, tell
me the dream, and I will know that you can interpret
it for me."*

*¹⁰The astrologers answered the king, "There is
no one on earth who can do what the king asks! No
king, however great and mighty, has ever asked such
a thing of any magician or enchanter or astrologer.
¹¹What the king asks is too difficult. No one can
reveal it to the king except the gods, and they do not
live among humans."*

*¹²This made the king so angry and furious that
he ordered the execution of all the wise men of
Babylon. ¹³So the decree was issued to put the wise
men to death, and men were sent to look for Daniel
and his friends to put them to death.*

*¹⁴When Arioch, the commander of the king's
guard, had gone out to put to death the wise men of*

Babylon, Daniel spoke to him with wisdom and tact.
¹⁵He asked the king's officer, "Why did the king issue
such a harsh decree?" Arioch then explained the
matter to Daniel. ¹⁶At this, Daniel went in to the king
and asked for time, so that he might interpret the
dream for him.

¹⁷Then Daniel returned to his house and
explained the matter to his friends Hananiah, Mishael
and Azariah. ¹⁸He urged them to plead for mercy
from the God of heaven concerning this mystery, so
that he and his friends might not be executed with
the rest of the wise men of Babylon. ¹⁹During the
night the mystery was revealed to Daniel in a vision.
Then Daniel praised the God of heaven ²⁰and said:

> *"Praise be to the name of God for ever and*
> *ever;*
> *wisdom and power are his.*
> *²¹He changes times and seasons;*
> *he deposes kings and raises up others.*
> *He gives wisdom to the wise*
> *and knowledge to the discerning.*
> *²²He reveals deep and hidden things;*
> *he knows what lies in darkness,*
> *and light dwells with him.*
> *²³I thank and praise you, God of my ancestors:*
> *You have given me wisdom and power,*
> *you have made known to me what we asked of*
> *you,*
> *you have made known to us the dream of the*
> *king."*

²⁴Then Daniel went to Arioch, whom the king
had appointed to execute the wise men of Babylon,
and said to him, "Do not execute the wise men of
Babylon. Take me to the king, and I will interpret his
dream for him."

²⁵Arioch took Daniel to the king at once and
said, "I have found a man among the exiles from
Judah who can tell the king what his dream means."

²⁶The king asked Daniel (also called Belteshazzar), "Are you able to tell me what I saw in my dream and interpret it?"

²⁷Daniel replied, "No wise man, enchanter, magician or diviner can explain to the king the mystery he has asked about, ²⁸but there is a God in heaven who reveals mysteries. He has shown King Nebuchadnezzar what will happen in days to come. Your dream and the visions that passed through your mind as you were lying in bed are these:

²⁹"As Your Majesty was lying there, your mind turned to things to come, and the revealer of mysteries showed you what is going to happen. ³⁰As for me, this mystery has been revealed to me, not because I have greater wisdom than anyone else alive, but so that Your Majesty may know the interpretation and that you may understand what went through your mind."

³¹Your Majesty looked, and there before you stood a large statue—an enormous, dazzling statue, awesome in appearance. ³²The head of the statue was made of pure gold, its chest and arms of silver, its belly and thighs of bronze, ³³its legs of iron, its feet partly of iron and partly of baked clay. ³⁴While you were watching, a rock was cut out, but not by human hands. It struck the statue on its feet of iron and clay and smashed them. ³⁵Then the iron, the clay, the bronze, the silver and the gold were all broken to pieces and became like chaff on a threshing floor in the summer. The wind swept them away without leaving a trace. But the rock that struck the statue became a huge mountain and filled the whole earth.

³⁶This was the dream, and now we will interpret it to the king. ³⁷Your Majesty, you are the king of kings. The God of heaven has given you dominion and power and might and glory; ³⁸in your hands he has placed all mankind and the beasts of the field and the birds in the sky. Wherever they live,

he has made you ruler over them all. You are that head of gold.

39After you, another kingdom will arise, inferior to yours. Next, a third kingdom, one of bronze, will rule over the whole earth. 40Finally, there will be a fourth kingdom, strong as iron—for iron breaks and smashes everything—and as iron breaks things to pieces, so it will crush and break all the others. 41Just as you saw that the feet and toes were partly of baked clay and partly of iron, so this will be a divided kingdom; yet it will have some of the strength of iron in it, even as you saw iron mixed with clay. 42As the toes were partly iron and partly clay, so this kingdom will be partly strong and partly brittle. 43And just as you saw the iron mixed with baked clay, so the people will be a mixture and will not remain united, any more than iron mixes with clay.

44In the time of those kings, the God of heaven will set up a kingdom that will never be destroyed, nor will it be left to another people. It will crush all those kingdoms and bring them to an end, but it will itself endure forever. 45This is the meaning of the vision of the rock cut out of a mountain, but not by human hands—a rock that broke the iron, the bronze, the clay, the silver and the gold to pieces.

46Then King Nebuchadnezzar fell prostrate before Daniel and paid him honor and ordered that an offering and incense be presented to him. 47The king said to Daniel, "Surely your God is the God of gods and the Lord of kings and a revealer of mysteries, for you were able to reveal this mystery."

48Then the king placed Daniel in a high position and lavished many gifts on him. He made him ruler over the entire province of Babylon and placed him in charge of all its wise men.

49Moreover, at Daniel's request the king appointed Shadrach, Meshach and Abednego

*administrators over the province of Babylon, while
Daniel himself remained at the royal court.*

❖ What did Nebuchadnezzar ask of his wise men? What was
their response?

❖ What was Nebuchadnezzar's reaction to their failure?
What was supposed to happen to Daniel and his friends
(2:13)?

❖ How did Daniel handle the news of the king's edict (2:14)?
What did he ask for (2:16)? For what did Daniel urge others
to pray (2:18)?

❖ Circle or highlight descriptions of God that Daniel gave in
   2:21–22 and summarize them. Why do you think Daniel
   praised God for these particular attributes?

❖ Describe the statue that Nebuchadnezzar dreamt about.
   What happened to it? List the four elements that represent
   the first four kingdoms that the dream depicted.

❖ What will be the final kingdom? How will it appear according to the dream?

❖ What was Nebuchadnezzar's response to Daniel's interpretation?

S **Seek counsel:** *What do wise people say?*

Review chapter 2 beginning on page 15 or watch a video presentation of this chapter. Access the QR (Quick Response) code that can be read by many smart devices using a scanning app. It allows you to immediately watch the video. If you do not have a QR code reader, you can access the same material at http://vimeo.com/74772468.
To the extent you have time and ability, read the relevant section from one of the recommended studies on page 325. Also check out the resources available on Bible.org.

D Develop your response: *What do I think?*

❖ What have you learned about The Big God from Daniel 2?

❖ What do you believe the Spirit of God is impressing on your heart? How can you grow in faith as Nebuchadnezzar did?

❖ How could you respond better to authorities in your life who make unreasonable demands or better respond to seemingly dreadful certainties such as Daniel faced?

◉ Openly discuss: *What do we think?*

1. How would you describe the chaos in your life right now? What chaos in the world is most disturbing to you?

2. Put yourself first in the shoes of Nebuchadnezzar and then in the shoes of his advisors. Describe the chaos each was feeling as the conflict mounted in Daniel 2:1–13.

3. Have you ever had advisors fail you? Ever trusted in someone or something that later proved to be false or fake? How did that feel? Has something like this happened to you in the spiritual realm?

4. Read 2:20–23 and describe the God that Daniel praised. What do we know about him?

5. What do you notice about how Daniel prayed? How did he pray once God revealed the vision? How would you compare your prayers to Daniel's prayer?

6. How do you typically respond when an authority in your life makes unreasonable demands? Contrast Daniel's response with that of the Babylonian enchanters. If you followed Daniel's model, how could you better respond to such demands?

7. What is most powerful to you about the dream and the interpretation (2:31–45)? To whom is "the Rock" referring and when will it likely crush all other kingdoms? How do you feel about the Rock?

8. How did Nebuchadnezzar respond (2:46–47)? How do you respond to a fresh understanding of the bigness of God from Daniel 2? How can what you have learned about The Big God help you overcome the chaos in your life and in the world?

M Move to action: *What will I do?*

In reflecting on your study of Daniel 2:1–49, how will you move to action? Write down what you will do differently. This could be a transformation in your mind, in your heart, or in your actions. Return to what you wrote in the "Develop your response" section. Now prayerfully choose how you will act differently in the power of the Spirit. For instance, how do you see God in a new way? How might you pray more like Daniel?

3

God Delivers through the Fire
Study Guide

Daniel 3

✝ Pray

W Work the issue: *What's really at stake?*

In Daniel 3, we come to a suspense-filled story in which Daniel's three companions, Shadrach, Meshach and Abednego find their allegiance to God threatened. What tests of loyalty are you facing or could you face in your life? As you study this week, pray you will come to a greater understanding of what it means to be faithful to Christ as you seek to strengthen your commitment to him.

A lot was at stake in this test of loyalties. Has anyone ever demanded your loyalty in a way that made you uncomfortable? It's one thing to quietly but resolutely refuse to compromise your faith. But when feeling the heat of the fire and staring into the eyes of the outraged king, it would take extraordinary courage to stand firm.

What's at stake? What is the central issue or issues being addressed? What is the biggest issue for you?

Write down the main issue(s):

Investigate Scripture: *What does God say?*

Daniel 3

> King Nebuchadnezzar made an image of gold, sixty cubits high and six cubits wide, and set it up on the plain of Dura in the province of Babylon. ²He then summoned the satraps, prefects, governors, advisers, treasurers, judges, magistrates and all the other provincial officials to come to the dedication of the image he had set up. ³So the satraps, prefects, governors, advisers, treasurers, judges, magistrates and all the other provincial officials assembled for the dedication of the image that King Nebuchadnezzar had set up, and they stood before it.
> ⁴Then the herald loudly proclaimed, "Nations and peoples of every language, this is what you are commanded to do: ⁵As soon as you hear the sound of

the horn, flute, zither, lyre, harp, pipe and all kinds of music, you must fall down and worship the image of gold that King Nebuchadnezzar has set up. ⁶Whoever does not fall down and worship will immediately be thrown into a blazing furnace."

⁷Therefore, as soon as they heard the sound of the horn, flute, zither, lyre, harp and all kinds of music, all the nations and peoples of every language fell down and worshiped the image of gold that King Nebuchadnezzar had set up.

⁸At this time some astrologers came forward and denounced the Jews. ⁹They said to King Nebuchadnezzar, "May the king live forever! ¹⁰Your Majesty has issued a decree that everyone who hears the sound of the horn, flute, zither, lyre, harp, pipe and all kinds of music must fall down and worship the image of gold, ¹¹and that whoever does not fall down and worship will be thrown into a blazing furnace. ¹²But there are some Jews whom you have set over the affairs of the province of Babylon—Shadrach, Meshach and Abednego—who pay no attention to you, Your Majesty. They neither serve your gods nor worship the image of gold you have set up."

¹³Furious with rage, Nebuchadnezzar summoned Shadrach, Meshach and Abednego. So these men were brought before the king, ¹⁴and Nebuchadnezzar said to them, "Is it true, Shadrach, Meshach and Abednego, that you do not serve my gods or worship the image of gold I have set up? ¹⁵Now when you hear the sound of the horn, flute, zither, lyre, harp, pipe and all kinds of music, if you are ready to fall down and worship the image I made, very good. But if you do not worship it, you will be thrown immediately into a blazing furnace. Then what god will be able to rescue you from my hand?"

¹⁶Shadrach, Meshach and Abednego replied to him, "King Nebuchadnezzar, we do not need to defend ourselves before you in this matter. ¹⁷If we are thrown into the blazing furnace, the God we serve is able to deliver us from it, and he will deliver us from Your Majesty's hand. ¹⁸But even if he does not, we want you to know, Your Majesty, that we will not serve your gods or worship the image of gold you have set up."

¹⁹Then Nebuchadnezzar was furious with Shadrach, Meshach and Abednego, and his attitude toward them changed. He ordered the furnace heated seven times hotter than usual ²⁰and commanded some of the strongest soldiers in his army to tie up Shadrach, Meshach and Abednego and throw them into the blazing furnace. ²¹So these men, wearing their robes, trousers, turbans and other clothes, were bound and thrown into the blazing furnace. ²²The king's command was so urgent and the furnace so hot that the flames of the fire killed the soldiers who took up Shadrach, Meshach and Abednego, ²³and these three men, firmly tied, fell into the blazing furnace.

If we are thrown into the blazing furnace, the God we serve is able to deliver us from it, and he will deliver us from Your Majesty's hand. ²⁴But even if he does not, we want you to know, Your Majesty, that we will not serve your gods or worship the image of gold you have set up.

Then King Nebuchadnezzar leaped to his feet in amazement and asked his advisers, "Weren't there three men that we tied up and threw into the fire?"

They replied, "Certainly, Your Majesty."

²⁵He said, "Look! I see four men walking around in the fire, unbound and unharmed, and the fourth looks like a son of the gods."

²⁶Nebuchadnezzar then approached the opening of the blazing furnace and shouted, "Shadrach, Meshach and Abednego, servants of the Most High God, come out! Come here!"

So Shadrach, Meshach and Abednego came out of the fire, ²⁷and the satraps, prefects, governors and royal advisers crowded around them. They saw that the fire had not harmed their bodies, nor was a hair of their heads singed; their robes were not scorched, and there was no smell of fire on them.

28Then Nebuchadnezzar said, "Praise be to the God of Shadrach, Meshach and Abednego, who has sent his angel and rescued his servants! They trusted in him and defied the king's command and were willing to give up their lives rather than serve or worship any god except their own God. 29Therefore I decree that the people of any nation or language who say anything against the God of Shadrach, Meshach and Abednego be cut into pieces and their houses be turned into piles of rubble, for no other god can save in this way."

30Then the king promoted Shadrach, Meshach and Abednego in the province of Babylon.

❖ Imagine and record your possible reaction if you had watched this event unfold as:

- A fellow Judean

- An average citizen of Babylon

- One of the palace guards

❖ Who was assembled on the plain of Dura? What were they commanded to do?

❖ How did the king find out that Shadrach, Meshach and Abednego were not worshipping the image?

❖ According to 3:16–18, what did Shadrach, Meshach and Abednego believe about God?

❖ How did Nebuchadnezzar respond to their refusal? What did he order?

❖ What did Nebuchadnezzar see when he looked into the fiery furnace?

❖ In what condition did Shadrach, Meshach and Abednego emerge from the fire?

❖ How did Nebuchadnezzar describe God in 3:26? What did he praise him for in 3:28?

S Seek counsel: *What do wise people say?*

Review chapter 3 beginning on page 31 or
watch a video presentation of this chapter.
Access the QR (Quick Response) code that
can be read by many smart devices using a
scanning app. It allows you to immediately
watch the video. If you do not have a QR
code reader, you can access the same
material at http://vimeo.com/74772469.
To the extent you have time and ability, read the relevant section
from one of the recommended studies on page 325. Also check out
the resources available on Bible.org.

D Develop your response: *What do I think?*

❖ What have you discovered about The Big God in Daniel 3
   that could enable you to hold to your loyalty to God when
   facing the fire?

❖ What situation are you facing or could you face where your loyalty might be tested? How will you handle it?

⬤ Openly discuss: *What do we think*?

1. What pressures have you felt in your life to honor another "god" or "idol" in your workplace, neighborhood, school or recreational setting?

2. We can fall into the same traps as Nebuchadnezzar. Analogous to what Nebuchadnezzar did, how have you seen people build statues to draw attention to themselves and get people to see how great they are? Get affirmation? How have you done this?

3. With such a massive crowd, how did Nebuchadnezzar discover that the three men did not worship the image (see 3:8–18)? Even kids hate anyone "telling" on them. Have you ever had someone say things against you to an authority? Do you have any concerns that someone might speak against you because of your faith?

4. Daniel 3:7 says that "all the nations and peoples of every nation fell down and worshiped the image" but the three men stood alone. How have you ever had to stand alone? How might you have to stand alone for Christ in the future?

5. How did God rescue them? How have you seen God rescue you or others *through* the fire rather than *from* the fire? How have you sensed God's presence with you when you were in the fiery furnace?

6. God supernaturally rescued the three men so that they were not even singed. How have you experienced God rescuing you from a situation that seemed impossible, especially one in which people were against you?

7. In the end, Nebuchadnezzar made an amazing declaration, "For no other god can save in this way" (3:29). How does God save us today in a way that no one else could? Do you believe God has saved you? How do you know that to be true?

8. Where in your life could you courageously resist honoring other "gods"?

M Move to action: *What will I do?*

In reflecting on your study of Daniel 3, how do you believe
God wants to transform you to greater spiritual maturity?
Return to what you wrote in the "Develop your response"
section. Now prayerfully choose how you will act differently
in the power of the Spirit. For instance, how do you see God
in a new way? How might you pray more like Daniel? Also
consider how God might use you to bless another person by
sharing what God is teaching you through Daniel. With
whom could you share?

4

God Humbles the Proud
Study Guide

Daniel 4

✝ **Pray**

W Work the issue: *What's really at stake*?

In this chapter, God gives a clear warning to Nebuchadnezzar. If God were to give you a warning, what do you think he would say? Are there any possible warnings in your life that you need to heed?

Have you ever tried to warn someone who was headed for disaster? You could see it coming and tried to steer them clear but they just wouldn't change course? It's a difficult position to be in when you are left with nothing to do but watch as the inevitable crash comes. Is there a friend that you need to warn of something?

Pride is a dangerous sin because it is so deceptive. It blinds us from seeing the reality of who God is and what a right relationship with him should be. Instead of acknowledging his place as Creator and King, we exalt ourselves. Instead of recognizing that everything we have is a gift, we act as if we've earned it. Instead of being thankful, we think we are owed and always deserve more. Prideful people have a distorted view of themselves, and this deception proved very costly to King Nebuchadnezzar. How do you struggle with temptations to be prideful?

What's at stake? What is the central issue or issues being addressed? What is the biggest issue for you?

Write down the main issue(s):

▌**I** Investigate Scripture: *What does God say?*

Daniel 4

> King Nebuchadnezzar,
>   To the nations and peoples of every language,
> who live in all the earth:
>   May you prosper greatly!
>   *²It is my pleasure to tell you about the miraculous signs and wonders that the Most High God has performed for me.*
>   *³How great are his signs,*

how mighty his wonders!
His kingdom is an eternal kingdom;
his dominion endures from
generation to generation.
⁴*I, Nebuchadnezzar, was at home in my palace, contented and prosperous. ⁵I had a dream that made me afraid. As I was lying in bed, the images and visions that passed through my mind terrified me. ⁶So I commanded that all the wise men of Babylon be brought before me to interpret the dream for me. ⁷When the magicians, enchanters, astrologers and diviners came, I told them the dream, but they could not interpret it for me. ⁸Finally, Daniel came into my presence and I told him the dream. (He is called Belteshazzar, after the name of my god, and the spirit of the holy gods is in him.)*

⁹*I said, "Belteshazzar, chief of the magicians, I know that the spirit of the holy gods is in you, and no mystery is too difficult for you. Here is my dream; interpret it for me. ¹⁰These are the visions I saw while lying in bed: I looked, and there before me stood a tree in the middle of the land. Its height was enormous. ¹¹The tree grew large and strong and its top touched the sky; it was visible to the ends of the earth. ¹²Its leaves were beautiful, its fruit abundant, and on it was food for all. Under it the wild animals found shelter, and the birds lived in its branches; from it every creature was fed.*

¹³*"In the visions I saw while lying in bed, I looked, and there before me was a holy one, a messenger, coming down from heaven. ¹⁴He called in a loud voice: 'Cut down the tree and trim off its branches; strip off its leaves and scatter its fruit. Let the animals flee from under it and the birds from its branches. ¹⁵But let the stump and its roots, bound with iron and bronze, remain in the ground, in the grass of the field.*

"'Let him be drenched with the dew of heaven, and let him live with the animals among the plants of the earth. ¹⁶Let his mind be changed from that of a man and let him be given the mind of an animal, till seven times pass by for him.

¹⁷"'The decision is announced by messengers, the holy ones declare the verdict, so that the living may know that the Most High is sovereign over all kingdoms on earth and gives them to anyone he wishes and sets over them the lowliest of people.'

¹⁸"This is the dream that I, King Nebuchadnezzar, had. Now, Belteshazzar, tell me what it means, for none of the wise men in my kingdom can interpret it for me. But you can, because the spirit of the holy gods is in you."

¹⁹Then Daniel (also called Belteshazzar) was greatly perplexed for a time, and his thoughts terrified him. So the king said, "Belteshazzar, do not let the dream or its meaning alarm you."

Belteshazzar answered, "My lord, if only the dream applied to your enemies and its meaning to your adversaries! ²⁰The tree you saw, which grew large and strong, with its top touching the sky, visible to the whole earth, ²¹with beautiful leaves and abundant fruit, providing food for all, giving shelter to the wild animals, and having nesting places in its branches for the birds—²²Your Majesty, you are that tree! You have become great and strong; your greatness has grown until it reaches the sky, and your dominion extends to distant parts of the earth.

²³"Your Majesty saw a holy one, a messenger, coming down from heaven and saying, 'Cut down the tree and destroy it, but leave the stump, bound with iron and bronze, in the grass of the field, while its roots remain in the ground. Let him be drenched with the dew of heaven; let him live with the wild animals, until seven times pass by for him.'

24"This is the interpretation, Your Majesty, and this is the decree the Most High has issued against my lord the king: 25You will be driven away from people and will live with the wild animals; you will eat grass like the ox and be drenched with the dew of heaven. Seven times will pass by for you until you acknowledge that the Most High is sovereign over all kingdoms on earth and gives them to anyone he wishes. 26The command to leave the stump of the tree with its roots means that your kingdom will be restored to you when you acknowledge that Heaven rules. 27Therefore, Your Majesty, be pleased to accept my advice: Renounce your sins by doing what is right, and your wickedness by being kind to the oppressed. It may be that then your prosperity will continue."

28All this happened to King Nebuchadnezzar. 29Twelve months later, as the king was walking on the roof of the royal palace of Babylon, 30he said, "Is not this the great Babylon I have built as the royal residence, by my mighty power and for the glory of my majesty?"

31Even as the words were on his lips, a voice came from heaven, "This is what is decreed for you, King Nebuchadnezzar: Your royal authority has been taken from you. 32You will be driven away from people and will live with the wild animals; you will eat grass like the ox. Seven times will pass by for you until you acknowledge that the Most High is sovereign over all kingdoms on earth and gives them to anyone he wishes."

33Immediately what had been said about Nebuchadnezzar was fulfilled. He was driven away from people and ate grass like the ox. His body was drenched with the dew of heaven until his hair grew like the feathers of an eagle and his nails like the claws of a bird.

34At the end of that time, I, Nebuchadnezzar, raised my eyes toward heaven, and my sanity was restored. Then I praised the Most High; I honored and glorified him who lives forever.

> *His dominion is an eternal dominion;*
> *his kingdom endures from generation to generation.*
> > [35]*All the peoples of the earth*
> > *are regarded as nothing.*
> > *He does as he pleases*
> > > *with the powers of heaven*
> > > *and the peoples of the earth.*
> > *No one can hold back his hand*
> > > *or say to him: "What have you done?"*

[36]*At the same time that my sanity was restored, my honor and splendor were returned to me for the glory of my kingdom. My advisers and nobles sought me out, and I was restored to my throne and became even greater than before.* [37]*Now I, Nebuchadnezzar, praise and exalt and glorify the King of heaven, because everything he does is right and all his ways are just. And those who walk in pride he is able to humble.*

❖ What subject does this story begin and end with?

❖ Notice the use of "I" in this chapter. Who is telling this story? Why is that significant?

❖ Look again at 4:3. For what did Nebuchadnezzar specifically praise God?

❖ Who did the king eventually summon to interpret his dream? What did he call the interpreter?

❖ What was the reason given for this judgment according to 4:17? How could you paraphrase 4:17?

❖ What was going to happen to Nebuchadnezzar (4:25)?

❖ What was Daniel's advice in 4:27?

❖ What did Nebuchadnezzar think as he gazed out on Babylon (4:30)?

❖ What happened to the king (4:33)?

❖ For what did Nebuchadnezzar praise God (4:34–35)?

S Seek counsel: *What do wise people say?*

Review chapter 4 beginning on page 45 or watch a video presentation of this chapter. Access the QR (Quick Response) code that can be read by many smart devices using a scanning app. It allows you to immediately watch the video. If you do not have a QR code reader, you can access the same material at http://vimeo.com/74772078.
To the extent you have time and ability, read the relevant section from one of the recommended studies on page 325. Also check out the resources available on Bible.org.

D Develop your response: *What do I think?*

❖ What lessons did God teach Nebuchadnezzar through the dream and resulting consequences?

❖ Over what kinds of things do you need to avoid pride and grow in humility?

❖ How could you praise God similar to how Nebuchadnezzar did?

⦿ **Openly discuss:** *What do we think?*

1. What are some of the worst examples of pride you have seen?

2. Obviously Nebuchadnezzar had confidence in Daniel as one in whom the "spirit of the holy gods" resides. Does your boss or someone you work with know that you are a spiritual person? Why or why not?

3. Daniel graciously but directly warned Nebuchadnezzar (4:19–22; 27). In the New Testament, we are called to speak with grace and truth as we admonish each other (Ephesians 5:1–5; Galatians 6:1–5; Colossians 3:16). Is there anyone in your life who you feel convicted to warn about something in their life? How and when could you warn them?

4. Nebuchadnezzar fell into terrible pride 12 months after the dream. When in your life have you said or thought something similar? Over what kinds of things are you most tempted toward pride?

5. God disciplined Nebuchadnezzar immediately until he acknowledged that the Most High is sovereign over all kingdoms on earth. When in your life have you experienced what you now realize may have been discipline from God? What did you learn from it?

6. How did Nebuchadnezzar describe God in the end of the chapter (4:34–37)? Which of his descriptions is most powerful or meaningful to you at this point in your life and why?

7. As you consider chapter 4, what do you sense the Spirit of God saying to you about pride, humility and his "bigness"? What changes is God convicting you to make in your life?

M Move to action: *What will I do?*

In reflecting on Daniel 4, how do you believe God wants to transform you to greater humility and greater recognition of who he is? Return to what you wrote down in the "Develop your response" section and prayerfully rework your responses to help you move from intention to action. How will you move to action this week? Also consider how God might use you to bless another person by sharing what God is teaching you through Daniel. With whom could you share? Maybe there is a person you need to warn, or to encourage.

5

God has the Last Word
Study Guide

Daniel 5

✝ Pray

W Work the issue: *What's really at stake?*

Every generation has some version of a certain song lyric. The song "Die Young" urges partiers to "make the most of tonight like we're gonna die young." In the 1980s, a popular song by Prince blared from stereo speakers promising that if the world was destined to end in the year 2000, they were "gonna party like it's 1999." Even the apostle Paul used this sentiment mockingly to make a point: "Let us eat and drink for tomorrow we die" (1 Corinthians 15:32). When we don't have the assurance of eternal life, people are inclined to stave off the fear of imminent death by indulging in the sensual pleasures of this world. How might you do this in your life?

King Belshazzar showed pride at his drunken party to the extent that he blasphemed God by using the holy goblets designed for worship. How do people dishonor or blaspheme God today in similar ways?

What's at stake? What is the central issue or issues being addressed? What is the biggest issue for you?

Write down the main issue(s):

I Investigate Scripture: *What does God say?*

Notice who is speaking in each section.

Daniel 5

> King Belshazzar gave a great banquet for a
> thousand of his nobles and drank wine with them.
> ²While Belshazzar was drinking his wine, he gave
> orders to bring in the gold and silver goblets that
> Nebuchadnezzar his father had taken from the
> temple in Jerusalem, so that the king and his nobles,
> his wives and his concubines might drink from them.
> ³So they brought in the gold goblets that had been
> taken from the temple of God in Jerusalem, and the

222

king and his nobles, his wives and his concubines drank from them. ⁴As they drank the wine, they praised the gods of gold and silver, of bronze, iron, wood and stone.

⁵Suddenly the fingers of a human hand appeared and wrote on the plaster of the wall, near the lampstand in the royal palace. The king watched the hand as it wrote. ⁶His face turned pale and he was so frightened that his legs became weak and his knees were knocking.

⁷The king summoned the enchanters, astrologers and diviners. Then he said to these wise men of Babylon, "Whoever reads this writing and tells me what it means will be clothed in purple and have a gold chain placed around his neck, and he will be made the third highest ruler in the kingdom."

⁸Then all the king's wise men came in, but they could not read the writing or tell the king what it meant. ⁹So King Belshazzar became even more terrified and his face grew paler. His nobles were baffled.

¹⁰The queen, hearing the voices of the king and his nobles, came into the banquet hall. "May the king live forever!" she said. "Don't be alarmed! Don't look so pale! ¹¹There is a man in your kingdom who has the spirit of the holy gods in him. In the time of your father he was found to have insight and intelligence and wisdom like that of the gods. Your father, King Nebuchadnezzar, appointed him chief of the magicians, enchanters, astrologers and diviners. ¹²He did this because Daniel, whom the king called Belteshazzar, was found to have a keen mind and knowledge and understanding, and also the ability to interpret dreams, explain riddles and solve difficult problems. Call for Daniel, and he will tell you what the writing means."

¹³So Daniel was brought before the king, and the king said to him, "Are you Daniel, one of the exiles my father the king brought from Judah? ¹⁴*I have heard that the spirit of the gods is in you and that you have insight, intelligence and outstanding wisdom. ¹⁵The wise men and enchanters were brought before me to read this writing and tell me what it means, but they could not explain it. ¹⁶Now I have heard that you are able to give interpretations and to solve difficult problems. If you can read this writing and tell me what it means, you will be clothed in purple and have a gold chain placed around your neck, and you will be made the third highest ruler in the kingdom."*

¹⁷*Then Daniel answered the king, "You may keep your gifts for yourself and give your rewards to someone else. Nevertheless, I will read the writing for the king and tell him what it means.*

¹⁸*"Your Majesty, the Most High God gave your father Nebuchadnezzar sovereignty and greatness and glory and splendor. ¹⁹Because of the high position he gave him, all the nations and peoples of every language dreaded and feared him. Those the king wanted to put to death, he put to death; those he wanted to spare, he spared; those he wanted to promote, he promoted; and those he wanted to humble, he humbled. ²⁰But when his heart became arrogant and hardened with pride, he was deposed from his royal throne and stripped of his glory. ²¹He was driven away from people and given the mind of an animal; he lived with the wild donkeys and ate grass like the ox; and his body was drenched with the dew of heaven, until he acknowledged that the Most High God is sovereign over all kingdoms on earth and sets over them anyone he wishes."*

²²*But you, Belshazzar, his son, have not humbled yourself, though you knew all this. ²³Instead, you have set yourself up against the Lord of heaven. You had the goblets from his temple brought to you, and you and your nobles, your wives and your*

concubines drank wine from them. You praised the gods of silver and gold, of bronze, iron, wood and stone, which cannot see or hear or understand. But you did not honor the God who holds in his hand your life and all your ways. ²⁴Therefore he sent the hand that wrote the inscription.

²⁵"This is the inscription that was written:
MENE, MENE, TEKEL, PARSIN
²⁶"Here is what these words mean:
Mene: God has numbered the days of your reign and brought it to an end.
²⁷Tekel: You have been weighed on the scales and found wanting.
²⁸Peres: Your kingdom is divided and given to the Medes and Persians."
²⁹Then at Belshazzar's command, Daniel was clothed in purple, a gold chain was placed around his neck, and he was proclaimed the third highest ruler in the kingdom.
³⁰That very night Belshazzar, king of the Babylonians, was slain, ³¹and Darius the Mede took over the kingdom, at the age of sixty-two.

❖ The author of Daniel gave us no description of Belshazzar but we can tell a lot about him from his actions. What kind of person was Belshazzar? How do you know?

❖ Daniel arrived on the scene in the middle of our story. Based on his actions, how was Daniel the same man that we've seen throughout the book? How was he different in his interaction with Belshazzar than with Nebuchadnezzar?

❖ What objects did Belshazzar want brought to him? What did he do with them?

❖ What happened "suddenly" according to 5:5? What was Belshazzar's immediate reaction?

❖ How did the queen describe Daniel in 5:12?

❖ What explanation did Daniel give for why Nebuchadnezzar "was driven away from people and given the mind of an animal" (5:21)?

❖ Which verse assures us that Belshazzar was aware of Nebuchadnezzar's experience with God? According to 5:23, of what was Belshazzar guilty?

❖ Summarize the message that was written on the wall.

❖ What happened to Belshazzar?

S **Seek counsel:** *What do wise people say*?

Review chapter 5 beginning on page 59 or watch a video presentation of this chapter. Access the QR (Quick Response) code that can be read by many smart devices using a scanning app. It allows you to immediately watch the video. If you do not have a QR code reader, you can access the same material at http://vimeo.com/74772077.
To the extent you have time and ability, read the relevant section from one of the recommended studies on page 325. Also check out the resources available on Bible.org.

D Develop your response: *What do I think?*

❖ What has this story taught you about God and your relationship to him?

❖ What warning do you think God would give you today?

⊙ **Openly discuss:** *What do we think?*

1. What is your personal history with drinking and partying? Have you ever been at a crazy party when all of a sudden something happened that quickly sobered up the room? Share the story. How is your story similar to what happened in Daniel 5?

2. Have you ever sensed God getting your attention in a way that scared you or unnerved you (such as the writing on the wall)?

3. How did the queen describe Daniel to Belshazzar (5:10– 12)? Which character traits of Daniel stand out to you? Why? What is your reputation at work? How would someone introduce you in a similar situation?

4. What are the five concerns that Daniel brought to Belshazzar in 5:22–23? How are we guilty of these today? Of all that Daniel said to Belshazzar, what did you hear as the most stinging? Why?

5. The consequences for Belshazzar were quick and severe which makes this chapter a bracing warning against prideful, immoral sin. In what areas of your life do you sense the Spirit of God warning you? What will you do about it?

6. How could God use you to courageously warn others as Daniel did?

M Move to action: *What will I do?*

In reflecting on Daniel 5, how do you believe God wants to transform you by warning you of sin and moving you to greater worship of him? Also consider how God might use you to bless another person by sharing what God is teaching you through Daniel. With whom could you share?

6

God Tames Lions
Study Guide

Daniel 6

✝ Pray

W Work the issue: *What's really at stake?*

What connections do you see between this chapter and the current issues in your life? While the book of Daniel continues, we've come to the final story that specifically records Daniel's experience in the court of Babylon. It's no wonder that this is such a beloved story. Daniel in the lion's den has so many elements of great drama including jealousy and intrigue, fear and regret, joy and triumph. But this story is more than a tale of suspense or even a lesson in courage. The account of Daniel and the lions shows us once again the dedicated faithfulness and awesome power of our Big God who reigns as the ultimate King.

A myth that we sometimes unintentionally promote in modern American Christianity is that the best way to serve God is by making it our vocation. The church certainly needs full-time missionaries, pastors and ministry workers, but everyone else can also make a significant impact for the kingdom of God. It is because we work and live as part of the world that we can reach people in the world. But to do this, we need to bless our culture without being assimilated into it.

Daniel made a name for himself in Babylon by serving the king with diligence, excellence and integrity. This made him a target for jealous colleagues, but it also put him in a position to be used to display the awesome power of God. How does it make you feel to see yourself as a representative of Christ in your workplace and home?

Once again Daniel's life was threatened and no one but God could save him. Imagine being lowered into a pit full of lions. Your feet hit the ground, the hole is sealed with a thud and you are surrounded by the sounds of beasts in the darkness. How do you think you would respond if you were in Daniel's place? Are you willing to hold to your convictions even if it means being "thrown into a den of lions" (6:7, 12)?

What's at stake? What is the central issue or issues being addressed? What is the biggest issue for you?

Write down the main issue(s):

▌I▐ Investigate Scripture: *What does God say?*

Read the chapter prayerfully asking God to show you himself and insight into yourself. Put yourself in Daniel's position.

Daniel 6

It pleased Darius to appoint 120 satraps to rule throughout the kingdom, ²with three administrators over them, one of whom was Daniel. The satraps were made accountable to them so that the king might not suffer loss. ³Now Daniel so distinguished himself among the administrators and the satraps by his exceptional qualities that the king planned to set him over the whole kingdom. ⁴At this, the administrators and the satraps tried to find grounds for charges against Daniel in his conduct of government affairs, but they were unable to do so. They could find no corruption in him, because he was trustworthy and neither corrupt nor negligent. ⁵Finally these men said, "We will never find any basis for charges against this man Daniel unless it has something to do with the law of his God."

⁶So these administrators and satraps went as a group to the king and said: "May King Darius live forever! ⁷The royal administrators, prefects, satraps, advisers and governors have all agreed that the king should issue an edict and enforce the decree that anyone who prays to any god or human being during the next thirty days, except to you, Your Majesty, shall be thrown into the lions' den. ⁸Now, Your Majesty, issue the decree and put it in writing so that it cannot be altered—in accordance with the law of the Medes and Persians, which cannot be repealed." ⁹So King Darius put the decree in writing.

¹⁰Now when Daniel learned that the decree had been published, he went home to his upstairs room

where the windows opened toward Jerusalem. Three
times a day he got down on his knees and prayed,
giving thanks to his God, just as he had done before.
[11] Then these men went as a group and found Daniel
praying and asking God for help. [12] So they went to
the king and spoke to him about his royal decree:
"Did you not publish a decree that during the next
thirty days anyone who prays to any god or human
being except to you, Your Majesty, would be thrown
into the lions' den?"

The king answered, "The decree stands—in
accordance with the law of the Medes and Persians,
which cannot be repealed."

[13] Then they said to the king, "Daniel, who is
one of the exiles from Judah, pays no attention to you,
Your Majesty, or to the decree you put in writing. He
still prays three times a day." [14] When the king heard
this, he was greatly distressed; he was determined to
rescue Daniel and made every effort until sundown to
save him.

[15] Then the men went as a group to King Darius
and said to him, "Remember, Your Majesty, that
according to the law of the Medes and Persians no
decree or edict that the king issues can be changed."

[16] So the king gave the order, and they brought
Daniel and threw him into the lions' den. The king
said to Daniel, "May your God, whom you serve
continually, rescue you!"

[17] A stone was brought and placed over the
mouth of the den, and the king sealed it with his own
signet ring and with the rings of his nobles, so that
Daniel's situation might not be changed. [18] Then the
king returned to his palace and spent the night
without eating and without any entertainment being
brought to him. And he could not sleep.

[19] At the first light of dawn, the king got up and
hurried to the lions' den. [20] When he came near the
den, he called to Daniel in an anguished voice,

*"Daniel, servant of the living God, has your God,
whom you serve continually, been able to rescue you
from the lions?"*
*21Daniel answered, "May the king live forever!
22My God sent his angel, and he shut the mouths of
the lions. They have not hurt me, because I was found
innocent in his sight. Nor have I ever done any wrong
before you, Your Majesty."*
*23The king was overjoyed and gave orders to lift
Daniel out of the den. And when Daniel was lifted
from the den, no wound was found on him, because
he had trusted in his God.*
*24At the king's command, the men who had
falsely accused Daniel were brought in and thrown
into the lions' den, along with their wives and
children. And before they reached the floor of the den,
the lions overpowered them and crushed all their
bones.*
*25Then King Darius wrote to all the nations and
peoples of every language in all the earth:*
"May you prosper greatly!
*26"I issue a decree that in every part of my
kingdom people must fear and reverence the God of
Daniel.*

> *"For he is the living God*
> *and he endures forever;*
> *his kingdom will not be destroyed,*
> *his dominion will never end.*
> *27He rescues and he saves;*
> *he performs signs and wonders*
> *in the heavens and on the earth.*
> *He has rescued Daniel*
> *from the power of the lions."*

*28So Daniel prospered during the reign of Darius, the
reign of Cyrus the Persian.*

❖   What do you most admire about Daniel? Why?

❖   How did Daniel distinguish himself according to 6:3?

❖   What did the other satraps try to discover about Daniel? What did they find out instead (6:4–5)?

❖ What plan did they come up with to get rid of Daniel?

❖ How did Daniel respond to news of the decree (6:10)?

❖ How did the accusers present their case to the king? What was the king's response?

❖ What did Darius find when he raced to the lion's den in the morning?

❖ How did Daniel explain his survival in 6:22–23?

❖ What happened to Daniel's accusers according to 6:24?

❖ What statements did Darius make about God?

S Seek counsel: *What do wise people say?*

Review chapter 6 beginning on page 73 or watch a video presentation of this chapter. Access the QR (Quick Response) code that can be read by many smart devices using a scanning app. It allows you to immediately watch the video. If you do not have a QR code reader, you can access the same material at http://vimeo.com/74772076. To the extent you have time and ability, read the relevant section from one of the recommended studies on page 325. Also check out the resources available on Bible.org.

D Develop your response: *What do I think?*

❖ Even if you are not currently employed, we all have responsibilities. If you were investigated based on your performance in an attempt to discredit you, what do you think would be discovered?

❖ Would your loyalty to Yahweh be something that you are so known for that it could be used against you? Why or why not?

❖ Because the first six chapters of the book of Daniel are arranged to give us six stories, let's review them. What name would you give each story, and what has each one taught you about God, his relationship with his people or our proper response to him?

Chapter 1:

Chapter 2:

Chapter 3:

Chapter 4:

Chapter 5:

Chapter 6:

◉ Openly discuss: *What do we think?*

1. Have you ever had people try to undermine you, investigate you, stab you in the back or falsely accuse you out of jealousy or some other motivation? How did you handle it?

2. Describe Daniel's character from the first nine verses of chapter 6. Why was he well-regarded by King Darius and why couldn't the other guys find dirt on him? How could you better demonstrate exceptional character at work?

3. Daniel faithfully prayed three times every day. How regular is your prayer life? What is your habit of prayer?

4. In what circumstances can you imagine that you or another Christian in America might one day have to decide to obey God rather than an authority—at work, at home, or in ordinary life? If the exercise of the Christian faith suddenly became illegal in this country, could you be arrested for going about your usual routine? If so, how? If not, why not?

5. According to Daniel 6:23, why was Daniel rescued without suffering a single wound? How can we grow in that trait?

6. Describe our Big God in view of Darius' final decree. What are some of your favorite characteristics of our Big God? Spend time praising The Big God for his greatness.

7. In reviewing our study through Daniel 1–6, how has your understanding of our Big God grown? What differences has that new understanding of God made in your life?

M Move to action: *What will I do?*

Considering not only chapter 6, but all of the first half of Daniel, prayerfully consider these questions and how you will move to action in the Holy Spirit's power:

❖ How are you developing your understanding of and relationship with The Big God to ensure your faithfulness to him?

❖ How are you encouraging fellow Christians to stand firm in a challenging culture?

In reflecting on Daniel 6, how do you believe God wants to transform you to become more like Jesus Christ, the model of spiritual maturity?

7

**Four Great Beasts
Study Guide**

Daniel 7

✝ Pray

W Work the issue: *What's really at stake*?

The biblical author is usually addressing a question, issue or
problem. At any given moment in our lives, we are facing
difficulties, asking questions and trying to make decisions. Your
study will be more transforming if you take time to consider what
is at stake in the passage and what is currently at stake in your life
to which the passage may speak.

Quickly scan the passage considering what underlying issues
may be present. Reflecting on what the author might be addressing
in his time, what about you today? What questions does this text
raise in your own mind? What do you wonder about?

The first six chapters of Daniel show us a Big God who, in spite of appearances, is in control. Stunning imagery, breathtaking drama and mind-bending prophecy await us in the second half of Daniel, and the reign of a powerful and righteous God is still the central theme. As we immerse ourselves in God-given visions and dreams, we will find strength and courage in the God who is revealed. As individuals, it is easy to feel at the mercy of forces we may not even understand, much less have control over. Although the future looks uncertain to us, Daniel assures us that we can trust our Big God who holds the future in his hands. What is our confidence in a chaotic world filled with nations and leaders who lack a moral compass?

What's at stake? What is the central issue or issues being addressed? What is the biggest issue for you?

Write down the main issue(s):

I Investigate Scripture: *What does God say?*

As you read today, try to experience the dream with your senses. What sights, sounds and smells does this vision bring to mind? How would you feel if this was your dream? (Daniel admitted in 7:28 that he was so afraid that all the color drained from his face!) Then record your initial thoughts and questions.

248

Daniel 7

In the first year of Belshazzar king of Babylon, Daniel had a dream, and visions passed through his mind as he was lying in bed. He wrote down the substance of his dream.

²Daniel said: "In my vision at night I looked, and there before me were the four winds of heaven churning up the great sea. ³Four great beasts, each different from the others, came up out of the sea.

⁴"The first was like a lion, and it had the wings of an eagle. I watched until its wings were torn off and it was lifted from the ground so that it stood on two feet like a human being, and the mind of a human was given to it.

⁵"And there before me was a second beast, which looked like a bear. It was raised up on one of its sides, and it had three ribs in its mouth between its teeth. It was told, 'Get up and eat your fill of flesh!'

⁶"After that, I looked, and there before me was another beast, one that looked like a leopard. And on its back it had four wings like those of a bird. This beast had four heads, and it was given authority to rule.

⁷"After that, in my vision at night I looked, and there before me was a fourth beast—terrifying and frightening and very powerful. It had large iron teeth; it crushed and devoured its victims and trampled underfoot whatever was left. It was different from all the former beasts, and it had ten horns.

⁸"While I was thinking about the horns, there before me was another horn, a little one, which came up among them; and three of the first horns were uprooted before it. This horn had eyes like the eyes of a human being and a mouth that spoke boastfully.
⁹ "As I looked,

"thrones were set in place,
    and the Ancient of Days took his seat.
His clothing was as white as snow;
    the hair of his head was white like wool.
His throne was flaming with fire,
    and its wheels were all ablaze.
10A river of fire was flowing,
    coming out from before him.
Thousands upon thousands attended him;
    ten thousand times ten thousand stood
        before him.
The court was seated,
    and the books were opened.
11"Then I continued to watch because of the
boastful words the horn was speaking. I kept looking
until the beast was slain and its body destroyed and
thrown into the blazing fire. 12(The other beasts had
been stripped of their authority, but were allowed to
live for a period of time.)

13"In my vision at night I looked, and there
before me was one like a son of man, coming with the
clouds of heaven. He approached the Ancient of Days
and was led into his presence. 14He was given
authority, glory and sovereign power; all nations and
peoples of every language worshiped him. His
dominion is an everlasting dominion that will not
pass away, and his kingdom is one that will never be
destroyed.

15"I, Daniel, was troubled in spirit, and the
visions that passed through my mind disturbed me.
16I approached one of those standing there and asked
him the meaning of all this.

"So he told me and gave me the interpretation
of these things: 17'The four great beasts are four kings
that will rise from the earth. 18But the holy people of
the Most High will receive the kingdom and will
possess it forever—yes, for ever and ever.'

19"Then I wanted to know the meaning of the fourth beast, which was different from all the others and most terrifying, with its iron teeth and bronze claws—the beast that crushed and devoured its victims and trampled underfoot whatever was left. 20I also wanted to know about the ten horns on its head and about the other horn that came up, before which three of them fell—the horn that looked more imposing than the others and that had eyes and a mouth that spoke boastfully. 21As I watched, this horn was waging war against the holy people and defeating them, 22until the Ancient of Days came and pronounced judgment in favor of the holy people of the Most High, and the time came when they possessed the kingdom.

23"He gave me this explanation: 'The fourth beast is a fourth kingdom that will appear on earth. It will be different from all the other kingdoms and will devour the whole earth, trampling it down and crushing it. 24The ten horns are ten kings who will come from this kingdom. After them another king will arise, different from the earlier ones; he will subdue three kings. 25He will speak against the Most High and oppress his holy people and try to change the set times and the laws. The holy people will be delivered into his hands for a time, times and half a time.

26"'But the court will sit, and his power will be taken away and completely destroyed forever. 27Then the sovereignty, power and greatness of all the kingdoms under heaven will be handed over to the holy people of the Most High. His kingdom will be an everlasting kingdom, and all rulers will worship and obey him.'

28"This is the end of the matter. I, Daniel, was deeply troubled by my thoughts, and my face turned pale, but I kept the matter to myself."

❖ Record your initial thoughts and reactions to this vision.

❖ What four beasts came out of the sea? What is disturbing about each of these beasts? What is unique about the horn?

❖ Summarize. What does each beast represent? What was the ultimate fate of each of these nations and who controls that fate?

❖ How is the Ancient of Days described?

❖ What happened to the beasts, particularly the one with ten horns?

❖ Who approached the throne? How is he described?

❖ From whom did Daniel ask for help?

❖ Which beast was Daniel concerned with? Why do you think that was so?

❖ What would happen to God's people according to 7:21 and 7:25?

❖ According to 7:26–27, what is the ultimate end of this evil kingdom? What about God's people?

![S] **Seek counsel:** *What do wise people say?*

Review chapter 7 beginning on page 87 or watch a video presentation of this chapter. Access the QR (Quick Response) code that can be read by many smart devices using a scanning app. It allows you to immediately watch the video. If you do not have a QR code reader, you can access the same material at. http://vimeo.com/74756869.
To the extent you have time and ability, read the relevant section from one of the recommended studies on page 325. Also check out the resources available on Bible.org.

D Develop your response: *What do I think?*

❖ Overall, what does this vision communicate to us about human kingdoms versus the divine one?

❖ Why should Daniel's vision matter to believers today? How should it affect our behavior?

❖ What stood out to you this week? What will you remember most from Daniel 7?

◉ **Openly discuss:** *What do we think?*

1. What about the future is most scary to you and why?

2. Good and bad, what have been your experiences with biblical prophecy, end-time teaching and predictions?

3. What is apocalyptic literature and how should we read its symbols and images differently than we read history or a letter, such as Romans?

4. What historical empires are the four beasts in Daniel's vision depicting? How does this accurate prophecy impact your confidence in God's Word?

5. Who is the little horn? What do we know about him from Daniel 7?

6. What did Daniel see in the "heavenly" part of his vision (7:9–14, 26–27)? Who is the "Ancient of Days" and who is the "Son of Man"? What will each one do in the future?

7. Daniel was deeply troubled by his thoughts in reaction to seeing this vision. How do you believe God wants you to respond to the vision?

M **Move to action:** *What will I do?*

Consider the following questions to prompt your prayerful decision on what action you will take.

❖ How does Daniel's dream about the four beasts help you deal with worry and anxiety about the future? How is your faith being strengthened?

❖ How could you be better prepared for Jesus' return by prioritizing his kingdom in your life?

❖ Knowing that evil will be allowed to reign for a time as we come nearer to the end, how can you help those around you by introducing them to Jesus? How could this vision increase your sense of urgency to share the gospel?

In reflecting on your study of Daniel 7, how will you move to action? Write down what you will do differently. This could be a transformation in your mind, in your heart, or in your actions. Revisit what you wrote in the "Develop your response" section. Now prayerfully choose how you will act differently in the power of the Spirit.

8

The Ram and the Goat
Study Guide

Daniel 8

✝ **Pray**

W **Work the issue:** *What's really at stake?*

Like the dream recorded in Daniel 7, this vision is highly symbolic, dramatic and rich in sensory detail. We will watch a fierce battle between two animals and encounter the angel Gabriel. We will marvel at the amazing accuracy of biblical prophecy. But we will also be challenged to both understand this vision and live according to what we learn.

What we have discovered in Daniel is that there is more to the course of history than meets the eye. The great kings in the first half of Daniel—Nebuchadnezzar, Belshazzar and Darius—were powerful rulers who commanded armies. Yet each was brought to power and deposed according to God's design. The lesson of the first half of Daniel, that God deserves worship as the ultimate ruler, certainly carries forward into the second half of the book. He is a very Big God. How does the bigness of God affect how your view the future?

What's at stake? What is the central issue or issues being addressed? What is the biggest issue for you?

Write down the main issue(s):

I Investigate Scripture: *What does God say?*

In your first reading, allow your imagination to get caught up in this incredible vision. Then read it a second time slowly, looking at the details.

Daniel 8

> In the third year of King Belshazzar's reign, I, Daniel, had a vision, after the one that had already appeared to me. ²In my vision I saw myself in the citadel of Susa in the province of Elam; in the vision I was beside the Ulai Canal. ³I looked up, and there before me was a ram with two horns, standing beside the canal, and the horns were long. One of the horns

*was longer than the other but grew up later. ⁴I
watched the ram as it charged toward the west and
the north and the south. No animal could stand
against it, and none could rescue from its power. It
did as it pleased and became great.*

*⁵As I was thinking about this, suddenly a goat
with a prominent horn between its eyes came from
the west, crossing the whole earth without touching
the ground. ⁶It came toward the two-horned ram I
had seen standing beside the canal and charged at it
in great rage. ⁷I saw it attack the ram furiously,
striking the ram and shattering its two horns. The
ram was powerless to stand against it; the goat
knocked it to the ground and trampled on it, and
none could rescue the ram from its power. ⁸The goat
became very great, but at the height of its power the
large horn was broken off, and in its place four
prominent horns grew up toward the four winds of
heaven.*

*⁹Out of one of them came another horn, which
started small but grew in power to the south and to
the east and toward the Beautiful Land. ¹⁰It grew
until it reached the host of the heavens, and it threw
some of the starry host down to the earth and
trampled on them. ¹¹It set itself up to be as great as
the commander of the army of the LORD; it took away
the daily sacrifice from the LORD, and his sanctuary
was thrown down. ¹²Because of rebellion, the LORD's
people and the daily sacrifice were given over to it. It
prospered in everything it did, and truth was thrown
to the ground.*

*¹³Then I heard a holy one speaking, and
another holy one said to him, "How long will it take
for the vision to be fulfilled—the vision concerning
the daily sacrifice, the rebellion that causes
desolation, the surrender of the sanctuary and the
trampling underfoot of the LORD's people?"*

¹⁴He said to me, "It will take 2,300 evenings and mornings; then the sanctuary will be reconsecrated."

¹⁵While I, Daniel, was watching the vision and trying to understand it, there before me stood one who looked like a man. ¹⁶And I heard a man's voice from the Ulai calling, "Gabriel, tell this man the meaning of the vision."

¹⁷As he came near the place where I was standing, I was terrified and fell prostrate. "Son of man," he said to me, "understand that the vision concerns the time of the end."

¹⁸While he was speaking to me, I was in a deep sleep, with my face to the ground. Then he touched me and raised me to my feet.

¹⁹He said: "I am going to tell you what will happen later in the time of wrath, because the vision concerns the appointed time of the end. ²⁰The two-horned ram that you saw represents the kings of Media and Persia. ²¹The shaggy goat is the king of Greece, and the large horn between its eyes is the first king. ²²The four horns that replaced the one that was broken off represent four kingdoms that will emerge from his nation but will not have the same power.

²³"In the latter part of their reign, when rebels have become completely wicked, a fierce-looking king, a master of intrigue, will arise. ²⁴He will become very strong, but not by his own power. He will cause astounding devastation and will succeed in whatever he does. He will destroy those who are mighty, the holy people. ²⁵He will cause deceit to prosper, and he will consider himself superior. When they feel secure, he will destroy many and take his stand against the Prince of princes. Yet he will be destroyed, but not by human power.

²⁶"The vision of the evenings and mornings that has been given you is true, but seal up the vision, for it concerns the distant future."

27I, Daniel, was worn out. I lay exhausted for several days. Then I got up and went about the king's business. I was appalled by the vision; it was beyond understanding.

❖ What physical features of the ram are mentioned? How is it described in 8:4?

❖ How is the goat described in 8:5 and 8:8? What happened to its horn? What did the goat do to the ram?

❖ What did the horn that came from the goat do, according to 8:10–12?

❖ What question is asked in 8:13? With what is it specifically concerned?

❖ According to Gabriel in 8:17, what did this vision concern?

❖ What timeframe is the vision referencing according to the angel (8:19)? How is the ruler described in 8:23?

❖ What will he do according to 8:24–25?

❖ What instructions are given to Daniel concerning the vision? What reason is given?

❖ How would you describe the Antichrist based on this vision?

❖ Who will ultimately defeat him?

S Seek counsel: *What do wise people say?*

Review chapter 8 beginning on page 99 or watch a video presentation of this chapter. Access the QR (Quick Response) code that can be read by many smart devices using a scanning app. It allows you to immediately watch the video. If you do not have a QR code reader, you can access the same material at http://vimeo.com/74419258.
To the extent you have time and ability, read the relevant section from one of the recommended studies on page 325. Also check out the resources available on Bible.org.

D **Develop your response:** *What do I think?*

❖ What did you learn about the end times?

❖ What does it look like to live in light of what God has said he will do in the future? In other words, what do you think it means to "be ready" as Jesus commanded (Matthew 24:44; Luke 12:40)?

❖ What will you take away from your study of Daniel 8?

◉ Openly discuss: *What do we think?*

1. Do you know anyone who has experienced persecution for their faith? What happened?

2. Who interpreted God's vision to Daniel? What else do we know about Gabriel (Luke 1:11, 19, 26–27)?

3. Who do the ram and the goat represent? How are those animals fitting representations? How does the accuracy of these predictions strengthen your faith?

4. How does Daniel 8 connect to the vision of the animals in chapter 7 and the vision of the statue in chapter 2? Draw a picture or create a chart that shows the parallels.

5. Who is the horn? Describe his character and his actions. When does he live (*Hint*: Time references are in the chapter)? How can we be tempted to similar kinds of behavior, such as being stern, using intrigue, deceit and considering ourselves superior?

6. What will happen to the horn in the end (see Revelation 19 for more)? Who is the Prince of princes (8:25)?

7. How can the ultimate, certain, divine defeat of the little horn, and all evil, encourage us today when we face difficult times, pain and suffering, often caused by others' actions?

M Move to action: *What will I do?*

In reflecting on your study of Daniel 8, how will you move to action in the Spirit's power? Revisit what you wrote in the "Develop your response" section. What will you do?

9

Daniel's Prayer
Study Guide

Daniel 9:1—21

✝ Pray

W Work the issue: *What's really at stake?*

As Christians, we know that prayer is important. So, how's your prayer life? Are you satisfied with the amount of time you spend praying and the content of your prayers? Do you feel they are effective? How do you know? The Bible teaches us that the Creator of the universe is available to us through prayer whenever we approach him. So why do many believers struggle in this area? Perhaps we could learn something about prayer from Daniel. We have already seen that Daniel was a man who prayed in times of need but also as part of his daily routine (see Daniel 2 and 6).

The prayer that he offered to the Lord in chapter 9 shows how well he understood the God he had spent his entire life serving. How do you approach God in prayer? Daniel approached God with unflinching honesty about the sins of his people. He didn't make excuses, justify their actions or get angry with God. He simply confessed the truth. How do you handle your sin with God?

You might imagine that under the weight of such obvious and staggering guilt, it would be difficult to approach a righteous and holy God. But Daniel knew that Yahweh had proven himself a faithful God of mercy as well as justice. How confident do you feel approaching the holy, merciful God?

What's at stake? What is the central issue or issues being addressed? What is the biggest issue for you?

Write down the main issue(s):

⬛ I Investigate Scripture: *What does God say?*

Daniel 9

In the first year of Darius son of Xerxes (a Mede by descent), who was made ruler over the Babylonia kingdom ²in the first year of his reign, I, Daniel, understood from the Scriptures, according to the *word of the L*ORD *given to Nehemiah the prophet, that the desolation of Jerusalem would last seventy years. ³So I turned to the Lord God and pleaded with him in prayer and petition, in fasting, and in sackcloth and ashes.*

*⁴I prayed to the L*ORD *my God and confessed:*

"Lord, the great and awesome God, who keeps his covenant of love with those who love him and keep his commandments, ⁵we have sinned and done wrong. We have been wicked and have rebelled; we have turned away from your commands and laws. ⁶We have not listened to your servants the prophets, who spoke in your name to our kings, our princes and our ancestors, and to all the people of the land.

*⁷"Lord, you are righteous, but this day we are covered with shame—the people of Judah and the inhabitants of Jerusalem and all Israel, both near and far, in all the countries where you have scattered us because of our unfaithfulness to you. ⁸We and our kings, our princes and our ancestors are covered with shame, L*ORD, *because we have sinned against you. ⁹The Lord our God is merciful and forgiving, even though we have rebelled against him; ¹⁰we have not obeyed the L*ORD *our God or kept the laws he gave us through his servants the prophets.*

¹¹All Israel has transgressed your law and turned away, refusing to obey you.

*"Therefore the curses and sworn judgments written in the Law of Moses, the servant of God, have been poured out on us, because we have sinned against you. ¹²You have fulfilled the words spoken against us and against our rulers by bringing on us great disaster. Under the whole heaven nothing has ever been done like what has been done to Jerusalem. ¹³Just as it is written in the Law of Moses, all this disaster has come on us, yet we have not sought the favor of the L*ORD *our God by turning from our sins and giving attention to your truth. ¹⁴The L*ORD *did not*

hesitate to bring the disaster on us, for the LORD our God is righteous in everything he does; yet we have not obeyed him.

¹⁵*"Now, Lord our God, who brought your people out of Egypt with a mighty hand and who made for yourself a name that endures to this day, we have sinned, we have done wrong. ¹⁶Lord, in keeping with all your righteous acts, turn away your anger and your wrath from Jerusalem, your city, your holy hill. Our sins and the iniquities of our ancestors have made Jerusalem and your people an object of scorn to all those around us.*

¹⁷*"Now, our God, hear the prayers and petitions of your servant. For your sake, Lord, look with favor on your desolate sanctuary. ¹⁸Give ear, our God, and hear; open your eyes and see the desolation of the city that bears your Name. We do not make requests of you because we are righteous, but because of your great mercy. ¹⁹Lord, listen! Lord, forgive! Lord, hear and act! For your sake, my God, do not delay, because your city and your people bear your Name."*

²⁰*While I was speaking and praying, confessing my sin and the sin of my people Israel and making my request to the LORD my God for his holy hill—²¹while I was still in prayer, Gabriel, the man I had seen in the earlier vision, came to me in swift flight about the time of the evening sacrifice.*

²²*He instructed me and said to me, "Daniel, I have now come to give you insight and understanding. ²³As soon as you began to pray, a word went out, which I have come to tell you, for you are highly esteemed. Therefore, consider the word and understand the vision:*

²⁴*"Seventy 'sevens' are decreed for your people and your holy city to finish transgression, to put an end to sin, to atone for wickedness, to bring in everlasting righteousness, to seal up vision and prophecy and to anoint the Most Holy Place.*

²⁵*"Know and understand this: From the time*
the word goes out to restore and rebuild Jerusalem
until the Anointed One, the ruler, comes, there will be
seven 'sevens,' and sixty-two 'sevens.' It will be rebuilt
with streets and a trench, but in times of trouble.
²⁶*After the sixty-two 'sevens,' the Anointed One will be*
put to death and will have nothing. The people of the
ruler who will come will destroy the city and the
sanctuary. The end will come like a flood: War will
continue until the end, and desolations have been
decreed. ²⁷*He will confirm a covenant with many for*
one 'seven.' In the middle of the 'seven' he will put an
end to sacrifice and offering. And at the temple he
will set up an abomination that causes desolation,
until the end that is decreed is poured out on him."

❖ How would you describe the tone of Daniel's prayer? What
was he specifically asking of the Lord?

❖ What did Daniel understand according to 9:2?

❖ What did he do with this information according to 9:3–4?

❖ How did Daniel address God? How did Daniel describe God (9:4)?

❖ What did Daniel confess? On whose behalf was he speaking (9:5–6)?

❖ What did Daniel say about the people of Israel in 9:7–11? What sins had they committed?

❖ What consequences had they suffered? How do we know they were warned beforehand (9:11–12)?

❖ In spite of this disaster, what had they not done according to 9:13–14?

❖ What act of God did Daniel reference in 9:15?

❖ What reasons did Daniel give for asking God to restore the people (9:17–19)?

❖ What did he ask of Yahweh in 9:19?

❖ What happened as Daniel was praying (9:20–21)?

S Seek counsel: *What do wise people say*?

Review chapter 9 beginning on page 111 or watch a video presentation of this chapter. Access the QR (Quick Response) code that can be read by many smart devices using a scanning app. It allows you to immediately watch a video presentation of this chapter by Pastor Rafe Wright of Christ Fellowship, McKinney, Texas. If you do not have a QR code reader, you can access the same material at http://vimeo.com/74756868. To the extent you have time and ability, read the relevant section from one of the recommended studies on page 325. Also check out the resources available on Bible.org.

D Develop your response: *What do I think?*

❖ What have you learned about our Big God from studying Daniel's prayer?

❖ How has Daniel's prayer encouraged you to pray in some new ways?

❖ Experiment with praying to God using Daniel's prayer as a model.

⊙ **Openly discuss:** *What do we think?*

1. Describe your prayer life. When was it the richest? Where do you struggle?

2. What Scripture led Daniel to pray (Daniel 9:1–3)? Has any Scripture passage you read led you to pray in a similar fashion? How much of your prayers are driven by: Life circumstance? God's Word? Daily discipline? Crisis?

3. Daniel prayed with fasting and in sackcloth and ashes. Have you ever engaged in fasting or some behavior parallel to sackcloth and ashes to express your heart to God? How might such physical acts relate to our prayerful interaction with God?

4. How did Daniel open his prayer? Scan his prayer to see other ways that Daniel praised and exalted God for his character. What character traits of God did Daniel highlight? What about God do you feel like praising today?

5. Daniel confessed his own sin and the sin of his people. To what extent is confession part of your prayer? How could we also confess sin for a group of which we are a part?

6. In what ways do you want to grow in your prayer life as a result of studying Daniel's prayer?

7. Using Daniel's model, pray for the body of Christ as he prayed for Israel.

M Move to action: *What will I do?*

❖ How has Daniel's prayer affected how you think about your own prayer life?

❖ Daniel prayed forcefully for the restoration of his people. Who can you pray for this week according to the promises of God in Christ? Pray for them.

In reflecting on your study of Daniel 9:1–21, how will you move to action in the Spirit's power?

10

The Seventy Sevens
Study Guide

Daniel 9:22—27

✝ **Pray**

W **Work the issue:** *What's really at stake?*

In the first part of chapter 9, we saw Daniel go boldly before God in prayer, confessing the sins of his people and asking for God to act. Suddenly the angel Gabriel was standing in front of him with an answer. What if you could know some details about what God is going to do in the future? How might that knowledge affect your choices and attitudes today?

The judgments of a holy God are always just. As human beings with limited perspective, we can be tempted to see them as harsh, but we are hardly in a position to judge the ultimate judge. The inconceivable lengths to which he went to save us from our sin should assure us that he is motivated by love, and we can trust in his ways. Should we fear God's judgment?

Speculations on when end-time events will occur and how they will unfold might fill your computer's hard drive. Those who thrive on sensational end-times speculation have much to say on Daniel 9, but even among respected scholars, there is no consensus on the details. However, the main outlines of the future are clear. Why is it important to understand what the Bible reveals about the future?

What's at stake? What is the central issue or issues being addressed? What is the biggest issue for you?

Write down the main issue(s):

▌I▐ Investigate Scripture: *What does God say?*

This is the shortest section we are studying by far. Read chapter 9:22–27 slowly, multiple times. The verses we consider this week look ahead to the Lord's plan for the future. To help focus your attention, underline references to time, places and specific events.

Daniel 9:22–27

He instructed me and said to me, "Daniel, I have now come to give you insight and understanding. [23]As soon as you began to pray, a word went out, which I have come to tell you, for you are highly esteemed."

[24]Seventy "sevens" are decreed for your people to finish transgression, to put an end to sin, to atone for wickedness, to bring in everlasting righteousness, to seal up vision and prophecy and to anoint the Most Holy Place.

[25]"Know and understand this: From the time the word goes out to restore and rebuild Jerusalem until the Anointed One, the ruler, comes, there will be seven "sevens," and sixty-two "sevens." It will be rebuilt with streets and a trench, but in times of trouble. [26]After the sixty-two "sevens," the Anointed One will be put to death and will have nothing. The people of the ruler who will come will destroy the city and the sanctuary. The end will come like a flood: War will continue until the end, and desolations have been decreed. [27]He will confirm a covenant with many for one "seven." In the middle of the "seven" he will put an end to sacrifice and offering. And at the temple he will set up an abomination that causes desolation, until the end that is decreed is poured out on him.

❖   What time periods are referenced?

❖ List the major events described in these verses. What events have already happened? What is yet to come?

❖ Who will be involved in those events?

❖ Why had Gabriel come to Daniel?

❖ What had been decreed by God? For what reason?

❖ What are the purposes of the seventy sevens (9:24)? How does Jesus' first coming relate to these?

❖ How is the Anointed One "cut off" (9:26)? Is this a defeat or a victory?

❖ Imagine being Daniel hearing this explanation. What do you think your reaction would be if you were in his place?

S Seek counsel: *What do wise people say?*

Review chapter 10 beginning on page 123 or watch a video presentation of this chapter. Access the QR (Quick Response) code that can be read by many smart devices using a scanning app. It allows you to immediately watch a video by Pastor Rafe Wright of Christ Fellowship, McKinney, Texas. If you do not have a QR code reader, you can access the same material at http://vimeo.com/74771164.

To the extent you have time and ability, read the relevant section from one of the recommended studies on page 325. Also check out the resources available on Bible.org.

D Develop your response: *What do I think?*

We've journeyed through another challenging chapter in God's Word! Spend some time reflecting on what you've learned about our Big God, and how you should shape your life around him.

❖ What understanding of Israel's past and glimpse into the future does Daniel 9:22–27 give us?

❖ How does knowledge of what God will do in the future impact how you live today?

◉ **Openly discuss:** *What do we think?*

1. What was Daniel doing when Gabriel came (Daniel 9:20–21)? How often are you engaged in such behavior?

2. What did Gabriel say he came to give Daniel (9:22)? Have you ever asked this from God? For what do you most want insight these days?

3. In the Old Testament, God often spoke through various means including dreams, visions, prophets and angels. Consider Hebrews 1:1–2, 1 Corinthians 2:12–14 and 2 Timothy 3:16–17. How is God communicating to us today?

4. How seriously does God take sin and rebellion in his people's lives (Leviticus 26:14–46)? What does Galatians 6:7–8 say about that?

5. When you hear the terms "prophecy" or "end times," what comes to mind (movies, books, people, etc.)? How does that background influence your view of biblical prophecy? What purpose do prophecies serve for the non-Christian? For the Christian?

6. Explain the timing of the seven sevens, the sixty-two sevens and the final one seven. What has already happened and what is still to happen in the future?

7. What will happen to the "ruler" who destroys the city and the sanctuary (9:27)? Relate this truth to what we have learned from previous chapters about the end of the world.

8. How does knowing this truth about the end times affect your attitudes and choices today?

M **Move to action:** *What will I do?*

❖ How is your understanding of the end times growing as you read Daniel 7–9? How is that knowledge impacting your understanding of God and your desire to live for him?

❖ Who do you know that needs both the warnings and assurances God gives us in these chapters? How can you share those with them?

❖ In reflecting on your study of Daniel 9:22–27, move to action in the Spirit's power.

11

Angels and Demons
Study Guide

Daniel 10

✝ Pray

W Work the issue: *What's really at stake?*

When you think of an angel, what picture pops into your head—a
long, flowing gown, enormous wings with a halo hovering above
her head and a harp in her hand? Popular culture has given us a
certain image of angels that is not necessarily rooted in Scripture.
This chapter gives us a glimpse into the hidden activities of the
supernatural beings when Daniel once again has an encounter with
one. There is an incredible realm beyond our view that affects our
reality. Daniel 10 shows us spiritual influences behind earthly
struggles. Yet, as we have seen throughout Daniel, our Big God
rules over all. Imagine if you could see into the invisible
supernatural activity happening around you.

Daniel sought God with intensity, including a three-week fast. Have you ever sought God with the intensity that Daniel did? Could you?

What's at stake? What is the central issue or issues being addressed? What is the biggest issue for you?

Write down the main issue(s):

▮ Investigate Scripture: *What does God say?*

As you read Daniel 10, try and imagine this supernatural experience through Daniel's eyes. Consider how he reacted to what he saw and ponder the implications of what he was told. Pay attention to the supernatural beings involved.

Daniel 10:1–11:1

> *In the third year of Cyrus king of Persia, a revelation was given to Daniel (who was called Belteshazzar). Its message was true and it concerned a great war. The understanding of the message came to him in a vision.*

²At that time I, Daniel, mourned for three weeks. ³I ate no choice food; no meat or wine touched my lips; and I used no lotions at all until the three weeks were over.

⁴On the twenty-fourth day of the first month, as I was standing on the bank of the great river, the Tigris, ⁵I looked up and there before me was a man dressed in linen, with a belt of fine gold from Uphaz around his waist. ⁶His body was like topaz, his face like lightning, his eyes like flaming torches, his arms and legs like the gleam of burnished bronze, and his voice like the sound of a multitude.

⁷I, Daniel, was the only one who saw the vision; those who were with me did not see it, but such terror overwhelmed them that they fled and hid themselves. ⁸So I was left alone, gazing at this great vision; I had no strength left, my face turned deathly pale and I was helpless. ⁹Then I heard him speaking, and as I listened to him, I fell into a deep sleep, my face to the ground.

¹⁰A hand touched me and set me trembling on my hands and knees. ¹¹He said, "Daniel, you who are highly esteemed, consider carefully the words I am about to speak to you, and stand up, for I have now been sent to you." And when he said this to me, I stood up trembling.

¹²Then he continued, "Do not be afraid, Daniel. Since the first day that you set your mind to gain understanding and to humble yourself before your God, your words were heard, and I have come in response to them. ¹³But the prince of the Persian kingdom resisted me twenty-one days. Then Michael, one of the chief princes, came to help me, because I was detained there with the king of Persia. ¹⁴Now I have come to explain to you what will happen to your people in the future, for the vision concerns a time yet to come."

¹⁵While he was saying this to me, I bowed with my face toward the ground and was speechless. ¹⁶Then one who looked like a man touched my lips, and I opened my mouth and began to speak. I said to the one standing before me, "I am overcome with anguish because of the vision, my lord, and I feel very weak. ¹⁷How can I, your servant, talk with you, my lord? My strength is gone and I can hardly breathe."

¹⁸Again the one who looked like a man touched me and gave me strength. ¹⁹"Do not be afraid, you who are highly esteemed," he said. "Peace! Be strong now; be strong."

When he spoke to me, I was strengthened and said, "Speak, my lord, since you have given me strength."

²⁰So he said, "Do you know why I have come to you? Soon I will return to fight against the prince of Persia, and when I go, the prince of Greece will come; ²¹but first I will tell you what is written in the Book of Truth. (No one supports me against them except Michael, your prince.

¹¹:¹And in the first year of Darius the Mede, I took my stand to support and protect him.)

❖ What did Daniel do to express the intensity of his prayer?

❖ When did Daniel receive this vision?

❖ What did Daniel see according to 10:5–6? What was his reaction?

❖ How did the angel comfort and reassure Daniel?

❖ What caused the angel to be delayed in coming to Daniel?

❖ What did the angel come to explain (10:14)?

❖ What was Daniel feeling according to 10:15–17?

❖ What did the angel do for him?

❖ What was the angel preparing to do according to 10:20–21?

S Seek counsel: *What do wise people say?*

Review chapter 11 beginning on page 137
or watch a video presentation of this
chapter. Access the QR (Quick Response)
code that can be read by many smart
devices using a scanning app. It allows you
to immediately watch the video. If you do
not have a QR code reader, you can access
the same material at http://vimeo.com/74771163.
To the extent you have time and ability, read the relevant section
from one of the recommended studies on page 325. Also check out
the resources available on Bible.org.

D **Develop your response:** *What do I think?*

❖ How would you describe Daniel's experience in chapter 10? What can we learn from this experience?

❖ How does it change your view of world events to know that there is a spiritual battle going on behind the scenes? How does knowing that encourage you to pray?

❖ Daniel models seeking God intensely. How could you do this?

◉ **Openly discuss:** *What do we think?*

1. In considering the people you know, what do you think are their common views of angels and demons?

2. How did Daniel express the intensity of his desire to hear from God (10:2–3, 12)? Have you ever mourned or fasted for something or someone? Daniel took three weeks to seek spiritual understanding. How could we take time to do the same, even if for not as long? Have you ever taken significant time to seek God? How did you do it and what were the benefits? How can we express our intensity in similar ways?

3. What was the impact of the vision of Daniel? Those with him? How did the angel strengthen him? Imagine an angel saying these words to you. How would you feel?

4. What was going on in the supernatural realm that affected the answer to Daniel's prayer?

5. How did Daniel struggle, and how did the angel encourage Daniel at the end of the chapter (10:15–19)? In what situations do you need to hear these words of encouragement in your life right now?

6. What can we learn about angels and demons from Daniel 10? How should we respond to their reality and interaction with our world?

7. The angel told Daniel to carefully consider the words he would tell him. What could we do to more seriously study God's Word? What new step will you take to study God's Word?

Ⓜ **Move to action:** *What will I do?*

❖ How has seeing spiritual realities beyond our sight in this chapter challenged and encouraged you to live for Christ? What will you do?

❖ How will you seek God intensely as Daniel did? When? For what?

❖ In reflecting on your study of Daniel 10, move to action in the Spirit's power?

12

The Big God Wins
Study Guide

Daniel 11—12

✝ Pray

W Work the issue: *What's really at stake?*

In this chapter, we will study Daniel's final recorded vision. Some of what is recorded there is now part of our past but within the prophecy. There are future events still on our horizon. What will we do with the knowledge of what is to come and how will we use it to affect our present?

This is a good time to really consider all that God has shown us in this amazing book. We should have a better understanding of our Big God. If you haven't already done so, prayerfully consider how this understanding changes the way you think about the world and how you live in it.

The vision Daniel received indicates that there would not be an end to conflict for some time. In fact, things would eventually get much worse. How do you deal with the worsening of our world?

What's at stake? What is the central issue or issues being addressed? What is the biggest issue for you?

Write down the main issue(s):

I Investigate Scripture: *What does God say?*

Because chapter 11 is long, read it to get the overall picture of the vision; then read chapter 12 slowly to hear the angel's parting words to Daniel. We will dig into the ways in which this prophecy has already been fulfilled and consider what events are still unfulfilled. As you read, think about how the language of the vision changes toward the end and how that might indicate a transition from events that have already happened to those that are yet to come.

Daniel 11

And in the first year of Darius the Mede, I took my stand to support and protect him.)

²"Now then, I tell you the truth: Three more kings will arise in Persia, and then a fourth, who will be far richer than all the others. When he has gained power by his wealth, he will stir up everyone against the kingdom of Greece. ³Then a mighty king will arise, who will rule with great power and do as he pleases. ⁴After he has arisen, his empire will be broken up and parceled out toward the four winds of heaven. It will not go to his descendants, nor will it have the power he exercised, because his empire will be uprooted and given to others.

⁵"The king of the South will become strong, but one of his commanders will become even stronger than he and will rule his own kingdom with great power. ⁶After some years, they will become allies. The daughter of the king of the South will go to the king of the North to make an alliance, but she will not retain her power, and he and his power will not last. In those days she will be betrayed, together with her royal escort and her father and the one who supported her.

⁷"One from her family line will arise to take her place. He will attack the forces of the king of the North and enter his fortress; he will fight against them and be victorious. ⁸He will also seize their gods, their metal images and their valuable articles of silver and gold and carry them off to Egypt. For some years he will leave the king of the North alone. ⁹Then the king of the North will invade the realm of the king of the South but will retreat to his own country. ¹⁰His sons will prepare for war and assemble a great army, which will sweep on like an irresistible flood and carry the battle as far as his fortress.

¹¹"Then the king of the South will march out in a rage and fight against the king of the North, who will raise a large army, but it will be defeated. ¹²When the army is carried off, the king of the South will be filled with pride and will slaughter many

thousands, yet he will not remain triumphant. ¹³For
the king of the North will muster another army,
larger than the first; and after several years, he will
advance with a huge army fully equipped.

¹⁴"In those times many will rise against the king
of the South. Those who are violent among your own
people will rebel in fulfillment of the vision, but
without success. ¹⁵Then the king of the North will
come and build up siege ramps and will capture a
fortified city. The forces of the South will be powerless
to resist; even their best troops will not have the
strength to stand. ¹⁶The invader will do as he pleases;
no one will be able to stand against him. He will
establish himself in the Beautiful Land and will have
the power to destroy it. ¹⁷He will determine to come
with the might of his entire kingdom and will make
an alliance with the king of the South. And he will
give him a daughter in marriage in order to
overthrow the kingdom, but his plans will not
succeed or help him. ¹⁸Then he will turn his attention
to the coastlands and will take many of them, but a
commander will put an end to his insolence and will
turn his insolence back on him. ¹⁹After this, he will
turn back toward the fortresses of his own country
but will stumble and fall, to be seen no more.

²⁰"His successor will send out a tax collector to
maintain the royal splendor. In a few years, however,
he will be destroyed, yet not in anger or in battle.

²¹"He will be succeeded by a contemptible
person who has not been given the honor of royalty.
He will invade the kingdom when its people feel
secure, and he will seize it through intrigue. ²²Then
an overwhelming army will be swept away before
him; both it and a prince of the covenant will be
destroyed. ²³After coming to an agreement with him,
he will act deceitfully, and with only a few people he
will rise to power. ²⁴When the richest provinces feel
secure, he will invade them and will achieve what

*neither his fathers nor his forefathers did. He will
distribute plunder, loot and wealth among his
followers. He will plot the overthrow of fortresses—
but only for a time.*

*25"With a large army he will stir up his strength
and courage against the king of the South. The king
of the South will wage war with a large and very
powerful army, but he will not be able to stand
because of the plots devised against him. 26Those who
eat from the king's provisions will try to destroy him;
his army will be swept away, and many will fall in
battle. 27The two kings, with their hearts bent on evil,
will sit at the same table and lie to each other, but to
no avail, because an end will still come at the
appointed time. 28The king of the North will return to
his own country with great wealth, but his heart will
be set against the holy covenant. He will take action
against it and then return to his own country.*

*29"At the appointed time he will invade the
South again, but this time the outcome will be
different from what it was before. 30Ships of the
western coastlands will oppose him, and he will lose
heart. Then he will turn back and vent his fury
against the holy covenant. He will return and show
favor to those who forsake the holy covenant.*

*31"His armed forces will rise up to desecrate the
temple fortress and will abolish the daily sacrifice.
Then they will set up the abomination that causes
desolation. 32With flattery he will corrupt those who
have violated the covenant, but the people who know
their God will firmly resist him.*

*33"Those who are wise will instruct many,
though for a time they will fall by the sword or be
burned or captured or plundered. 34When they fall,
they will receive a little help, and many who are not
sincere will join them. 35Some of the wise will
stumble, so that they may be refined, purified and*

made spotless until the time of the end, for it will still come at the appointed time.

36 "The king will do as he pleases. He will exalt and magnify himself above every god and will say unheard-of things against the God of gods. He will be successful until the time of wrath is completed, for what has been determined must take place. 37 He will show no regard for the gods of his ancestors or for the one desired by women, nor will he regard any god, but will exalt himself above them all. 38 Instead of them, he will honor a god of fortresses; a god unknown to his ancestors he will honor with gold and silver, with precious stones and costly gifts. 39 He will attack the mightiest fortresses with the help of a foreign god and will greatly honor those who acknowledge him. He will make them rulers over many people and will distribute the land at a price.

40 "At the time of the end the king of the South will engage him in battle, and the king of the North will storm out against him with chariots and cavalry and a great fleet of ships. He will invade many countries and sweep through them like a flood. 41 He will also invade the Beautiful Land. Many countries will fall, but Edom, Moab and the leaders of Ammon will be delivered from his hand. 42 He will extend his power over many countries; Egypt will not escape. 43 He will gain control of the treasures of gold and silver and all the riches of Egypt, with the Libyans and Cushites in submission. 44 But reports from the east and the north will alarm him, and he will set out in a great rage to destroy and annihilate many. 45 He will pitch his royal tents between the seas at the beautiful holy mountain. Yet he will come to his end, and no one will help him."

Daniel 12

"At that time Michael, the great prince who protects your people, will arise. There will be a time of distress such as has not happened from the beginning of nations until then. But at that time your people—everyone whose name is found written in the book—will be delivered. ²Multitudes who sleep in the dust of the earth will awake: some to everlasting life, others to shame and everlasting contempt. ³Those who are wise will shine like the brightness of the heavens, and those who lead many to righteousness, like the stars for ever and ever. ⁴But you, Daniel, roll up and seal the words of the scroll until the time of the end. Many will go here and there to increase knowledge."

⁵Then I, Daniel, looked, and there before me stood two others, one on this bank of the river and one on the opposite bank. ⁶One of them said to the man clothed in linen, who was above the waters of the river, "How long will it be before these astonishing things are fulfilled?"

⁷The man clothed in linen, who was above the waters of the river, lifted his right hand and his left hand toward heaven, and I heard him swear by him who lives forever, saying, "It will be for a time, times and half a time. When the power of the holy people has been finally broken, all these things will be completed."

⁸I heard, but I did not understand. So I asked, "My lord, what will the outcome of all this be?"

⁹He replied, "Go your way, Daniel, because the words are rolled up and sealed until the time of the end. ¹⁰Many will be purified, made spotless and refined, but the wicked will continue to be wicked. None of the wicked will understand, but those who are wise will understand.

> ¹¹*"From the time that the daily sacrifice is*
> *abolished and the abomination that causes*
> *desolation is set up, there will be 1,290 days.* ¹²*Blessed*
> *is the one who waits for and reaches the end of the*
> *1,335 days.*
> ¹³*"As for you, go your way till the end. You will*
> *rest, and then at the end of the days you will rise to*
> *receive your allotted inheritance."*

❖ An angel said that a king was coming from Greece. How is
he described? What would happen to him?

❖ From 11:5–20, summarize the conflict between the kings of
the North and those of the South. How will Israel be affected?

❖ How is the next king described in 11:21? How do the actions described in the rest of the passage support that title? What contemptible things does the king do to the Jews?

❖ What was the king's attitude toward God?

❖ What is Michael's role in 12:1?

❖ According to 12:2–3, what are the two possible futures for those who "sleep in the dust of the earth"?

❖ What questions did Daniel ask in 12:6 and 12:8? What answers did he get?

❖ What are the angel's parting words to Daniel in 12:13?

❖   What do you think it means to "go on your way" (12:13)?

S   Seek counsel: *What do wise people say?*

Review chapter 12 beginning on page 151 or watch a video presentation of this chapter. Access the QR (Quick Response) code that can be read by many smart devices using a scanning app. It allows you to immediately watch the video. If you do not have a QR code reader, you can access the same material at http://vimeo.com/74756870.

To the extent you have time and ability, read the relevant section from one of the recommended studies on page 325. Also check out the resources available on Bible.org.

D Develop your response: *What do I think?*

❖ Briefly summarize the events of Daniel 11–12.

❖ How does knowing the end of the Antichrist encourage you?

❖ What has been your biggest takeaway from the book of Daniel?

You've done it! You have made it through a very challenging book in the Bible. Today reflect on what you've learned about our Big God and how that knowledge can make a difference in your life.

O Openly discuss: *What do we think?*

1. What has your experience been with biblical prophecy about the Antichrist?

2. Daniel's vision in chapter 11 was fulfilled exactly in history. How does the fulfillment of biblical prophecy increase your faith?

3. What is going on with the kings of the South and North in the first part of chapter 11? Who is the king at the end of the chapter (11:36–45), and what does he do? How does this vision add to our knowledge about end times and the Antichrist?

4. Who will be delivered (12:1)? What are two destinies of all people (12:2)? How do you know which destiny is yours? What can we do to be the "wise" who shine forever?

5. What are the characteristics of "the wise" in 11:32–35 and 12:3, 10? How could you grow in these characteristics? Which one do you need the most?

6. Until the times described in Daniel chapters 11–12, what is our opportunity and responsibility as followers of Jesus Christ (Daniel 12:3)? With whom specifically can you share the promise associated with the Book of Life described in Daniel 12:1?

7. What have you learned about The Big God in our study? How would you describe The Big God as he is portrayed in Daniel?

M Move to action: *What will I do*?

❖ What have you learned about the end times and how we are to live today in light of them?

❖ How has a study of Daniel given you confidence in The Big God? How does that confidence affect how you see the world and act toward others?

❖ How has Daniel challenged you to share Christ with those who don't know him and help them grow in Christ?

❖ What do you believe God is telling you to do to grow spiritually and to make an impact in the lives of others?

In reflecting on your study of Daniel 11–12, how will you move to action in the Spirit's power? Prayerfully think back over your entire study of Daniel to identify what God has taught you and how he wants to change you to become more spiritually mature.

Final thoughts

Way to go finishing an in-depth study of Daniel's 12 chapters!

I hope and pray that the Holy Spirit has opened your eyes to see how big our God really is and that he is The God that we can trust in all circumstances of our lives.

In his stories and visions, Daniel displays for us the all-powerful Big God who raises up empires, and rescues his people from the furnace and the lion's pit. Since God revealed the future to Daniel, he was able to write the future before it happened. As we learned, Daniel wrote about even more to come that hasn't yet happened. And we know with confidence that God has the whole world in his hands, including us and our eternal destiny.

While there will be dark, chaotic days ahead, we will not fear because we trust in The God who is bigger than every trial, greater than any king and will certainly deliver us one day into his eternal kingdom of peace.

May you grow in your faith and knowledge of our Big God as you continue to study his Word.

In worship and honor of our Big God,

Bruce

Acknowledgments

My greatest thanks goes to my wife, Tamara, who insisted that I rest from a minor surgery, and it was in that "rest" time that I composed this book. Tamara, thank you for loving me enough to make me stay home. And she urged me to finish this book during the summer of our thirtieth wedding anniversary. Thank you, Tamara, for your prayers and your love. Here's to 30 more years.

Thanks to Rafe Wright, my fellow pastor at Christ Fellowship who wrote the first drafts on Daniel 9. He delivered those sermons while I was recovering from surgery and graciously offered them to be included in this book.

I also appreciate the solid work of Barry Applewhite and Lisa Scheffler in preparing a different type of Study Guide for Christ Fellowship from which I drew to create the WISDOM Study Guide you have in this book. Some of the questions and material in the "Work the issue" sections comes from that previous guide. Thanks also to Barry for researching and writing the first draft of the section on the historical background.

I also thank the people of Christ Fellowship and especially my fellow elders and pastors for their encouragement to write this book.

Thanks to Iva Morelli for editing this book with me, and walking with me to complete this project. Without you, this book would not exist. Finally, thanks to Dave and Judy Buckert who helped launch me into publishing with the first edition of this book.

Recommended studies

Stephen R. Miller, *Daniel, The New American Commentary*, vol. 18 (Nashville: Broadman & Holman, 1994).
    This commentary was written for pastors and Bible students but keeps the technical details in the footnotes. It gives solid answers to critical and anti-supernatural attacks on the book for those who need them.

Leon J. Wood, *A Commentary on Daniel* (Eugene: Wipf and Stock Publishers, 1998).
    This commentary was first published in 1973 but remains one of the best on history, language, exposition and theology.

Robert B. Chisholm, Jr., *Handbook on the Prophets* (Grand Rapids: Baker Academic, 2009).
    This book does an exceptionally good job of summarizing the teachings of the Old Testament prophets on a book-by-book basis while also dealing with crucial issues. Aimed at college level.

Now to the King of the ages, immortal, invisible, the only God, be honor and glory forever and ever. Amen (1 Timothy 1:17, ESV).

About the author

BRUCE B. MILLER

God has given Bruce the privilege of serving as husband to his wife, Tamara, since 1983 and father to their five children. They are also blessed with their grandchildren. God used Bruce to plant Christ Fellowship in McKinney, Texas where he currently serves as senior pastor (CFhome.org). In his spare time, he loves spending time with Tamara, playing racquetball, using a chainsaw and sitting by an open fire with his chocolate Labrador, Calvin.

His passion for leadership development led to his first book, *The Leadership Baton*, written with Jeff Jones and Rowland Forman. Bruce's heart to see people live more fulfilled lives sparked the writing of *Your Life in Rhythm*, the forerunner to *Your Church in Rhythm* which applies the concepts of rhythmic living to local churches (BruceBMiller.com).

Bruce developed the innovative six-step WISDOM Process© which serves as a learning engine in the study guides for his other books *When God Makes No Sense—A Fresh Look at Habakkuk; Same-Sex Wedding—Should I Attend?* and *Sexuality—Approaching Controversial Issues with Grace, Truth and Hope.*

Bruce graduated Phi Beta Kappa from the University of Texas at Austin with a B.A. in Plan II, the Honors Liberal Arts Program ('82); received a master's degree in Theology from Dallas Theological Seminary ('86); and did doctoral work at the University of Texas at Dallas in the History of Ideas (focus on philosophical hermeneutics, Hans-Georg Gadamer, and post-modernism). He taught theology for four years at Dallas Theological Seminary.

Bruce speaks and consults around the world. He founded the Centers for Church Based Training and served as Chairman of the Board for 12 years (http://ccbt.org). Bruce founded and leads Dadlin ministries, an organization committed to helping people develop wisdom for life. You can follow Bruce on:

Twitter (http://twitter.com/Bruce_B_Miller) or
Facebook (https://www.facebook.com/BruceBMillerAuthor)
Blog (BruceBMiller.com)
To invite Bruce to speak, contact him at:
Website (BruceBMiller.com)

Other resources

The publishing ministry of Dadlin ministries—an organization committed to helping people develop wisdom for life.

Dadlin Media
— *wisdom for life* —

Resources by **Bruce B. Miller**:

The Leadership Baton
Equips you with a solution to the need for quality leaders in local churches. Miller provides you with a biblical vision, a holistic approach and a comprehensive plan.

Your Life in Rhythm
Offers a realistic way to overcome our crazy, overly busy, stressed lives. Exposes the myth of living a "balanced" life. Miller presents "rhythmic living" as a new paradigm for relieving guilt and stress, so we can accomplish more of what matters most in life—with more freedom, peace, fulfillment and hope.

Your Church in Rhythm
Most pastors try to do everything at once, and they feel guilty if even one aspect of their church ministry is neglected in the process. Instead, Miller proposes replacing this exhausting notion of "balance" with the true-to-life concept of "rhythm." Churches, just like people, should focus on the seasons and the cycles of ministry programs. That way, leaders can avoid burnout by focusing only on each issue at the time that it matters most.

Big God in a Chaotic World—A Fresh Look at Daniel
Shows we can live faithfully in this sinful, out-of-control world when we get a fresh vision of our big God. Daniel opens our eyes to see the God who is bigger than the problems in our world, bigger than all our fears, fires and lions.

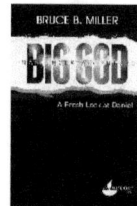

329

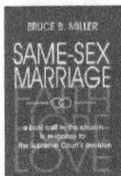

Same-Sex Marriage—A Bold Call to the Church in Response to the Supreme Court's Decision

In response to this cultural crisis, the church should step up with a Christlike response that stuns the world, and draws people to Jesus Christ with counter-cultural love.

Sexuality—Approaching Controversial Issues with Grace, Truth and Hope
Addresses the purposes of sex in marriage, singleness, cohabitation, homosexuality (and more), with fresh biblical insights filled with grace.

When God Makes No Sense—A Fresh Look at Habakkuk
When life is shaking you like a leaf in a storm, learn how to hold on to the unshakeable God who controls the storm.

Never the Same—A Fresh Look at the Sermon on the Mount
A fresh reading of Jesus' famous Sermon on the Mount helps us feel the shock and offence his original audience felt because Jesus turns upside down how most people view life.

Coming Soon:
Miracles—A Fresh Look at Jesus

For more information on current and upcoming books, go to BruceBMiller.com.

http//brucebmiller.com_MyStory

Dadlin Media
— *wisdom for life* —
McKinney, TX 75070

From the author

Thank you for taking time to read this book. My hope is that you have found wisdom for your life. I love hearing from my readers. Feel free to contact me if you have any questions or thoughts you'd like to share. Email me at author@brucebmiller.com.

If you enjoyed this book, there are several things you can do to help others:

- Consider leaving a review on Amazon, and on Goodreads or your favorite online retailer. Honest reader reviews help others decide whether they'll enjoy a book.

- You can lend this book to a friend who might enjoy it.

- Check my website (BruceBmiller.com) or Facebook page (BruceBMillerAuthor) to find my other books and new releases. You can sign up for my newsletter to receive the latest news.

Sincerely,
Bruce

Notes

1. Stephen R. Miller, *Daniel, The New American Commentary: An Exegetical and Theological Exposition of Holy Scripture,* vol. 18 (Nashville: Broadman & Holman, 1994), 57.
2. Christopher Torchia, "Archeologists explore site on Syria-Turkey border," *Bloomberg Businessweek, AP News* (November 8, 2012), 1.
3. Leon J. Wood, *A Commentary on Daniel* (Eugene: Wipf and Stock Publishers, 1973), 29.
4. John E. Goldingay, *Daniel, Word Biblical Commentary,* vol. 30 (Dallas: Word, 1998), 9.
5. Wood, *A Commentary on Daniel,* 31.
6. Ibid., 33.
7. Ibid., 40.
8. Miller, *Daniel,* 95.
9. Ibid., 92.
10. Ibid., 108.
11. Wood, *A Commentary on Daniel,* 80.
12. Beth Moore, *Daniel: Lives of Integrity Words of Prophecy* (Nashville: LifeWay Press, 2006), 66.
13. Wood, *A Commentary on Daniel,* 117.
14. Ibid., 119.
15. Tremper Longman III, *Daniel: The NIV Application Commentary* (Grand Rapids: Zondervan, 1999), 122.
16. Ibid., 124.
17. Wood, *A Commentary on Daniel,* 129.
18. Ibid., 130.
19. Ronald S. Wallace, *The Message of Daniel,* ed. J. A. Moyter (Downers Grove: InterVarsity Press, 1971), 96.
20. Wood, *A Commentary on Daniel,* 135.
21. Miller, *Daniel,* 156.
22. Longman, *Daniel,* 146.
23. Miller, *Daniel,* 165.
24. Ibid., 167.
25. Longman, *Daniel,* 167.
26. Ibid., 199.
27. Ibid., 221.
28. Ibid., 222.
29. Wood, *A Commentary on Daniel,* 211.

30. Longman, *Daniel*, 203.
31. The Jews used a lunar 360-day calendar, also called a "prophetic years" calendar.
    - ❖ 69 x 7 x 360 = 173,880 days.
    - ❖ The difference between 444 BC and AD 33 then is 476 solar years.
    - ❖ 476 x 365.242219879 = 173,855 days.
    - ❖ This leaves only 25 days to be accounted for between the fourth decree delivered on March 5, 444 BC and AD 33.
    - ❖ By adding the 25 days to March 5 (of 444 BC), one comes to March 30 which was Nisan 10 in AD 33. This is the time of the triumphal entry of Jesus into Jerusalem.
    - ❖ Jesus' crucifixion then occurred on Friday of Passover, Nisan 14, AD 33. According to our calendar, Friday April 3, AD 33.
32. Joyce G. Baldwin, *Daniel: An Introduction & Commentary* (Downers Grove: InterVarsity Press, 1978), 180.
33. Longman, *Daniel*, 254.
34. Wood, *A Commentary on Daniel*, 282.
35. Ibid., 283.
36. Miller, *Daniel*, 319.
37. Ibid., 302.
38. Longman, *Daniel*, 299.